WE ARE PILGRIMS

Mission from, in and with the Margins of our Diverse World

Edited by **Darren Cronshaw**
and **Rosemary Dewerse**

© UNOH Publishing, 2015

Published 2015 by UNOH Publishing
2/6–12 Airlie Avenue, Dandenong
Victoria 3175, Australia
www.unoh.org/publishing

National Library of Australia Cataloguing-in-Publication entry (pbk)

Creator:	AAMS Conference (2014: Adelaide, S Aust.)
Title:	We are pilgrims: mission from, in and with the margins of our diverse world / Darren Cronshaw, Rosemary Dewerse, editors.
ISBN:	9780994202345 (paperback)
Subjects:	Missions--Congresses
	Evangelistic work--Congresses.

Other Creators/Contributors:
    Cronshaw, Darren, editor.
    Dewerse, Rosemary, editor.
    Australian Association of Mission Studies.

Dewey Number: 266.023

Editors: Darren Cronshaw and Rosemary Dewerse
Design: Les Colston at Urban Zeal

Appreciation to CBM Australia

We appreciate the generous sponsorship of CBM Australia of this book, and of the fourth annual Australian Association for Mission Studies conference, October 2014, which inspired and gave content for the book.

Formerly known as Christian Blind Mission, over time CBM's work has widened from serving just people with vision impairment to giving all people with disabilities access to basic healthcare services and restoring life. They are also involved in providing immediate aid in times of emergency, long-term support where needed, and advocacy, all in partnership with local organisations, governments and agencies. Today CBM is the world's largest Christian organisation working in over 70 countries with people with disabilities in the most marginalised places.

Committed also to working with Australian local churches and other Christian organisations interested in ministry on the margins and with people of diverse abilities, CBM's sponsorship of this volume is a logical and welcomed partnership.

Because of CBM's sponsorship, *We are Pilgrims* is available for free distribution as an EBook. Go to https://www.cbm.org.au

Dedicated to

Dr Ross Langmead

Professor of Mission Studies, Whitley College, University of Divinity

Convenor and Founding Secretary, Australian Association for Mission Studies

Ross was married to Alison (for 40 years),

proud father to Benjamin and Kia,

and grandfather to Sage and Zara, those who miss him most;

but those of us who appreciated his warm interest,

thoughtful mind and his commitment to journeying Jesus' way of love also miss him,

and continue to be inspired by his life well lived.

Contents

Foreword
Alison Langmead   9

Introduction
Darren Cronshaw and Rosemary Dewerse   13

Margins and Mission

1. **Standing Fast and Breaking Through: Challenges and Possibilities for Marginal Ministry**
   Anthony J. Gittins, CSSp.   27
2. **Finding the Centre at the Margins: Renewing the Call to Mission**
   Anthony J. Gittins, CSSp.   39

A. Indigenous Reconciliation

3. **Finding our Soul, Finding my Soul: Walking the Long Journey of Reconciliation in Australia**
   Rosemary Dewerse   57

B. A Multicultural Vision

4. **Finding Communitas in Liminality: Invitations from the Margins in the New Testament and in Contemporary Mission**
   George Wieland   71
5. **Growing a Truly Multicultural Australian Catholic Church**
   Noel Connolly   83
6. **A Mission of the Second Generation (Australian Born Chinese) in South Australian Migrant Churches: Dealing with Unintentional Marginalisation due to Confucian Values**
   Samuel Chan with Kim Chan   97
7. **Becoming a Diverse Multicultural Church in Central Adelaide. A Case Study**
   Elizabeth Vreugdenhil   111

C. Mission in a Post-Christian Society

8. But is it Church?
   Karyl Davison — 127
9. Where the Margins Meet: An Exploration of the Prophetic Dimensions of a Church Willing to Embrace
   Jasmine Dow — 139
10. Grappling for Christ: Incarnational Mission at the Margins of the Church
    Mick Pope — 151
11. On the Journey to New Creation: Mission with People with Disabilities
    Immanuel Koks — 165

D. Engaging the postmodern mind

12. A Mutual Understanding, Emerging Spirituality and the Christian Church
    Christy Capper — 179
13. There is No Public Square, The Secularist Myth of Neutral Ground
    Lewis Jones — 193
14. Indie-Rock And Mission: Challenges and Possibilities of De-centred Mission in the 21st Century
    T. Mark McConnell — 207

E. The Asian Horizon

15. Christians in the City: Challenges to Faith and Mission in the First "Urban Century"
    Ash Barker — 225
16. A World of Peripheries
    Scott Litchfield — 233
17. Contextual Theologising on the Doorstep of Asia: Mission and Marginalisation among the Irupara Hula People of PNG
    Graeme Humble — 245
18. "God called us here for a reason" Karen and Chin Baptist Churches in Victoria: Mission from the Margins of a Diaspora Community
    Darren Cronshaw, Stacey Wilson and Meewon Yang, with Ner Dah, Si Khia, Arohn Kuung, and Japheth Lian — 263
19. A Korean Woman: A Marginal Perspective for a Multicultural Society
    Pauline Kim van Dalen — 279

Contributors — 293

Foreword
Alison Langmead

I am most encouraged that a book is emerging out of the 2014 AAMS Conference, "Margins, Mission and Diversity". As I read through the amazing range of topics, approaches, reality-facing questions, issues, needs and insights-from-experience covered in the papers that were presented, now becoming chapters in this book, I was deeply moved to realise how the seed planted when Ross helped to form the Australian Association of Mission Studies so that just such interchange and encouragement could occur here in our Australian context – multi-various as it is – has been clearly watered into a fruit-bearing tree.

Living with Ross for almost 40 years was a very down to earth and heart-warming way of exploring what it means to be open and thoughtful while living the life-giving challenge of the way of Jesus.

I did not marry a missiologist as such, but I did meet and marry a man who was already grappling with: the nature of church (having lived and breathed 18 of his first 24 years in a deeply committed Salvation Army family before suddenly leaving); the nature of better communication, whatever the realm; how religious education could have greatest integrity within secondary education (he was a maths teacher thinking of training towards teaching religious education); the nature and concept of God (philosophically speaking) which brought him to a crisis of faith while doing a Master of Education in our first year of marriage; and, for example, how a newly-wed husband could take his turn at cooking meals, fixing what breaks and so on!

My father was a Baptist minister who became a Chaplain in a Baptist school while gaining his education qualification. He had been grappling with many similar questions which he often shared at the tea-table, so I found lots of common ground for long talks with Ross and I loved that he was also writing and singing songs that echoed his journey in its different stages.

When Ross completed his research for the western suburban Baptist churches, culminating in the Western Suburbs Conference Report in 1978 it was clear to both of us that we should commit to living in the area so we could put into practice at least some of the recommendations Ross had made. I can say without hesitation that this commitment deeply shaped our lives and the lives of those who moved to the area to share the journey. With the deep and often surprising movements of God's Spirit, even though we were grappling with the ups and downs of working with people who are struggling most with life's complexities and adverse circumstances, there has been a beauty in the journey which often produces deep wells of gratitude.

Athol Gill was an influential mentor in Ross's life when he was studying theology and considering its implications. Athol's life, and then especially his sudden death in 1992, gave Ross deep pause to consider how the inspiration of Athol's combination of theological reflection and teaching with radical application on the ground could best be continued. When encouraged by a friend to apply for the first Whitley Baptist Theological College appointment of a lecturer in Missiology, Ross wondered if this could be the way to do so. But as it has so often been throughout the ages in the lives of God's people, I remember witnessing in Ross that deep mix of human uncertainty as to whether he had what it would take, yet sensing the fire that he was being called to take the step anyway! Despite his feelings of inadequacy he applied and found the role to be increasingly fruitful. He was clear however that, as with so many before him, it would be God's mission and all he could do would be to make himself available and to follow God's lead.

That is true for all of us and it takes the rest of our lives to learn the daily rhythm of what that means in practice. Ross was no exception. The songs he wrote through those years clearly articulate the journey into the hope of the good news of Jesus at the heart of the struggle for life and freedom that becomes apparent when the light of God's love and grace pierces the darkness yet again. His last song was one he managed with tearful gratitude, despite wondering if he could possibly write anything that came near the feelings he was experiencing in considering it. He wrote these words for our daughter Kia's marriage to Thierry: *"Love Surround You (love from within and behind and before: love be constant like the waves breaking upon the shore"* – a prayer for all of us perhaps?!) In the week before Ross's heart attack, while having a break at our favourite Wye River (where he wrote Kia's wedding song), he was sharing with me the inspiration of Richard Rohr's book *Falling Upward* and his desire that in this "second half of life", he looked forward to becoming more contemplative. Though his song-writing was a deeply contemplative process, there was something more to grow into ... and always will be.

As with Athol's death, Ross's sudden death came as a shock to many of us, his loved ones, friends and colleagues – here in Australia and around the world. I have been touched over and over again and been given precious strength by the outpouring of love that has accompanied that sorrowful time and the ongoing journey. Thank you.

I also want to express my gratitude for the way the AAMS community and 2014 Conference organisers consulted and included me in their desire to honour Ross through the Ross Langmead Memorial lecture, the use and performance of his songs and in this book being dedicated to the memory of his life and work. It seemed most fitting that the first presenter of this lecture, included as a chapter below, was Ash Barker with whom Ross worked so closely in supervision via Skype while Ash was living, working, reflecting and writing for his PhD in the Bangkok slums with Urban Neighbours of Hope.

As Athol Gill's death inspired Ross in exploring God's missional journey, may all of us who have benefited from particular aspects of Ross's commitment continue to discover the fire within that will be feet, voice and wings to the work of God's Spirit present among us and ahead of us in the whole creation – even though our feet must so often remain in the mud!

Introduction
Darren Cronshaw and Rosemary Dewerse

We are pilgrims, we are strangers,
we are orphans, we are widows,
Is there anyone who will shelter us in this land?
On the hard road, in a strange place,
needing comfort, feeling lonely,
Will we find a roof and a welcoming hand?

We're restless till we find our home in you, O Lord
Find our resting place in you.
A place we're never alone. A place where we are known.
May we find our home in you.

If we're hungry, if we're thirsty,
if we're shivering, if we're prisoners,
Is there anyone who will take us out of the cold?
If we're wandering like a lost sheep,
without shelter or direction,
Will we find the shepherd and sleep in the fold?

You are homeless and rejected,
and you send us into byways
Calling anyone who will take on what you went through.
Yet you call us to your mansions,
to your fireside, to your ballroom,
Will we come and celebrate living with you?

("Finding our Home", Ross Langmead, 1982)

Dr Ross Langmead, in his songs as well as his writing and teaching on mission, reflected the heart of God for mission from, with and in the margins. His deep and broad contribution as a missiologist and activist was, and still is, something that many of us appreciate and honour.[1]

Missional life and ministry

An early and significant research project Ross undertook was a survey of churches and needs in *The Western Suburbs Conference Report* (Baptist Union of Victoria 1978). In his research and advocacy he identified a disparity of resources allocated to the Western suburbs of Melbourne, and in response Ross and Alison moved into the South Kingsville manse just ahead of Benjamin's birth in '78 (followed by Kia in '80) to work with the local Baptists and became founding members of Westgate Baptist Community which was formed by three churches coming together. Ross served on Westgate's pastoral team 1980-1992 and remained an active member while teaching at Whitley. He is remembered especially for composing and leading songs that emerged out of local mission projects, important celebrations and the many challenges and hope of being God's people. He is also remembered for his teaching and work for justice, and for his practicality on the ground. Ross and Alison actively explored the nature of Christian Community in small groups with the many who came to join them in serving their neighbourhood. They were active in many arenas of parent and community life and embraced, along with their Community, whole new areas of friendship and sharing as Karen and Chin refugees from Burma (Myanmar) began to arrive at Westgate after years in refugee camps in Thailand and Malaysia.

Ross became the first lecturer in mission studies at Whitley College, the Baptist Theological College of Victoria in 1993, and later Director of the School of World Mission and Dean of the Theological School. As a missionary statesman, Ross was founding convenor and secretary of Australian Association for Mission Studies (AAMS) and convenor of the first AAMS conference in Melbourne in 2005,[2] the precursor to the conference this book draws from. His championing of missiology in Australia and his friendship with other Australian, Pacific and Asian missiologists, including many of the contributors of this volume, leaves us an example for thoughtful reflection and practice of mission.

---

1 These first few paragraphs of tribute draw on Darren Cronshaw, "Mission Studies Obituary – Dr Ross Oliver Langmead," *Mission Studies* 31:1 (Spring 2014), 7-8.
2 Proceedings of the first AAMS Australian Missiology Conference was published as: Ross Langmead (ed.), *Re-Imagining God and Mission: Perspectives from Australia* (Adelaide: Australian Theological Forum, 2007).

Ross' teaching and research interests included multicultural ministry, contextual mission, church in Australian society, ecotheology, justice, peace-making, interfaith dialogue, reconciliation, and incarnational mission. His research interests always overlapped with ministry passion. As a Victorian Baptist, Ross was actively engaged in reconciliation with Indigenous Australians, advocating for action on climate change, and supporting refugees especially Karen and Chin from Burma. He regularly taught in Myanmar because he was eager to teach in and learn from Majority World Contexts as well as Australia.

Yet of everything we have read or learned from Ross, we most appreciate his strong commitment to integration, holding together mission as word and deed, dialogue as conviction and openness, training as action and reflection, spirituality as action *and* contemplation, and reconciliation encompassing relationships in all directions – with God, with creation, in international peacemaking, and with others including indigenous and non-indigenous peoples.

One of our favourite paragraphs of Ross' writings came from an article on "theological reflection for mission." In it he encouraged grassroots engagement with places of the world that needed shalom but also made space for fostering reflection on our practice of mission and spirituality. He was a person of good news who realised mission drew him to areas in need of transformation, but he warned (and here are some of his words we return to often, for our own sanity and balance):

> If mission were all action, with no reflection, we would go off the rails. We would 'hard sell' the gospel, organise our way to being an international brand name, manage the church and cram every living moment with mission activity. But it's mission with mystery, and waiting is as important as outreach, listening as speaking, responding as pro-active planning. The reflective and meditative dimension of mission is central.[3]

Space for contemplation and worship were not optional extras for Ross as an activist.

Those who sang his songs will have experienced how the issues close to his heart overflowed into his song-writing – on radical discipleship, social justice, care for creation, inclusive community, authentic spirituality, and enjoying and sharing the grace and goodness of God. His song writing, as much as his other missiological

---

3   Ross Langmead, "Theological Reflection in Ministry and Mission," *Ministry, Society and Theology* vol.18 (2004), 25-26, accessible at http://www.buv.com.au/witness/entry/vale-ross-langmead; drawing on Donald Messer, *Contemporary Images of Christian Ministry* (Nashville: Abingdon, 1989); discussed previously in Darren Cronshaw, "Reenvisioning Theological Education, Mission and the Local Church," *Mission Studies* 28:1 (June 2011), 107, 91-115.

writing and teaching, embodies an attentiveness to God and the world, and to people on the margins.

Hospitality as a metaphor for mission

Whenever Ross was asked to summarise the essence of mission and identify what image or model was most helpful, he emphasised hospitality. In one of his final conference presentations at the International Association for Mission Studies in Toronto in 2012, which became an article published posthumously, he developed a framework for informing a theology of mission for refugees and argued that hospitality is the most appropriate metaphor for a theology of mission.[4]

As helpful background, he explained that the marginalised were at the centre of Jesus' life and teaching. Jesus promised that God's realm was good news for people persecuted for seeking justice (Matt 5:10) and for those who are poor, weeping or hungry (Lk 6:21). He commented on the parable of the sheep and goats and how that obviously connects to the marginalised lives of refugees:

> Only when serving those who are hungry, thirsty, sick, naked, imprisoned and foreigners – what better summary could there be of the extremities faced by so many refugees? – are the people of all nations worshiping God (serving Christ himself) and living into God's gracious realm (Mat. 25:31-46)[5]

Similarly, he reminded his readers of the proximity and need for hospitality of our "neighbour", drawing on another famous teaching passage of Jesus:

> If the command to love our neighbor is seen through the eyes of the story of the Good Samaritan (Lk. 10:29-37), the neighbor is clearly the friendless stranger [Bretherton], one who is beaten up and abandoned by the side of the road, or perhaps left for years in a refugee camp or left to drown on the high seas in a leaky boat.[6]

---

4   Ross Langmead, "Refugees as Guests and Hosts: Towards a Theology of Mission among Refugees and Asylum Seekers," *Exchange: Journal of Missiological and Ecumenical Research* 43:1 (2014), 29-47. The IAMS conference paper is accessible at http://rosslangmead.50webs.com/rl/Downloads/Resources/RefugeesIAMSAug12ShortPresentation.pdf

5   Langmead, "Refugees as Guests and Hosts," 35.

6   Langmead, "Refugees as Guests and Hosts," 36; drawing on Luke Bretherton, *Hospitality as Holiness: Christian Witness Amid Moral Diversity* (Aldershot: Ashgate, 2006), 139.

Moreover, to make another biblical connection that should be obvious Ross sang:

> In Jesus God was a refugee
>
> The pain of God has set us free
>
> In God we'll find our home.[7]

Mission has often been seen as centrifugal to other nations (as in foreign mission) or as incarnational and outward focused (as in the missional church), but there is also an attractive and inviting element to mission. The world is coming to the door of Western countries through migration and the only appropriate Christian response is to practice hospitality by welcoming migrants and refugees.[8]

Ross wrote that such hospitality, towards refugees, has ten dimensions:

1. Defense of human rights
2. Political action
3. Settlement assistance
4. Sanctuary
5. Being welcoming multicultural churches
6. Intercultural learning
7. Interfaith dialogue
8. Awareness of the ethics of welcome
9. Meals and personal friendship
10. Openness to a transforming divine presence.[9]

He expanded on these, for we need much more research and practice of each of them. An element that captures our imagination is seeing hospitality as "embrace" and allowing our hospitality to be mutually transformative. This is not just one-way ministry. Langmead quoted Anthony Gittins:

> It is fairly natural, and easy (at least in theory) to see the other as stranger, guest, outsider, needy, or outcast. But such astigmatism distorts, and may produce a theology of control, a 'magisterial' approach, and a tendency to indoctrinate.[10]

---

7   Langmead, "Refugees as Guests and Hosts," 34-35.

8   Mortimer Arias, "Centripetal Mission, or Evangelization by Hospitality," in *The Study of Evangelism: Exploring a Missional Practice of the Church*, ed. Paul W Chilcote and Laceye C Warner (Grand Rapids: Eerdmans, 2008), 429-30; discussed in Langmead, "Refugees as Guests and Hosts," 38.

9   Langmead, "Refugees as Guests and Hosts."

10 Anthony Gittins, "Beyond Hospitality? The Missionary Status and Role Revisited," *International Review of Mission* 83 (1994), 398; discussed in Langmead, "Refugees as Guests and Hosts," 45.

Colonial paradigms view mission as a one-way flow from the West to the rest, rather than fostering partnerships and collaboration in mission and learning. Terry Veling, in contrast, suggests that we have a lot to learn from marginal voices:

> The rabbinic tradition provides a strong legitimation and rich resources for supporting the interpretive activity of intentional communities whose voices sound out from the margins of tradition.[11]

Ross pointed us in this direction of listening to those on the margins of our tradition, to being attentive to what God is doing among people that the hierarchy or institutional powers or we in our pride ignore. Those voices include women, children, indigenous people, people with different abilities, people at different stages of faith or no faith, and people from diverse cultures and diasporas. These people do not often readily get a voice at the table of Western church and scholarship. In our research and practice of mission, we too – Rosemary and Darren – have been freshly challenged to learn all we can from the experience and insights of people on the margins. This is part of hospitality – receiving as well as giving.

Miroslav Volf describes hospitality as being like an embrace, with four movements:

- open arms in offer (or open our door),
- wait for free acceptance
- close arms in embrace (inviting others into our home to help them feel at home)
- and then open our arms again (and let the guest go).

Thus we welcome and embrace, but also release the person to be themselves and find their own new space.[12] This is an imagination-grabbing vision, about which we appreciate some final words from Ross' article on hospitality:

> If the churches in the "receiving" country catch the vision of mission as hospitality, strangers will become guests, and then hosts. Those without defenders in their old country will have advocates in the new. Those on the margins will, at least in faith communities, become "insiders" "at home". Our

---

11 Terry A Veling, *Living in the Margins: Intentional Communities and the Art of Interpretation* (New York: Crossroad Herder, 1996), 152; in Steve Taylor, "Baptist Worshp and Contemporary Culture: A New Zealand Case Study," in *Interfaces, Baptists and Others: International Baptist Studies*, ed. David Bebbington and Martin Sutherland (Milton Keynes: Paternoster, 2013), 305.

12 Miroslav Volf, *Exclusion & embrace: A theological exploration of identity, otherness, and reconciliation* (Nashville: Abingdon, 1996), 140-47; discussed in Langmead, "Refugees as Guests and Hosts," 45.

welcome will in some way reflect God's abundant welcome. We should not underestimate how countercultural this vision is, or how challenging it is to live out in a fearful and often selfish society.[13]

The third triennial conference of the Australian Association of Mission Studies

In October 2014 the Australian Association of Mission Studies gathered for its triennial conference in Adelaide. Participants came from most Australian states and capitals, and from New Zealand, Papua New Guinea, Zambia and Myanmar (Burma). The chair of the conference organising committee, David Turnbull, had come up with the inspired idea of having "Margins, Mission and Diversity" as the theme. He was mindful of the 2013 statement on mission from the World Council of Churches, "Together Toward Life: Mission and Evangelism in Changing Landscapes" but also very aware, as he wrote in the call for papers, that "mission has traditionally been to the margins but the time has come to consider mission from the margins also."

As we have already noted, Ross had been appreciating this truth for many years in this context and was very enthusiastic about the theme, which David discussed with him fully expecting that Ross would deliver a paper and be a key participant.

We invited Emeritus Professor Anthony Gittins, a colleague of Ross' in the International Association of Mission Studies (IAMS), and a writer he himself had engaged with, to be the keynote speaker. Like Ross, Anthony is one who not only writes about the gifts and challenges of margins, mission and diversity, but who lives and engages with it in his everyday life. We felt it was important to hear what this senior Roman Catholic anthropologist and missiologist had to say.

Before the conference could begin, Ross was gone.

The desire then grew to create within the program and beyond, activity by way of plenary and publication that would honour him, his passions and commitment. This book, gathering up papers that we believe resonate with Ross' priorities, and including the text of the public lecture held during the conference in his memory, is one result.

---

13 Langmead, "Refugees as Guests and Hosts," 39.

The book itself

Two of Tony Gittin's keynote addresses are reproduced here, with his permission. They consider the first two elements of the conference theme: theme, "Margins" and "Mission." "Standing Fast and Breaking Through: Challenges and Possibilities for Marginal Ministry" discusses a number of understandings and types of marginality before critically reflecting on the problems but more particularly the possibilities margins and marginal people offer to mission. Tony points out that Jesus himself was marginal by choice and by example and his second chapter explores this in more depth. In "Finding the Centre at the Margins: Renewing the Call to Mission" Tony describes the distinctions created within human societies across two intersecting axes, "insider"/"outsider" and "participant"/"non-participant," producing four quadrants representing possible social and cultural locations. He indicates which one Jesus occupied and argues that participants in mission today should operate from that same space.

Beyond these two chapters papers from the conference have been selected to complete this book, which honours the person who was Ross Langmead. Between them they model, display and discuss diversity, mindful of the margins and of mission. The voices include women and men, older and younger, people from across the theological spectrum and Christian traditions, people with greatly varying personal experience and cultural perspectives, and people based in Australia, New Zealand and Cambodia.

As a framework for the rest of the book we are drawing from a 2009 paper Ross himself delivered at a conference of the Aotearoa New Zealand Association of Mission Studies in 2009.[14] In it he considered the changing landscape of mission since the 1910 World Missionary Conference in Edinburgh, highlighting a number of points of continuity and discontinuity with the world of the early 20th century. He went on to speak of five areas challenging effective contextual mission in the Australian context in particular: indigenous reconciliation; a multicultural vision; mission in a post-Christian society; engaging the postmodern mind; and the Asian horizon.

This thinking was not entirely new. Ross had pondered most of these areas in a conference paper he presented in 2005 called "Rethinking Mission in Australia" and they would recur across the years in other writing also, sometimes grouped, sometimes

---

14   Ross Langmead, "Contextual Mission: An Australian Perspective" (Auckland: Paper presented to the ANZAMS mini-conference, 2009).

given sole focus in their own right.[15] The important thing to note is that while he spoke as a person with some authority to do so, born out of personal encounter as well as scholarly foresight, he approached each of these with the humble stance of a learner. Ross genuinely understood the importance of listening to the Spirit of Jesus Christ and of listening to others and the privilege and mutuality inherent in that. In choosing papers to fit the five areas we have been mindful of this commitment, especially because it is an integral stance and practice in marginal spaces and fundamental to incarnational missional endeavour.

The first of these further papers, "Finding Our Soul, Finding My Soul" charts the thinking and story of Rosemary Dewerse as she has sought to engage with justice with indigenous peoples in South Australia. Ross was deeply concerned that non-indigenous Australians in particular understand how diminished their hopes for a sense of home and mission in this place are until the journey of justice and reconciliation is being undertaken. He pondered this in an IAMS conference paper in Hungary in 2008 concluding that while the church has much to offer theologically, she has much to learn morally and practically.[16]

Four papers speak into Ross' belief in the importance of a multicultural vision for the church today, a vision he lived and breathed, spoke into, sang and wrote about for many years.[17] George Wieland, in "Communitas in Liminality," begins with a case study of a migrant New Zealand Chinese church alongside the story of Peter and Cornelius and challenges host churches to leave the comparative security of a perceived centre and join immigrant churches in liminal space, which is the place of potential transformation. Noel Connolly ponders what is needed for "Growing a Truly Multicultural Australian Catholic Church," drawing upon the history and theology of migration as he reflects. Samuel Chan and Kim Chan then detail something of the tensions created within migrant Asian communities with the birth of subsequent generations and dare to suggest to young people that they adopt the attitude of a missionary in "A Mission of the Second Generation (Australian Born Chinese) in South Australian Migrant Churches." A case study detailing a Uniting Church's story

---

15 Ross Langmead, "Rethinking Mission in Australia" (paper presented at the Australian Missiology Conference, 2005).

16 Ross Langmead, "Indigenous Reconciliation: What Can the Church Offer and Receive?" (conference paper presented at IAMS Balaton, Hungary, 2008); see also Ross Langmead, Transformed Relationships: Reconciliation as the Central Model for Mission, *Mission Studies* 25 (2008), 5-20.

17 For example, Ross Langmead, "The Multicultural Vision in Christian Mission," *South Pacific Journal of Mission Studies* 23 (April), 1-6; and "From Around the World" [song], 2006.

in "Becoming a Diverse Multicultural Church in Adelaide," by Elizabeth Vreugdenhil, offers insights into lessons learned and possibilities discovered when Anglo, Sudanese and Chinese people gather for worship.

Ross was very aware that church in a post-Christian society often struggles to embody a gospel that no longer defines people's worldview or figures significantly in their conversations, except perhaps in a negative way. He wrestled with this across his life, before the turn of the millennium and after.[18] Four chapters join his wrestling and offer possibilities for "the path of change."[19] In "But is it Church?" Karyl Davison delves into historical understandings of church, tracing a narrowing of views across time and calling for a necessary reclaiming of hospitality as missional church. Meanwhile Jasmine Dow invites renewed understanding of the Eucharist as both a prophetic act and a movement of embrace in "Where the Margins Meet." Mick Pope, in "Grappling for Christ," explores the impact of three Martial Arts gyms seeking to incarnate Christ in a community often left on the margins of both society and church. And in the fourth chapter Immanuel Koks calls for the reframing of Trinitarian theology to help us move from a "cult of normalcy" asking God to change *them* to a true appreciation of mutuality and the desire for God to change *us*. Immanuel is particularly interested in the implications of such a theology for those living today with disabilities.

The fourth area Ross saw as challenging effective contextual mission is that of engaging the postmodern mind. He called for careful understanding of difference as well as potential contribution. Here three chapters respond, beginning with Christy Capper's "A Mutual Understanding," which invites us to understand the issues and priorities of Gen Y and engage in "constructive narrative dialogue." Lewis Jones then explores the notion of common good and neutral ground in "There is No Public Square," pointing out that in a society that values tolerance, liberal truth, objectivity and pluralism, leaving little room for what it perceives to be the totalitarianism of religion, Christian mission needs to strive for a coherent and respectful community with a strong sense of its identity. Mark McConnell offers a very different perspective in his article "Indie-Rock and Mission," in which he asks how a music band "who are to Gen Y what U2 is to Gen X" might in fact be of help to the church.

---

18 Ross Langmead, "Future Church – Changing Patterns of Mission," in *Future Church: A Baptist Discussion*, ed. Ken Manley (Hawthorn, Vic: Baptist Union of Victoria, 1996), 45-49; Ross Langmead, "Not Quite Established: The Gospel and Australian Culture," *The Gospel and Our Culture* 14:3/4 (2002), 7-10; and Langmead, "Contextual Mission".

19 Ross Langmead, "Future Church" (song), accessible at http://rosslangmead.50webs.com/rl/songs.html

Ross was also very aware of the Asian horizon, born as he was to a mother who herself was born in Beijing and having himself spent some of his childhood in Hong Kong and adult years backpacking around South East Asia and later teaching in Burma. He called strongly for cooperation and a growing appreciation of what our Asian brothers and sisters can teach us about the gospel and mission.[20] The text of Ash Barker's public lecture in honour of Ross exhorts us to get engaged in the "new urban world," a world of cities increasing in size, along with their slums, not just for their transformation but for our own also. Scott Litchfield, living in Cambodia, offers us challenges and lessons for mission he has been discovering from the borderlands of South East Asia in "A World of Peripheries." Writing from Melanesia, Graeme Humble details careful ethnographic work done in search of themes for contextual theology for the Hula people and discovers in the process lessons for us all. Darren Cronshaw, Stacey Wilson, Meewon Yang and a number of senior Chin and Karen pastors bring their insights in this regard to within the borders of Australia where Chin and Karen refugees have migrated and live and worship in "God Called Us Here for a Reason." Finally, Pauline Kim van Dalen offers us a work of autobiographical theology from her story as a multiply marginalised Korean New Zealand woman, leaving us with questions for personal reflection.

You will discover that at the beginning of each section we have given Ross the first say. Because he was a man of many means of "speech" we will draw from his songs as well as his writings. In this way we hope to give you, the reader, a little more of a sense of this man who stood tall and strong in our mission studies community before drawing your attention to the writing and critical reflection of others.

Ross was passionate about empowering others. If he had been here he would have pointed far more quickly away from himself, but because this book is seeking to honour his wisdom as well as this particular passion of his, we offer both. We think doing so rings truer to the man.

---

20 Langmead, "Contextual Mission."

Margins and Mission

There is an increasing number…who see the link between mission on the margins and the cultural location taken up by Jesus.

Ross Langmead, "Not Quite Established: The Gospel and Australian Culture"
Gospel and our Culture 14.3/4 (2002), 10.

1. Standing Fast and Breaking Through: Challenges and Possibilities for Marginal Ministry

Anthony J. Gittins, CSSp.

The related words "margins" and "marginality" are polysemic and ambiguous, elusive and sometimes subtly shape-shifting, and by no means user-friendly to large numbers of people. Yet we must also note that what is problematic or offensive to some can be life-giving and wholesome, even attractive, to others. Jesus himself, our teacher and model, deliberately adopted a marginal lifestyle and lived for those who people who subsisted at the margins. But the phrase "comfortably marginal" would be a near-oxymoron; so we begin with a few clarifications of terminology and usage, lest we find ourselves creating more confusion than clarification.

Boundaries, Definitions and Margins

Thinking missiologically, we recall first that a **boundary** is a marker or dividing line serving primarily to separate but also thereby to connect, spaces or people; significantly, some boundaries are porous while others are impermeable, some hardly noticeable yet others patrolled and stoutly defended. Second, a **definition** is itself a form of boundary-creation identifying the limits or limitations, the edges that clearly exclude what, or who, is not clearly included. And third, a **margin** is an edge, but it also draws immediate attention to a centre, against which it is polarised and by reference to which it is defined. The word **marginal** – implicitly "hegemonic" because it rests on the perspective of the person at the centre – refers to something or someone judged unimportant, of minimal significance, and not included in the main part of something else; marginal people are by definition, incompletely assimilated into the mainstream, at the lower limits of someone else's standards of acceptability, and liminal. But how they become or remain marginal is also highly significant. And since the word *marginalise* in its verbal or adjectival form can carry very different connotations and denotations, we must distinguish imposed and chosen marginality, then active and passive marginality, and third, make a brief reference to liminality.

Imposed and chosen marginality

Socially speaking, marginality, as a condition of being judged far from the centre – of power, influence, orthodoxy or lifestyle – is most often a label attached to or a condition imposed upon people. By whatever social or religious agencies, such people are forced into a situation in which they are perceived – by those at the centres and sometimes even by themselves – as irrelevant, inferior, and often culpable. Most people do not choose the appellation "marginal." But some do; there <u>are</u> people who, for various reasons, actually choose to leave the centres of power and seek an "eccentric" or marginal status. Such are some dedicated individuals who leave their home or centre and seek the margins where other people – who are themselves "at home," such as it may be – live. Insofar as those who choose marginality dedicate themselves to "the other," they are outsiders in the new social world they enter and yet they can, with the gradual development of appropriate mutuality and the assistance of the insiders, become outsider-participants rather than outsider-nonparticipants, as is the case of tourists or sojourners (*nokri* in Hebrew). The outsider-participant, by contrast, would be the sociological stranger (*gēr* in Hebrew). This describes Jesus himself and his chosen ministry as a "marginal Jew," in the striking phrase of Biblical scholar John Meier,[1] and we will look more closely at the relevant dynamics later. Anyone who attempts to follow the example of Jesus as a disciple and intentionally takes up the daily cross in order to follow the Teacher, thereby chooses marginality. Yet relatively few seem to take this sociological identity seriously to heart as the major driving force of their ministerial and missionary lives. Nevertheless, it is critically important for us to mark the distinction between imposed and chosen marginality.

Active and passive marginality

Some people choose a marginal status or even lifestyle, while it is imposed on others, so we distinguish active and passive marginality. Active marginality may take the form of an initiative or a response. As an initiative it is essentially the same as chosen marginality. But there are some people, initially marginalised against their will, who manage to turn this imposition into a mark or symbol of new significance. One thinks of people who are gay or lesbian, bisexual or transgendered. By asserting their legitimate identity they gained wide currency in social service circles and beyond for the designation LGBT, thus removing some social stigma. More widely, active marginality describes what any counter-cultural Christian is committed to as a path to discipleship.

---

1   John P Meier, *A Marginal Jew: Rethinking the Historical Jesus*, 4 vols (New York: Doubleday, 1991-2009).

Classically, through Georg Simmel a century ago, and Everett Stonequist thirty years later, the social sciences described the marginal person as one who lives in two societies but is a member of neither, "poised in psychological uncertainty," in Stonequist's words.[2] But there is much more to marginality than this. In his influential 1995 book on Marginality, Korean-American Jung Yung Lee discusses its positive and negative aspects, and offers a helpful scheme or scale. He distinguishes between passive or even pathological marginality, and other, more productive forms. Because, as he says, "to be in-between two world means to be fully in neither[3]; therefore one must strive for more than becoming a non-being living in "existential nothingness."[4] There are, fortunately, a number of possibilities. One may learn to live "in-both," but only by affirming both one's roots and one's branches, one's original home and one's current domicile or sojourn. But it is also possible to live "in-beyond," which describes the perspective of the Letter to the Hebrews (13:14): "We have here no abiding city, but seek one which is to come," by keeping our focus on our ultimate destination and aspiration. Lee says that being "in-between" and "in-both", "embodies a state of being in both of [these] without either being blended. This new *marginal person* has the ability to be continuously creative."[5] Here is an insight to work with as we explore possibilities and challenges that are posed by margins, marginality, and marginalisation.

Economist and Social Justice theorist Amartya Sen speaks of active and passive "social exclusion."[6] The former happens when immigrants or refugees are "not given a usable political status," while passive exclusion happens "when there is no deliberate attempt to exclude,"[7] but poverty and unemployment create conditions that produce such exclusion. This can be just as harmful, as when the government or church has a responsibility to examine the effects – direct and indirect – of its policies or procedures but fails to do so. But whether missionaries create or perpetuate the marginalisation of people actively or passively is less important than the fact that to contribute to either form of marginalisation is immoral, reprehensible, and completely contrary to the spirit of the mission of Jesus. In short, social exclusion describes any process that causes people to be relegated to the social margins by depriving them – individually

---

2   Everett Stonequist, *The Marginal Man: A Study in Personality and Culture Conflict* (New York: Russell and Russell, 1961), 8.
3   Jung Young Lee, *Marginality: The Key to Multicultural Theology* (Minneapolis: Fortress Press, 1995), 45.
4   Lee, *Marginality*, 45.
5   Lee, *Marginality*, 62.
6   Amartya Sen, "'Social Exclusion': Concept, Application, and Scrutiny," *Social Development Papers*, 1 (Office of Environment and Social Development, Asian Development Bank, Manila, 2000).
7   Sen, "Social Exclusion," 14-15.

or collectively – of their basic human rights through discrimination on whatever grounds.

Positive and negative marginality (liminality)

One form of marginality well known to us all is *liminality*. From the Latin word for threshold or boundary, it describes a state of in-between-ness in a rite of passage as one is moved from a former social status to a new one. The middle or *liminal* stage places initiates in transition, identified with both danger and great promise. The intended outcome of the *liminal* stage is the re-incorporation of individuals as a group into society, but with a new, enhanced, social identity. As a transitional stage in a ritual, *liminality* is positive if it leads initiands to the intended outcome; but it becomes negative if it fails to do so, leaving an individual in an ongoing state of status-confusion, anguish, and often real and enduring fear. The theories of Arnold van Gennep and Victor Turner,[8] which built on the ethnography of *liminality*, are not beyond lively critique but have afforded us very useful language and concepts.

Marginality and *liminality* have similar connotations of the transitional, or an experience of something between life and death. Positively, the move needs to be towards life: working through a death-like struggle to a transformation of status and the beginning of new life such as experienced in the Rites of Christian Initiation. They move a person, via submersion and symbolic death-by-drowning, to emergence to a new life in Christ. Traditional initiation rites, the original focus of Victor Turner's studies, have a similar function, with particular emphasis on new life as both the ascription of a completely new status and incorporation into a new group. But if *liminality* emphasises the positive, marginalisation is most commonly used with negative connotations, signifying a gradual or dramatic fall from grace, a passage from life to social death. Yet while acknowledging the dreadful effects of imposed marginalisation, it is particularly important missiologically to identify the potential benefits of positive marginalisation, not only on the person who chooses it, but on the beneficiaries of that choice.

Margins: Problems and possibilities

An exploration of margins or boundaries discloses that they serve a triple function, each component of which has an essential purpose: to keep in; to keep out; and to serve as contact points, bridges, or meeting-places. To consider not only associated

---

[8] Arnold van Gennep, (1908) *The Rites of Passage* (London: Routledge and Kegan Paul, 1977); Victor Turner, *The Forest of Symbols* (Ithaca, NY: Cornell University Press, 1967).

problems therefore, but real pastoral possibilities, we might begin by noting that every person is situated in a particular place or centre that is itself defined in relation to an edge, boundary or margin. Each of us is a microcosm within a macrocosm, and we live in a series of microcosms nesting within their respective macrocosms. Our own body is a microcosm, a little world, bounded visibly by our skin and invisibly by our social space. This microcosm encapsulates something autonomous and sacred: our personal physical integrity. But the bodily or physical microcosm is not an isolate in total independence; it exists in relation to a macrocosm, a bigger world beyond the boundaries of the self, in which other entities and other persons exist.

Each person here constitutes an individual microcosm existing within the broader macrocosm that is the physical reality of this room. But if we were to start walking around blindly, we would either bump into each other, or blunder into a table or a wall. We exist, in other words, within a web of boundaries and margins. There are personal boundaries, visible and invisible, between each of us; and structural boundaries – brick walls and closed doors – between ourselves and the world beyond this room. If these are negotiated appropriately, we can hope to live with dignity and harmony. Then we can assume responsibility for maintaining our personal integrity, and encounter others – or "the other" – in a wholesome and mutually respectful manner. Then, boundaries or margins, personal and interpersonal, serve a positive function of protecting human dignity and enabling wholesome interaction. But whenever something or someone inhibits the appropriate negotiation of personal and social boundaries or margins, people's lives are endangered and their human dignity impugned. Then, either people exploit others' physical integrity by failing to respect mutual boundaries or margins, or they constrain or restrain others within spatial or territorial boundaries, as in a prison or custodial area. Then, boundaries become the locus of rank injustice and oppression.

According to "Together Towards Life" (TTL), the recent Statement on Mission of the World Council of Churches, "Mission has been understood as a movement taking place from the centre to the periphery, and from the privileged to the marginalized."[9] This common understanding located the missionary, the one who was sent, at the centre, and "the other" or the recipients of the message, as marginal. But TTL does not pursue a highly significant point: that one who moves from the centre to the margin is thereby now located at, or on, the margin itself. Instead, it implies, without further development, a unidirectional movement, as a result of which, the marginal,

---

9 "Together Towards Life: Mission and Evangelism in Changing Landscapes," (World Council of Churches, 2013), paragraph 6.

or marginalised person (which is not quite the same thing), becomes assimilated to the centre. Had the point been developed, there might have been a consideration of the reciprocal movement whereby the person from the centre now becomes marginal, in two possible ways. First, by "contagion" or stigma: simply by being located among the people designated "marginal" (as in "He eats with tax collectors and sinners"); and second, by now being marginal oneself, relative to the people who, after all, occupy the centre of their own world, which the missionary patently does not.

Paragraph 6 of TTL continues: "Now people at the margins are claiming their key role as agents of mission," noting that "there is a shift in the mission concept, from 'mission *to* the margins' to 'mission *from* the margins.'" This theme is then pursued and developed in Part Two of the document, and I have two thoughts about this.

First, to talk about margins and marginal ministry with any degree of relevance, we need to keep in the forefront of our minds that we do not simply minister "at the margins" or "to the marginalised." Such phrases as "the marginalised" or "the privileged" reduce people to a category and can depersonalise and even dehumanise them, as do phrases like "the homeless", "the poor," or "prostitutes." We cannot talk generically, because there are no generic people, only particular people: women, and men, and children. So our language needs to become sensitised to human persons as individuals and agents. "Homeless woman," 'unemployed man" or "marginalised people" is a more appropriate way of identifying our sisters and brothers. After all, ministry is, first and last, communication and relationship with real flesh-and-blood people, some of whom happen to be marginalised and to live, or subsist, at the margins.

Second, according to this categorisation, we ourselves are not typical of such people – though each of us here can probably identify some situations in which we are, or feel marginalised, relative to church or society. Therefore, the marginal ministry we undertake implies and entails outreach across – or indeed at – whatever margins or boundaries separate or insulate us from those who are. Before returning to the matter of whether, and in what ways we ourselves might be or become marginal, however, I need to pursue the line of reasoning developed in TTL, which contrasts "mission to the margins" with "mission from the margins," as a contemporary way of imagining mission.

Perhaps this pendulum shift – from "mission to" to "mission from" – is rather more dramatic than it need be. Is it too dialectical to be of the greatest practical and pastoral value? Perhaps a more analogical[10] or balanced relationship between "mission to" and "mission from" may be more realistic, more helpful, and better reflect the mission of Jesus. So to add "mission with" or "mission for" would highlight the mutuality or reciprocity mission in a global church requires. A most telling aspect of the mission and ministry of Jesus is that he came not simply *to*, but *for* and indeed to be *with* the recipients of the Good News; discipleship is essentially collaboration with Jesus and responsibility for living and spreading the Good News: co-responsibility or co-missioning. A radical shift from "mission to" to "mission from," might make us overlook the very locus of all missional encounters: at the margins themselves where I and Thou, Us and Them, can meet. We need to focus on those very margins, on marginal and marginalised people, and on the dynamics of the encounters taking place there, as people from both sides of the margin converge and are called to conversion.

Unquestionably, we who have often spoken too much and too loudly and listened too little and too late need to be converted and to listen to the voices from the margins, especially the cries of the poor. But to move from speech to silence is not to facilitate conversation. Only when both parties listen attentively and speak sequentially is there conversation and dialogue. So when paragraph 38 of TTL speaks of mission from the margins as "an alternative missional movement," my instinct is that it should be complementary rather than alternative. Then paragraph 45 says it very well: "Participation in God's mission follows the way of Jesus … characterized by mutuality, reciprocity, and interdependence." This avoids the polarisation or opposition between a variety of approaches to mission, as found, for example, in paragraph 41 which again opposes marginalised people "as recipients" *rather than* "active agents of missionary activity." Each person should strive to be <u>both</u> a giver and receiver. If the world were only composed of givers, there would be nobody to receive, and vice versa. But in a world of interdependence, we must become both.

Jesus: Marginal by choice and by example

Many people at the margins are victimised and treated sinfully. But others, including most conventional missionaries, are not forced into anything; and Jesus himself exemplifies one who chooses marginality precisely as a way of doing mission, and as an example to those who presume to follow his missionary example. It always strikes me as curious and deeply saddening that, having read the words of Jesus, "I was a stranger" (Mt 25:35), we have concluded they mean that we should in turn embrace

---

10 As in David Tracy, *The Analogical Imagination: Christian Theology and the Culture of Pluralism* (New York: Crossroad, 1981).

and show hospitality to the stranger. That is only one implication, but not perhaps the most important. Applying those other words of Jesus at the Last Supper, "As I have done, so you must do" (Jn 13:14), we would need to conclude that Jesus is asking us to be like him in *actually embracing* the role and status of a stranger ourselves. To show hospitality to the stranger is to identify *the other* as stranger and oneself as host – a position of superiority and control. The stranger, by definition, is in an inferior position and not at all in control, which is perhaps why we have been considerably quicker to opt for the role of host than to embrace the role of stranger.

The Letter to the Philippians is memorable here:

> Though he was in the form of God, he did regard his equality with God as something to be exploited, but emptied himself, taking the form of a slave, being born in human likeness. And being found in human form, he humbled himself and became obedient to the point of death – even death on a cross" (2:6-8, NRSV).

This is precisely to embrace the role and status of a stranger, the palpably marginal person! It seems to me that, as Jesus' disciples in mission, we have, as Jesus did, two tasks then: first, to acknowledge that we do indeed have a choice and that we must make that choice and undertake to learn to become marginal; and second, to focus on the margins themselves as places of exploitation, committing ourselves to an active marginal ministry with the people to be found there. The whole life of Jesus was poured out in marginal ministry or ministry at the margins. Born outside the city and raised in marginal circumstances – of poor, migrant, and later refugee parents – he lived continuously in such circumstances "with no place to lay his head" and at odds with authorities, and died outside the city, having been branded variously as out of his mind, a blasphemer, Beelzebul, and a criminal. But at every step, Jesus made choices in favour of the margins and the women and men caught there because of circumstances, economic, political or religious. This was his preferential option for the poor. He warned his disciples explicitly that to follow him would lead them to commit themselves to, for and with the dregs of society: people living either on the margins of society or even beyond, and even marked, as many were, by various forms of "social death." The Twelve, slow learners looking for privilege and seats on his right and left, were warned of the persecutions to come (Mk 10:30), and told that what he asked was "impossible" for them, but not for God's grace (Mk 10:27). As descendants of those disciples, we are instructed as they were, to reach out to the margins and the people who live there.

So much for the first task, to become people of the margins rather than cling to authority and status. The next chapter will elaborate on this and the second task, to work at and on the margins themselves, in relation to the centres of power and influence.

The missionary potential of marginal people

Having rather polarised "mission to" against "mission from" and strongly endorsed the latter, paragraph 38 of TTL makes an extremely important point: "Living on the margins however, can provide its own lessons. People on the margins have agency, and can often see what, from the centre, is out of view." But "people on the margins" cannot be restricted to those actively marginalised by social or religious forces; they also include people – like Jesus himself, and every disciple – who choose some form of marginal living as a faith commitment. Sociologically they are "strangers," the word Jesus applies to himself. Assuming that they remain with the people they serve over a considerable period of time and with due commitment to their well-being, they can make a unique contribution in half a dozen significant ways:[11] from the sharing of lives to the pooling of their respective resources; from a commitment of solidarity and moral support to a mutual opening-up of microcosms; and from mediating factional hostilities to forging real fraternal interdependence.[12] Engagement between people marginalised by circumstance and people who choose to become marginal – as outsider-participants in a world and community in which they can never and need not become fully assimilated or incorporated – can be life-saving literally and figuratively. As a missionary commitment, it creates a new space where, in encountering the other, we encounter a hitherto unknown and unrecognised face of God.

This brings us back to Jung Young Lee. An ever present danger is that we lose our bearings as we struggle at and with margins and marginalised people. Then we would become *liminal* in a negative or pathological way, leaving us "in-between" worlds, in his term. But if we are truly committed to Jesus' mission and the people we meet at the margins, we can learn to live integrated and healthy lives, as Lee says, "in-both" worlds. We must remember though, that as outsider-participants we cannot be fully "at home" with those in whose home we find ourselves – any more than we can ever become fully at home even when we return to the home we left. If we are intentionally marginal people for the Kingdom or Realm of God, we will come to realise that indeed we have here no abiding city. That, theologically, in Lee's term, is to live "in-beyond."

---

11 Anthony, J. Gittins, *Ministry at the Margins: Strategy and Spirituality for Mission* (Maryknoll: Orbis, 2002), 121-160.
12 Gittins, *Ministry at the Margins*, 135-141.

Bringing it close to home

As a result of the Royal Commission or Ecclesiastical Tribunals or Offices, no Christian can fail to be keenly aware and ashamed (by contact or implication) of the scandal of sexual abuse perpetrated on minors by ostensibly trustworthy adults, many of whom are professed Christians themselves. Because our topic is margins and marginality, I offer a word of reflection on this matter which is far from over and the consequences of which will be with us for many years, to fester unless they are healed. This abuse is of course, significantly related to the control of boundaries or margins, and the violent breaching of personal boundaries and bodily margins. A parallel can be seen in attitudes to refugees and migrants who reach or seek refuge beyond the margins of their own territory and at the borders of another nation.

As opposing forces threaten to create or perpetuate a devastating riptide in the church in which our faith flourishes and the world in which our survival depends, one current seems to be driving people to give up or walk away, to keep their heads down and turn inward – or perhaps to turn to prayer and the pious hope that the present multiples crises will pass and life will somehow return to "normal." This current is driven by desperation, fuelled by fear, and carried forward by cowardice, and many people caught in it can make no headway and are close to panic. But there another current that moves some people, not to desist but to resist and persist in their commitments to God and neighbor in the church and the world, to move forward with courage and conviction, and to look these crises straight in the eye. This one is driven by fierce faith and abiding hope in God's covenant, the Word incarnate in Jesus, and the Spirit who is within and around the chaos we experience.

Paralyzing fearfulness, panic-driven immobility, capitulating retreat are clearly not legitimate pastoral options for believers, any more than homophobia or xenophobia. So how to face the future remains a constant challenge. Legitimate answers must be sought and can only be found in specific contexts: generic bromides are no substitute for compassion that is incarnated in each of us and directed at real people.

Every person should learn – though some fail to do so – to identify and respect a range of margins: social, personal, interpersonal, religious or national; the list can easily be extended. Self-abuse, in whatever way we choose to understand that term, bespeaks a breakdown of *self* respect, just as the abuse of others, whether sexually, physically or by neglect, is a desecration of the physical or moral integrity of individuals or groups of people. The abuse of other things – of property, of space, of earth, air, fire or water

– is a social sin of structural proportions. Tragically, self-respect, mutual respect, and respect for nature are at a premium in many human communities and cultures today.

Respect for boundaries or margins however, is only part of our responsibility to each other. It must be balanced with committed outreach, engagement, and human contact. People must discover new ways to reach out, to encounter, to engage at their respective boundaries, in order to establish authentic human connections of appropriate intimacy. Then they can build amicable and loving relationships and create new communities, lest human society break down and people become isolated and antisocial. True intimacy is intrinsic to true humanness; and margins are precisely the points of contact between individual persons.

Christians, since we are talking in a particular context here, must identify various margins, understand their functions, and then learn whether, how, and under what circumstances to attempt to bridge or cross them, in order to connect with whoever or whatever is just on the other side. Those who lack such finesse will fail to honour or claim their personal integrity or to respect that of others. Then people may overstep appropriate margins, causing grave harm, or they may become so fearful of encounters that they withdraw and cower within the margins of their own little world. Our challenge today – and in the particular circumstances of this country and this place – is first to respect and then appropriately to cross or erase the boundaries or margins that mark our world and separate or segregate people who need each other. It is a huge challenge and it is vitally necessary that we meet it, as an expression of our faith, compassion, and solidarity.

Conclusion

The institutional Church in recent years has been thoroughly confused and compromised over boundary issues. People in positions of trust have violated others, and some still fail to understand the scandal, the sin, and the cost. Victims – by no means all of them "survivors" – have been betrayed and cheated. Appropriate sanctions have not been imposed, nor has adequate repentance been shown. Secretiveness and cover-ups have protected the guilty. A corrupt system operated by some authorities and hierarchy who closed ranks and refused to be accountable, hiding within the boundaries of clerical privilege, has re-victimised already damaged victims.

When the volcano erupted, chaos ensued, producing systemic breakdown of communication and trust, and deep anger with the realisation of how widespread was the breaching of personal boundaries. The outraged reaction on the part of the People of God including many clergy is producing a quite unchristian stalemate between bishops and clergy on the one hand and children and parents on the other. Meanwhile, seminarians and some clergy seem paralyzed, or appear to be running away, hiding, or determined never again to reach out, to encounter, to negotiate interpersonal margins in a loving and respectful way – all of which is a direct threat to the essential Christian ministry which is always a call to the margins, the interstices that separate and unite us, in order to heal rather than hurt, to connect rather that confront.

This behaviour is absolutely no remedy and will only produce a caricature of authentic ministry. We are not monads, but dyads, triads and communities; we need each other. Therefore we must, always and urgently, work toward the establishment or re-building of trust and credibility. As public agents, believers and ministers in our various ways, we must be seen to be committed to integrated and integral ministry which can be realised only when the inner and the outer aspects of life, the pastoral and the missional, the microcosmic and macrocosmic are appropriately related; and this always entails work on personal and interpersonal margins.

Trust can only be established through actual face-to-face encounters, which require that people meet at their respective bodily or territorial margins where they can reach out, make contact, and embrace, tentatively at first, but wholesomely and humanly. Mission is boundary-crossing outreach and pastoral encounters always demand willingness to allow boundaries to become places for mutual encounter rather than the site of enmity and mutual destruction. We are called both to stand fast in our integrity and to break through lines of division and margins of discrimination or privilege. For standing fast and breaking through are two sides of a single coin, the currency of ministry and mission.

2. Finding the Centre at the Margins: Renewing the Call to Mission

Anthony J. Gittins, CSSp.

Who's calling? Who's responding?

Mission, as we have reminded ourselves almost *ad nauseam* for 80 years, is not primarily our initiative or something we do as executives. Mission is God's work and we seek to respond to God's initiative as instruments of the *Missio Dei,* God's eternal mission, still very active in our own particular times and circumstances. We try to respond to both the suffering and the smiling faces of God, particularly as they appear in people who are broken, silenced and marginalised. This, after all, was the way of Jesus and his preferential option for the poor was not merely optional but an urgent imperative. Therefore it is for us a choice that we must choose, as he did. In the words of Jacques Dupuis:

> Jesus not only shows a 'preferential option' for the poor, he is not simply 'on their side,' but he personally identifies and associates preferentially with them: he is not simply 'for' the poor, but belongs to them and is with them.[1]

Since the word mission is simply one more inadequate label that we try to attach to the dynamic activity of God's outreach and inreach, it applies to humanity only derivatively or by extension. Because we are made in God's image, however, it can apply to us directly and legitimately if we are truly making the choices Jesus made. It is precisely as the incarnate one – Emmanuel, God-with-us, the human face of God – that Jesus shows each of us how to be authentically human. But if we are to grow towards the full potential of our humanness – *theosis* or divinisation (or, to use a vivid biblical word, restoration) – if we are to be restored rather than broken and unfulfilled, we must necessarily express, through our actions, that Godly dimension of our lives that we call missional.

Pastoral ministry has historically been identified with boundedness or the maintenance of an established community within fixed territorial boundaries, while mission has emphasised movement *beyond* or *across* boundaries. As a simplification there is some merit in this distinction, though pushed too far it evidently becomes false and

---

1 Jacques Dupuis, *Christianity and the Religions* (Maryknoll: Orbis, 2002), 30.

dangerous. But the common factor is the word "boundary" or margin and that is our present concern. It is one thing to approach a boundary or margin and then stop, and quite another to breach it. In each case the boundary or margin is seen negatively, as a barrier forbidding progress or challenging one, but boundaries and margins are themselves in-between places, ambiguous, liminal areas of both peril and potential: both dangerous and powerful. They are precisely the places where people exist, living or dying, subsisting or surviving, and are therefore the primary sites of the missional ministry of Jesus and therefore of all would-be followers.

Over forty years ago, Victor Turner was studying pilgrims and pilgrimages – but he might have been studying mission and missionaries. In a seminal article entitled "The Centre Out There," he identified a pilgrim's *need* to move from the usual centres of activity to find a more significant or relevant centre on the edge of previous experience, and, significantly, in the company of strangers who could become friends.[2] A century ago, sociologist Georg Simmel had spoken of adventure as something that starts on the very periphery of one's life but works its way to the very centre. In a classic essay he wrote that adventure is "a particular encompassing of the accidentally external by the internally necessary."[3] I understand the "accidentally external" to refer to whatever is contingent – geographical location or social circumstances – and the "internally necessary" to refer to an inner conviction, a sense of vocation or mission.[4] He speaks of "a characteristic daring with which [a certain kind of person] continually leaves the solidities of life," and the certain conviction of an "unknown and unknowable element in [that person's] life. For this reason, to the sober person," says Simmel, "adventurous conduct often seems insanity."[5] He then states that only youth are really adventurous and that "the old person usually lives either in a wholly *centralised* fashion, peripheral interests having fallen off and being unconnected with their essential life and its inner necessity; or the centre atrophies and existence runs its course only in isolated, petty details, accenting mere externals and accidentals."[6] Of course I disagree with this gloomy picture (painted by a mere 53 year old!), but do take very seriously the observation that certain people – not limited to the old – do live in a very centralised or self-focused fashion. The missionary movement calls young and old alike to seek the centre precisely *at the margins*. We may have been drawn into that movement,

---

2   Victor Turner, "The Center Out There: Pilgrim's Goal," *Journal of the History of Religions*, Vol 12/3 (February 1973).
3   In Donal Levine (ed.), *Georg Simmel On Individuality and Social Forms* (Chicago: University of Chicago Press, 1971), 187-98.
4   Levine, *George Simmel*, 191-192.
5   Levine, *George Simmel*, 194.
6   Levine, *George Simmel*, 198.

as Simmel suggests, when what began as peripheral worked its way to our life's very centre, becoming "internally necessary." Whatever our age or circumstances, however, our commitment must remain solid and serious.

I want to reflect on how Jesus lived and remained faithful to the mission, using him as an example of how mission and margins are intrinsically related, and of how commitment to both remains "internally necessary" for each of us today.

From paradise to brokenness: "The Cultural Flaw"[7]

The twin Genesis creation myths paint a picture of initial chaos transformed into order, in which God and all creation – including the man and the woman, created equal because equally in the Divine image (Gen 1:27) – live in peace and harmony; "and God saw that it was very good." In the second story we are first reminded of the mutuality or complementarity of the couple: together they are one body, one flesh (Gen 2:24). Disobedience by eating the fruit of the tree of the knowledge of good and evil brings disaster, disharmony and dispersal. And yet, there are two critically significant and positive by-products of the Fall: first, "The Lord God said, 'See! The man (that is, male *and* female) has become *like us*, knowing what is good and what is evil'" (Gen 3:22); and second, though the human ones were disgraced, they did not lose grace entirely. These two things, conscience and moral knowledge contain the potential both for humanity's greatness and its shame.

In the story, God brought animals and birds to the man and permitted the man to name them: "And whatever the man called each of them would be its name" (Gen 2:19). This power – astonishingly and gratuitously granted to the man – will also become a measure of human control and discrimination: it represents what I call the "cultural flaw." The ability to use language to name and define gives the user great power. "Light!" says God, and there <u>was</u> light. "I name this ship *Invincible*, says the Queen, and it becomes reality; "I declare you husband and wife" says the minister, and the words actually make it happen. This is the "performative" power of words, as J.L Austin demonstrated brilliantly in his classic *How to Do Things with Words*. But when we use language to define something or someone, we do so by distinction as well as by inclusion, as God separated light from darkness and sea from dry land. An Englishman is *not* a woman, English or not; *not* Australian or Vietnamese, and so on. I am *not* you; Catholics are *not* Protestants, and Christians are *not* Muslims. In the mythical

---

[7] This is dealt with in greater detail in Anthony J Gittins, *A Presence That Disturbs: A Call to Radical Discipleship*. (Ligouri, MO: Liguori, 2002), 94ff.

harmony of paradise there was inclusion and a community of "we"; after the Fall there was exclusion, confrontation, discrimination, and polarisation. By identifying oneself as the norm we can then identify others as abnormal. This is dangerous and demeaning. If I am a literate, white, British, Catholic, I can too quickly label others as illiterate, non-white, non-British or non-Catholic, thereby defining them negatively, where identifying someone as an oral, Chinese-American Presbyterian would be both more correct and more respectful, but we often define other by assumed deficiency as a matter of course.

Every culture and language, by naming and taming, labeling and bringing under verbal control, distinguishes, separates, opposes and excludes every bit as much as it includes, joins, or harmonises. God's multiform and diverse creation is good, but the cultural flaw is the perverse tendency to see difference through the distorting lenses of discrimination, distinction, dissimilarity, divergence, discord or disparity. In their native Persia, the *magi* were revered as the most influential and respected people; by their neighbors the Jews, they were defined as foreigners, idolaters, and both ignorant and contemptuous of God's ways. The Law served to mark and maintain the boundaries between them, lest Israel and its people became contaminated and fell from grace.

Culture is what humanity does to the world in which it lives and cultures produce, to some degree, the sundering of nature, creating the very separation and division that Genesis warned about. Explicitly or not, from the raw materials in Genesis and the gospels, from "have dominion" or "be masters" (Gen 1:28), from "the two become one body" (Gen 2:24) and from "what God has joined together, humans must not separate" (of Mk 10:9 and Matt 19:6), human cultures have remade the world and often ridden rough shod over the earth and its people. As soon as "We" is split, ruptured, riven and then re-named as "me" and "you, "mine" and "yours" or "us" and "them," the cultural flaw or tendency to reconstruct by deconstructing, and to advance by avoidance or competition rather than encounter and collaboration, is revealed.

Four quadrants

#1 Insider Participants	#3 Outsider Participants
#2 Insider Non-Participants	#4 Outsider Non-Participants

In order to create and maintain an inner identity or social order, a culture or community will define itself first by drawing a real but vertical line between itself and the other, so that "insiders" are clearly distinguished from "outsiders," natives from foreigners. In some cases the line may be as concrete as the Berlin Wall or the architectural monstrosity that forms the border between USA and Mexico, but it may also be a natural feature like the sea or a mountain range. In other cases the line may be invisible but no less real, marked for example by differences of language, ethnicities or cultures within the borders of a single nation, as in this country and many others. The more porous the line, the more likely it will have both a conjoining and a separating function; the less porous and the more tightly patrolled, the more its exclusionary function becomes evident.

Within the "insider" community itself, every society draws another line, horizontal this time, sometimes very visible and sometimes less obvious but no less real. This line separates "insider participants" from "insider non-participants"; and different societies create and maintain it in such a way that it divides these into two equal or unequal groups. In some cultures, the "insider-participants" are the majority, while the minority, substantial or not, are "insider non-participants."

If that horizontal line were projected to cut across the vertical line, it would create a figure of four quadrants. Top left (#1) would be "Insider Participants" and bottom left (#2) "Insider non-participants." Bottom right would be "Outsider non-participants" (#3) and top right, "Outsider-participants" (#4). The diagram illustrates this social construct, created by the insiders and – implicitly but very dangerously – from the patriarchal perspective, two facts that are of enormous importance for our understanding of mission.

Human cultures are patriarchal. There is no record of a truly matriarchal culture, in which women alone would exercise authority and control and men would be subordinated. One may think of a "default matriarchy" in extreme and atypical circumstances (the men are all away at war, deported, imprisoned or incapable), or indeed of matrilineal societies that constitute about 16% of the world's cultures. Matriliny, however, is about tracing descent and some privileges through the maternal line and not about the control of authority. Moreover, even though there may be some very high status women in a society (like a Queen Mother), men still exercise authority, though it is the brother rather than the husband of the influential woman. Sadly the truism holds universally: "It's a man's world." Accounts of true matriarchies are thoroughly discredited by academic anthropologists. Even when women do occupy the pinnacle of power, they become, in traditional societies, "sociological men": they must be beyond childbearing age, and can sometimes become the sociological father (*pater* rather than *genitor*) of children born to women obtained as their fictive wives. This is rare but real. I lived in such a culture in Sierra Leone. It is attested long before the gay marriage question arose.

Turning to the diagram, quadrant # 1 is occupied by the holders of authority who, in principle, are adult males. Some have moral and/or legal authority, predominantly at the domestic or local level and some have the authority associated with public law-keeping, such as military or religious figures. These are the "participant insiders", VIPs responsible for the maintenance of domestic and public order.

Quadrant #2 consists of the people regarded in a particular society – by, of course, the VIPs or "number ones," and there will be variation here from one society to another – as expendable, useless, or without authority within the community. There are three primary groups: first, the immature (the as yet unborn, infants, and children); second, those regarded as deviant (physically, mentally or morally); and third, women. Some of these "have their uses" as is sometimes said: the unborn ("non-viable") can be brought to term, be born, and grow to maturity; infants (literally, "those without language") can acquire language; and children ("those lacking sexual identity") can become sexually mature adults. Likewise, criminals might reform, and some others, deemed "deviant," may become rehabilitated. But those who do so can only graduate into quadrant #1 if they are, or become, adult males. Throughout history, women have never – or only very rarely and under socially prescribed conditions – been able to cross from quadrant #2 to quadrant #1. They do, of course, have a place within the domestic sphere, but their primary function is considered to be their contribution to the honour of their menfolk, for they cannot accrue honour for themselves. Women are also deemed dangerous, however, because they may bring shame upon their menfolk and for this reason they must be controlled and kept in their place.

Contemporary instances of so-called "honour killings" exemplify this social fact perfectly: men are in control. (This is not to say women are totally powerless, as every woman, and some men, are well aware, but to pursue this here would take us too far afield). In short, women are confined within, or certainly on the margins of, their quadrant, for the simple reason that they can never become men.

There is one other group identifiably in quadrant #2: "non-participating males." This would include everyone, even able-bodied men, who contribute nothing whatever to the common good; they are effectively social parasites. It is important to identify such people because they can, and do, exist universally. Unlike many women, who live thankless and unacknowledged lives of service, or some of those identified as "deviant" or with other disparaging names – who are not capable of contributing more – these non-participating men are a burden and a bad example.

This portrayal – especially my identification of many women and other "non-participants" – may seem bleak or even cynical but it is simply an attempt to sketch *"la condition humaine,"* the cultural lot of people throughout history and across cultures: it is the "cultural flaw," the 'original sin', the universal cultural bias, Its existence or reality poses a direct challenge to anyone committed to the Christian mission.

The two quadrants on the right side of the diagram contain the people – seen as such, of course, from the perspective of the insiders – as "outsiders."

In quadrant #3 they are identified as "non-participating outsiders." In those cultures whose boundaries or borders are non-porous and whose members are extremely xenophobic, there may be virtually no such people, They are either irrelevant or simply unknown. Even today, there are some small social groups virtually cut off from contact with or concern about who or what might exist beyond their own little world, but in today's globalised world there are three categories that deserve mention. One includes outsiders who are social parasites and perhaps transients. A second category is tourists who pay their way. Most tourists are clearly non-participating though in the sense that their purpose is entirely selfish if relatively harmless. They may be said to be important contributors to local economies but that is certainly not their *raison d'etre*: they arrive, remain, and leave, entirely on their own terms. A third category we can identify as unwanted outsiders: invaders, imperial agents, or interfering busybodies, including, sadly but historically, some missionaries.

In these days of short mission trips this raises a question: given both the good intentions of those who take such trips and the patent fact that they are outsiders to the people they seek to encounter, how do the insiders perceive them? It takes time to be granted the status of "outsider participant" and such status is ascribed rather than simply achieved. So, what is the social identity of are those undertaking short "mission trips," largely on their own terms? Are they outsider participants or outsider non-participants? And what are the implications here?

We now look more closely at quadrant #4: "outsider-participants." Their specific purpose is to contribute – *precisely as outsiders and with their particular perspectives and the gifts they bring* – to the well-being of the insiders, especially the "nobodies" or "number twos" – the "non-participant insiders." Such people can become their champion when many insider-participants exploit or ignore this underclass. In quadrant #4, the operative words – "outsiders" and "participant" or "participating" – are held together in tension, as each component contributes something very particular to the interaction between insider and outsider, "us" and "them." Sociologically, the classic outsider-participant is the person initially identified by the insiders as one of "them" (a rank "outsider") but who, through a discernible and chartable process, passes, by structured stages – identified as preliminal, liminal and postliminal – to a new status. No longer simply "the outsider," nor an interloper or tourist, they now have the new ascribed sociological status of "stranger."

"The stranger" here, is different from the sojourner or bird-of-passage and now has the status of permanent resident, and as such fulfills prescribed and appropriate roles that are both clearly delimited and structurally and socially different from any role or status occupied by the insiders. Biblically, this is the stranger or "resident alien" (gēr), who has specified rights and duties, quite different from the biblical *nokri*: the sojourner or transient, who is accorded safe passage but who must not tarry and who has no permanent status within the community. Would-be strangers or resident aliens (gēr) cannot force or foist themselves on the community and must of necessity pass through the period of trial and testing before becoming accepted by the host community. One very significant reason for the insiders' caution is that although the stranger's contribution can be life-giving for the community, experience shows that strangers can also be deadly. ("I fear the Greeks bearing gifts" is the well-known opening line of Virgil's *Aeneid*). Both the insiders and the stranger must, for a long time, act with caution. The stranger lives in a state of some ambiguity precisely because they are not entirely integrated, are never an insider, and are thus inherently marginal. Yet, to repeat, the potential of the ambiguous or marginal stranger is enormous.

In paragraphs 70 and 71 of the recent Statement on Mission from the World Council of Churches entitled "Together Towards Life" (TTL) it is worth noting that the stranger is identified with someone from outside, but not with ourselves as the outsiders in other communities.[8] The paragraphs assume that "we" are the insiders and "they" are the outsiders and urges us to treat them, the migrants, with kindness and respect. This is commendable, appropriate, and quite biblical, as far as it goes. But it does not go far enough because it does not go as far as Jesus went. Paragraph 71 identifies God as the host and ourselves as guests, invited into God's mission, but Jesus went much further, identifying his own *kenotic,* self-emptying role and status: "I was a stranger," said Jesus (Matt 25:35). Because he became a stranger himself, this puts Jesus in quadrant #4 or on its margins, whereas, if he were only and always the host, he would be only and always in quadrant #1. This has profound implications for his way of doing mission and for our way of imitating him.[9]

The mission and ministry of Jesus the stranger

We can briefly explore the mission and ministry of Jesus specifically as an outsider-participant, and as an example to anyone who aspires to follow him in being committed to God's mission.

It is important to differentiate between "host" and "guest" or "stranger." The host is always the person with superior status, even through the guest may be very distinguished and, in other circumstances, the social equal or superior. But the host, specifically as host, is in control and holds authority and power. Host and guest constitute a dyadic pair: like knife and fork or night and day, each one completes the other. There can be no host unless there is a guest, and *vice versa*. In this dyad, the host is socially superior.

There is another dyad, however: host and stranger. In fact, in many languages, the word for "stranger" or "guest" is one and the same word but its referent is evidently two very different social statuses. All we need do here, is reflect on how much more congenial it is to be treated as a guest than as a stranger. The English word "guest"

---

8 "Together Towards Life: Mission and Evangelism in Changing Landscapes" (World Council of Churches, September 2012).

9 See Kosuke Koyama, "'Extend Hospitality to Strangers' – A Missiology of *Theologia Crucis*," *International Bulletin of Missionary Research* LXXXII (1993), 283-295; Anthony J. Gittins, "Beyond Hospitality? The Missionary Status and Role Revisited," *Currents in Theology and Mission* (1994), 164-182.

connotes one who is treated much better than the "stranger" would be. The stranger may be ignored or treated disrespectfully, unlike the guest who will be pampered and indulged – at least for a relatively short time. But no community can treat an outsider as a guest indefinitely; unless that person moves on quite quickly the host's tolerance will fade as the resources are stretched or run out. Unless the guest leaves, he or she must contribute to the common good, which necessitates a change of social status from privileged "guest" to far-from privileged "stranger" who must manifest vulnerability, willingness to learn and to reciprocate, and the patient endurance of continual scrutiny for as long as it takes the community to determine his or her acceptability as an outsider participant to the community. A stranger is not self-defined: that social identity is conferred on an outsider by the insiders. So how does this shape our understanding of Jesus as a marginal stranger and ourselves as not simply hospitable hosts (and therefore in a superior position) but actually becoming strangers ourselves (and therefore neither in total control nor in a superior position)? As Henri Nouwen wrote:

> Being poor and a stranger is what Jesus invites us to, and that is much, much harder than serving the poor. The unnoticed, unspectacular, unpraised life in solidarity with people who cannot give anything that makes us feel important is far from attractive. It is the way of poverty. Not an easy way, but God's way, the way of the Cross.[10]

Jesus: marginal by circumstance and by choice

To identify events surrounding his birth is to underline a series of circumstances that place Jesus very far from the norm, the normal or the ordinary. The Incarnate One of God, begotten not conceived, is born "on the road," beyond civilization's margins, among animals rather than human society, and welcomed by angels, shepherds and magi – three of the most abnormal or marginal categories of beings imaginable. The recipients of the angels' message were not the insiders – the Chief Priests or King Herod – but those judged by them as unclean and irreligious (shepherds) or unclean and idolaters (the Magi).[11] The story continues with death threats and flight-by-night, and this is only the beginning. Jesus' end is no less marginal: again he is outside the city walls and crucified as a criminal blasphemer – a classic "outsider non-participant" from the perspective of the "Number Ones," the religious and civil authorities.

---

10 Henri J. M. Nouwen, *The Road to Daybreak: A Spiritual Journey* (New York: Doubleday, 1988), page unrecorded.
11 Scott Hahn sketches a helpful vignette of shepherds, angels, and Magi, in *Joy to the World: How Christ's Coming Changed Everything (And still does).* (New York: Image, 2014), 107-125.

If Jesus was marginal and marginalised by circumstance, he was no less marginal by choice. An itinerant preacher and teacher with no official credentials, he associated not only with people who were patently "non-participant *insiders*", but with "non-participant *outsiders*" like the Syrophonecian or Samaritan women and other "lost sheep" beyond the House of Israel. The very people he chose as his closest companions were largely rough and ready, far from people of probity, and so numerous and motley a crew as to bring ridicule on his ostensible status as a rabbi, since no self-respecting rabbi would ever have had more than two or three disciples at one time – and they would have been intelligent, focused, and definitely upright people: "number ones." Apart from saying that he had no place to lay his head – even less so than foxes or birds – he did not aspire to respectability as defined by religious or civil authorities and in fact challenged the leaders' understanding of legitimate authority and appropriate status and power. He left the centres and chose the margins, as he challenged and sometimes condemned the behavior of people at the centres while distinctly favouring the people at the margins. So much so that he was publicly criticised because "he eats with tax collectors and sinners." Looking his accusers straight in the eye, he affirmed their judgment, as much as saying, "Yes! And so should you." I think we need not gild the lily here, or romanticise; Jesus was a marginal man, but he was also very much one who participated, as an outsider, among and with the insiders.

Jesus: a double focused ministry

The mission and ministry of Jesus was to reach out and embrace everyone. Although his initial outreach was to "the lost sheep of the House of Israel" – whom scholars now identify as every Jewish person, including both Israel and Judah, since they were all living at a time of confusion, struggling faith, a history of being scattered in exile, and God's apparent dilatoriness – before long (and pointedly, with the urging of the Syrophonician woman) his net was thrown as wide as geographical and chronological constraints would allow. Given this inclusiveness, though conscious of the "preferential option for the poor," which he identified as God's own attentiveness (Psalm 34s "God hears the cry of the poor"), we can identify his outreach by superimposing or mapping it on to the diagram of the four quadrants. If the itinerant ministry of Jesus the stranger places him consistently along the margins that both connect and separate the insiders and outsiders – and given the palpable fact that he was considered marginal, an outsider, and even mad by his peers – we can see that his first outreach starts from the vantage point of somewhere in quadrant #4, and is directed diagonally, to the people in quadrant #2 (often called simply "the crowds" [ochloi] or "the poor" [ptochoi]).

John Dominic Crossan aptly calls them "the nobodies," and they consist precisely of: the immature (children and infants); the deviant (crippled, sick, possessed, tax-collectors, prostitutes and sinners); and, pointedly, the largely invisible women, socially and religiously speaking. (We recall that the women and children were not counted with the 5000; that when Jesus was in conversation with the woman at the well, "the late-arriving disciples were astonished that he was talking to a woman, but nobody asked why" (Jn 4:27); and that not a single woman in the gospels is given the title of "disciple."[12]) Crossan says that Jesus surrounded himself with a crowd of nobodies – and indeed called his disciples to accept that appellation themselves.

TTL paragraph 45 is good here. Having spoken in the previous paragraph of our participation in God's mission of "deconstructing patriarchal ideologies," it says that God's mission "entails the restoration of right relationships between God and humanity and all of creation" by "following the way of Jesus, who came to serve, not to be served, who exalts the lowly, and whose love is characterised by mutuality, reciprocity and interdependence." This is precisely the *kenotic* ministry of the outsider-participant.

Jesus also has a second, simultaneous outreach, however, directed laterally or horizontally, to those who occupy quadrant #1. They are the "number ones," or those whom Jesus sometimes refers to as "the first," warns that they will be "the last," and excoriates as "the haves" in Luke's addition to the Beatitudes: "Woe to you who are rich, who have your fill, who laugh, and of whom the world speaks well" (cf Lk 6:24-26). In the diagram they are identified as those men in authority or those who wield power: teachers, police or military forces and, in Jesus' case, civil and religious authorities.

If, in approaching the "nobodies," Jesus is attempting to restore them to society, then in approaching the "number ones" he is reproaching them insofar as they exclude and oppress the "nobodies" in the name of the emperor and even in the name of God. "Unless you turn, change, repent," and become as little children (obvious "nobodies"), you will not enter the Kingdom of God" (Matt 18:3). TTL paragraphs 37-40 focus on this, but emphasise only the advantages of quadrant #1 ("access to systems that lead to one's rights, freedom, and individuality being affirmed and respected") and only the disadvantages of quadrant #2 ("exclusion from justice and dignity"). Because Jesus actually chose the margins and a marginal lifestyle, we must try to understand its own advantages or potential. TTL 38 does acknowledge some of this: "People on the margins have agency and can often see what, from the centre (quadrant #1), is out

---

12 The only woman identified by the feminine form of the word disciple (*mathētria*), is Tabitha in Acts 9:36.

of view. Paragraph 37 notes that "Jesus relates to and embraces those who are most marginalised, *in order to confront and transform all that denies life*" (which would put the blame on those in quadrant #1), and 39 recognises that "marginalised people have God-given gifts." Yet it is not only those marginalised by others who have gifts of their own, but those who, like Jesus, actively seek and embrace the margins and the people who live there.

Paragraph 41 boldly admits the imperialistic style of some missionary approaches, stating that "mission from the centre is motivated by an attitude of paternalism and a superiority complex"; but either this fails to acknowledge that people at the centres *are able* to use their position – like St Francis – deliberately to move from the centres to the margins and become examples of real missionary discipleship, and/or it paints everyone with high social status or *cachet*, as incapable of personal conversion. True, there is no way for people who protect their position at the centres of power and influence to participate in the Kingdom, unless they move, from the centres they currently occupy, to the margins they currently defend and protect. But that must always remain a possibility, as paragraph 33 affirms: "The cross calls for repentance in the light of misuse of power and use of the wrong kind of power."

We have identified two distinguishable margins: first, between quadrants #1 and #2, the participant and non-participant insiders, and then between the insiders and outsiders. The centre of mission is always at the margins, wherever they may be found, and those who refuse to move, not simply to the margins but specifically to engage with those who live there, are, says Jesus, "not worthy," including "whoever prefers father or mother to me," and whoever does not take their cross and follow me" (Mat 10:37-8).

Mission in the Spirit of Jesus

I want to finish by reflecting that some of the distinctions commonly found in missiological writings may be rather too arcane and abstract for non-academics striving to follow Jesus. Terms like *kerygma, koinonia, diakonia* and *leitourgia*, or even *proclamation, witness, dialogue* and *liberation* can be rather forbidding. So I offer a much simpler – even perhaps simple-minded – way for us to approach mission in the spirit of Jesus himself; a way for us to emulate his own very practical pastoral approach and something that anyone, young or old, academic or not, can attempt. The four elements that constitute what I understand as integral evangelisation as lived by Jesus seem both to embrace his whole ministry and, as he himself did, to bring God's eternal mission down to earth. They are *encounter, table-fellowship, foot-washing* and *boundary-crossing*, and if "integral" or "integrated" is opposed to "partial" or "disintegrated," then, like Jesus, we must attend to each and every one, and not simply pick and choose.

Encounter. One of Viktor Frankl's aphorisms was, "to love, you must encounter." This is precisely how Jesus lives his mission: he encounters real people, one by one, excluding nobody and including everybody. Because there are no generic people, it is impossible to love people in general. One cannot love "the poor" or "the disenfranchised," because one cannot love a category, only a person. So, as I reflect on the encounters of Jesus, their extent and authenticity, I am left to ponder: whom do I encounter and whom do I avoid? What is the quality of my encounters: casual, rushed, perfunctory? Whom do I never encounter, since they live on the margins of society – the very margins I avoid? And how do I measure up to Jesus in this respect?

Table-fellowship. In recent years, many scholars have identified this as the most important single reason for Jesus' death. He chooses to eat with all the wrong people, at all the wrong times, and in all the wrong places, flouting religious rule and convention, and practicing "reverse contamination." Rather than being contaminated by other people's putative pollution, he contaminates the world, as it were, with his own holiness and wholesomeness. That accusation, that "he eats with tax-collectors and sinners" (Mk 2:15-17) not only fails to deter him, but serves as a rallying call for anyone who would follow him – even to Jerusalem and to death. Jesus knows that you must eat with two kinds of people; not only your friends but – if you hope ever to become friends – with those from whom you are currently alienated. So, with whom do I eat and whom do I avoid? With whom do I like to be seen, and who would I consider an embarrassment? And how do I measure up to the practices of Jesus? An ecclesial policy that drives a wedge into the community of "us" who share "one Lord, one Faith, on Baptism," judges and condemns people in broken marriages, or members of other Christian denominations as "them," and then excludes them from the Eucharistic table in the name of the one who excluded nobody, is particularly difficult to fathom and shameful to experience.

Foot-washing. One of the greatest challenges to Peter and the Apostles was Jesus' example at the Last Supper. Having washed Peter's feet, thereby ensuring that his own head was lower than Peter's – a patent and palpable act of self-abasement – Jesus said unequivocally that unless the Twelve did the same in relation to other people they could not remain his disciples. So, whose feet do I wash, literally or figuratively? Whose feet would I never think of washing? And whom do I expect to wash my feet? How do I treat people in service industries – caregivers, hotel maids, bus drivers or supermarket workers? When Pope Francis washed the feet of a dozen people on Maundy Thursday last year and this, his response to those who were offended because some of the feet were not priestly, male, or even Christian, but the feet of women and Muslims was that he was only doing what Jesus commanded. This, of course, failed to satisfy a number of pious people.

Boundary-crossing. Finally, we return to where we started, perhaps, in the words of T.S. Eliot, "to know the place for the first time."[13] Jesus' entire life was spent in encountering and transcending boundaries and margins, in order to encounter, embrace, and restore those who existed there. Bad theology persuaded many that this was God's will or their own fault, and a central component of Jesus' mission was to identify and expose bad theology. Boundaries and margins offer opportunity as well as danger, but Jesus, never cowed by danger, used them as a way of including the excluded and showing God's love and concern by putting his own life on the line. He has set the bar very high for us, but not impossibly so. He warned the Twelve that for them, his call to discipleship was impossible, but all things are possible with God (Mk 10:27), and for those who trust, follow, and, by God's grace, remain faithful.

---

13 T.S. Eliot, *Little Gidding*, part 5.

A. Indigenous Reconciliation

Lord, let me see, see more and more:
See the beauty of a person, not the colour of the skin,
See the faces of the homeless with no one to take them in,
See discouragement because she'll never win,
See the face of our Lord in the pain.
Lord, let me see.

...

Lord, let me learn, learn more and more:
Learn that what I know is just a speck of what there is to know,
Learn from listening to my neighbour when I'd rather speak and go,
Learn that as we live in faith and trust we grow;
Learn to see, hear and care, with our Lord.
Lord, let me learn.

...

Ross Langmead, Extract from "Lord, let me see" (1981)

3. Finding our Soul, Finding my Soul: Walking the Long Journey of Reconciliation in Australia

Rosemary Dewerse

This chapter discusses the first area Ross Langmead highlighted for effective missional engagement in this contemporary context: indigenous reconciliation. It explores where the roots of injustice toward the indigenous peoples of Australia have come from and how they have played out, before considering how one might live in a way that seeks reconciliation. The author's own personal story of working with local Indigenous leaders, and one in particular, is told to illustrate her journey toward finding her soul in this land.

In 2009 Ross Langmead delivered a paper at a symposium held by the Aotearoa New Zealand Association of Mission Studies. In it he discussed five areas the church needed to address if "Australian Christians are to engage with their contemporary context." The first area he highlighted was that of needing to work on reconciliation with indigenous peoples. He said:

> A fundamental aspect of the Australian context is that we are a nation founded on an unacknowledged invasion and appalling treatment of the Indigenous peoples. I'm not sure that the average non-indigenous Australian Christian appreciates how deeply this affects who non-indigenous Australians are and whether they can feel at home in the Australian continent…I agree with Norman Habel that Australia will only find its soul as a nation when the long journey of reconciliation is taken.[1]

These words, which I heard in person, have stayed with me.

As a Kiwi who has been living in Australia since 2012, my observation is that this journey is one most individuals I meet are still needing to take, and certainly the nation as a whole. Aboriginal peoples are still waiting to be named in the Constitution of Australia and the government's Intervention in the Northern Territory, carried out by the army in 2007-2008 and set to continue via the Stronger Futures Policy until at least 2022, has created more scars on an already scarred landscape. Reconciliation on many levels seems a distant dream. According to Ross' logic this constrains the ability of Australian Christians to engage with their contemporary context.

---

1 Ross Langmead, "Contextual Mission: An Australian Perspective" Auckland (October 2009).

In 2013 my family and I took part in a workshop led by Australian Children's Laureate, Boori Monty Pryor, a Birri-gubba/Kunggandji man from Queensland. When my husband commented that it was great to experience his culture Pryor replied that for anyone who has chosen to make Australia their home this becomes their culture also. And so, as a non-indigenous person seeking to engage in mission here, the journey of reconciliation is thus one that even a newcomer like myself needs to travel for my soul is also now caught up in the story of this land. In order to do so I have been learning that it becomes important to understand where the roots of injustice toward the indigenous peoples of this country have come from and how they have played out, but more importantly to learn exactly how one might live in a way that seeks reconciliation. For me, my main teachers in this have been Aboriginal elders (and one in particular), people marginalised in their own land yet offering me a way to find my soul in a nation that for the most part has lost it and has much work to do to recover it.

Roots and Shoots of Injustice

There are very few tourist brochures that I have read that tell much, if anything, of the story of Aboriginal people in the place one is looking to holiday in, unless they have been written by Aboriginal people themselves. In that industry at least there seems to be a conspiracy of silence or a tyranny of ignorance at work. It has only been in talking with local Aboriginal elders that I have discovered where, for example, it would be sacrilegious to climb, to walk or to visit. While the education system is making an effort to teach local Aboriginal and Torres Strait Islander histories, for my own children this work is confined to NAIDOC observances once a year.[2] Moreover, every week they sing, to the ironic strains of a didgeridoo, "Australians all let us rejoice, for we are young and free."

When I look at politics, state policy, and social needs the reality gets uglier. There is much one could speak of. The following examples have particularly struck me of late.

A recent review of indigenous education conducted in the Northern Territory concluded that bi-literacy should not be encouraged in the education of Aboriginal young people but rather an education only in the English language be provided.[3] It also recommended that remote secondary school students should have residential education provided for them in provincial towns. This sits in the broader context of

---

[2] http://www.acara.edu.au/curriculum/cross_curriculum_priorities.html Accessed 27 August 2014. NAIDOC: National Aboriginal and Islander Day Observance Committee.

[3] Bruce Wilson, "A Share in the Future: Review of Indigenous Education in the Northern Territory" (released May 2014).

the Intervention. It seems little has changed since the days of the Stolen Generations and Mission stations.[4] Meanwhile the campaign for recognising Aboriginal peoples in the Constitution of Australia continues to wait for a date to be set for a national referendum, while deaths in custody and health challenges occur at unacceptable levels.[5] The infant mortality rate is three times higher than the national average and life expectancy is 10+ years lower for indigenous than for non-indigenous peoples.[6] Compensation for Stolen Generations children is slow in coming and somewhat contentious. The first person to receive compensation in Australia was Bruce Trevorrow in 2007, 49 years after being taken from his family as a 13 month old, but processes for others, including in South Australia where Bruce was from, have been painful and unwieldy.[7] These state and national details are only a small part of the reality Aboriginal people live with.

The question is: Where has such a systematic and ongoing denial of the worth and integrity of people descended from 390+ ancient nations in this land come from?[8] A superb documentary series by the Australian Broadcasting Corporation in 2013, "First Footprints," displayed the work of contemporary archaeologists and Aboriginal elders in uncovering 50,000 years of sophisticated history, art, environmental knowledge, spiritual understandings and ritual, and cultural life in this place. And yet for the last 200+ years Aboriginal peoples have been "refugees in our own country",[9] unrecognised, written out of the narratives of this place, and disrespected.

A friend and colleague, Dr Ian Coats, recently visited one of my classes and read to us from Chapter Nine of *The City of God*, by Augustine, one of the most influential works to shape Western civilisation. In that chapter Augustine writes about the Antipodes, a concept inherited from Plato, and the notion of "men on the opposite side of the

---

4 Missions were run by different church denominations and were places where local Aboriginal people were "sent" to live. They were mostly places of disempowerment rather than empowerment. Cf James Miller, *Koori, A Will to Win: The Heroic Resistance, Survival and Triumph of Black Australia* (Sydney: Angus and Robertson, 1985), 99.

5 Twenty-one Aboriginal people died in custody in 2010-2011 alone. See Martin Cuddihy, "Aboriginal Deaths in Custody Numbers Rise Sharply Over Past Five Years," ABC The World Today (May 2013), http://www.abc.net.au/news/2013-05-24/sharp-rise-in-number-of-aboriginal-deaths-in-custody/4711764, accessed 29 August 2014.

6 See the Australian Institute for Health and Welfare, http://www.aihw.gov.au/deaths/life-expectancy/, accessed 27 August 2014.

7 Jens Korff, "Compensation for Stolen Generation Members" (22 August 2014), http://www.creativespirits.info/aboriginalculture/politics/compensation-for-stolen-generation-members, accessed 27 August 2014.

8 Around 391 nations are shown on a map created by David R Horton, Aboriginal Studies Press, AIATSIS and Auslig/Sinclair, Knight, Merz. 1996, which does not include clans and smaller groups.

9 Denise Champion, *Yarta Wandatha* (Adelaide: Denise Champion, 2014), 23.

earth."[10] He dismisses the idea of them as "on no ground credible."

> For Scripture, which proves the truth of its historical statements by the accomplishment of its prophecies, gives no false information; and it is too absurd to say, that some men might have taken ship and traversed the whole wide ocean, and crossed from this side of the world to the other, and that thus even the inhabitants of that distant region are descended from that one first man.[11]

It is possible to trace through history the adoption and development of this incredulous and othering thread. When laid alongside notions of Terra Australis, the South Land, or Terra Australis Incognita, the Unknown South Land, inherited from such philosophers as Aristotle, and initially drawn without accuracy on early European maps, logic argued that if those living there cannot be descended from Adam then they must be monsters, and inhuman. When one adds reinforcing threads in the form of the doctrine of Terra Nullius (The Land Belonging to No One), which Captain Cook claimed Australia to be when he arrived in 1770 on the basis of eighteenth century European "international law," Western Enlightenment notions of "civilisation," social Darwinianism and the pseudoscience of phrenology, which was popular in Britain in the 1800s, the treatment of Aboriginal peoples in this place becomes sadly and lamentably unsurprising. No wonder the histories of Aboriginals being hunted, shot and poisoned for sport, and women raped.[12] No wonder the histories of forced labour akin to slavery. No wonder the harsh commitment on the part of those in power to making Aboriginals "white." No wonder the assumption that Aboriginal women would not be able to feel the loss of children stolen. No wonder it was 1967 before Aboriginal peoples were legally counted human, rather than flora and fauna.

Chris Budden, in his book *Following Jesus in Invaded Space*, notes the church's support of racist practices and policies since "invasion" through its silence, its teaching when it did speak, and its institutions.[13] By and large it chose to interpret the biblical meta-narrative through the historic lens of a denial of the humanity of the Antipodeans, and in favour of colonial agendas. Anne Pattel Gray's historico-theological analysis of the

---

10 Ian noted that the earliest mention of the word "Antipodes" (opposite feet) that he knows of is in the writing of Plato.

11 Augustine, *City of God*, chapter nine.

12 See Henry Reynolds, *This Whispering in Our Hearts* (Sydney: Allen and Unwin, 1998), especially chapter 5; and Reynolds, *Why Weren't We Told? A Personal Search for the Truth About our History* (Sydney: Penguin, 2000).

13 Chris Budden, *Following Jesus in Invaded Space: Doing Theology on Aboriginal Land*. Princeton Theological Monograph Series (Eugene, Oregon: Pickwick, 2009), 29-36.

church's choices in *The Great White Flood* is damning.[14]

In 2009 the Uniting Church in Australia adopted a Revised Preamble to its constitution. This significant document owns that

> many in the uniting churches [ie Methodist, Presbyterian and Congregationalist]...shared the values and relationships of the emerging colonial society including paternalism and racism towards the First Peoples. They were complicit in the injustice that resulted in many of the First Peoples being dispossessed from their land, their language, their culture and spirituality, becoming strangers in their own land.[15]

The Preamble notes also that "Some members of the uniting churches approached the First Peoples with good intentions, standing with them in the name of justice." This other, significantly weaker, thread running through the history of the church in this place draws from the belief that all people are made in the image of God and a belief in creation's original goodness.[16] Unfortunately it underpinned the commitment of only a few in the early history of colonised Australia who risked reputation, economic viability, their safety and the safety of their families to befriend and learn from Aboriginal peoples and speak out against their destruction.[17]

It is the adoption and outworking of this weaker but theologically and socially crucial thread that offers me a way to find my soul in this place.

Principles and Factors of Reconciliation

Theologically the adoption of a belief that all have been made in the image of God can look like the opening lines of that Revised Preamble, which declares that this land was created and sustained by the Triune God who has been revealed by the Spirit to the people over thousands of years through their law, custom and ceremony. It also states that the love and grace of God "finally and fully revealed in Jesus Christ" gave them "particular insight into God's ways." This is significantly different thinking from that espoused by the colonial church. It requires that Aboriginal peoples be granted

---

14 Anne Pattel Gray, *The Great White Flood: Racism in Australia; Critically Appraised from a Historico-Theological Viewpoint* American Academy of Religion Cultural Criticism Series (Atlanta: Scholars, 1998).

15 Taken from a poster: "The Uniting Church in Australia Revised Preamble to the Constitution" (Sydney: Communications Unit of the Uniting Church in Australia Assembly, 2011).

16 Interestingly, it too in fact lies within Augustine's work, as Ian Coats pointed out to my class, but was not included in his writing about the Antipodes.

17 For stories of some of these people see Reynolds, *This Whispering in our Hearts*. See also Tracy Spencer, *White Lives in a Black Community: The lives of Jim Page and Rebecca Forbes in the Adnyamathanha Community* (unpublished thesis, Flinders University, Adelaide, 2011).

the deep respect, let alone the human rights, that an equal under God deserves, not because they think or operate the same as a person from another people group but because their unique perspective, wisdom and understanding has much to offer to all. Practically this requires from non-indigenous peoples a way of living that allows for genuine curiosity, mutuality, justice and love.

In 1999 Norman Habel introduced in a book three principles and two factors that he believed crucial to an "advocacy of authentic reconciliation," which he argued was the answer to finding Australia's lost soul.[18] The principles were truth, justice and identity. The factors were forgiveness and suffering.

The truth principle Habel explained as allowing suppressed stories to be told in public, particularly by the oppressed, researching our history and reading it with new eyes as the historian Henry Reynolds has bravely done, and listening to local histories as Aboriginals tell them.

The justice principle then seeks to address past wrongs "by a mutually agreed procedure."[19] It rebalances power, restores rights long removed, and stops placing the blame for their plight on the victims of the injustice. It cannot be achieved through a one-off act, like a public apology given by a Prime Minister, but is a long-term commitment to building a different kind of community.

The identity principle, meanwhile, asserts the equality of all parties. In the Australian context this is of vital importance because of a long history of assimilationist policies intent on making Aboriginal peoples "white." It requires learning to understand and value "the mythic, spiritual and ritual tradition of Aboriginal peoples as integral to their identity."[20]

In speaking of the forgiveness factor, Habel notes the ability of forgiveness to "heal past hurts" and mentions ritual as a useful medium for its realisation. Regarding suffering, he observes that without "suffering through" the pain of truth–telling, justice and forgiveness, "reconciliation" can prove to be false.

While these principles and factors are all true and important, I am left with the sense that something is missing. It is clear in Habel's writing that the use of the pronoun "we" and the angle from which the principles and factors are approached is the voice,

---

18   Norman C Habel, *Reconciliation: Searching for Australia's Soul* (Sydney: HarperCollins, 1999), 28ff.
19   Habel, *Reconciliation*, 37.
20   Habel, *Reconciliation*, 41.

perspective and activity of the non-indigenous person. Their thinking, words and actions are his concern: his own thinking, words and actions are his concern. He suggests that public rituals led by the church and other bodies can bring forgiveness and speaks of "my advocacy." But is not forgiveness a gift bestowed on the wrong-doer by the wronged? Is not reconciliation a two-way process that needs the active will and involvement of all parties if it is to be effected, and so "my advocacy" for it is not enough? How, if the action is initiated and in large part controlled by the powerful ("my", "we"), might change come in soul-full ways that create space for deep respect, genuine mutuality of engagement and a truly just society?

Perhaps the answer to these questions is implicit in Habel's thinking and I have missed something.

My sense is that there is a precondition for truth, justice, identity, forgiveness and suffering and it is **relationship**. And I would suggest that because of the colonial history of which I am part, to build relationship in the interest of finding my soul in this land, three practices will first be required of me if "authentic reconciliation" is ever to become possible: listening, humility, and patience, or the ability to wait. In these practices power is set aside, even given away. In essence this is mission-in-reverse.

Mission-in-Reverse

Where mine is the assumption that I, as a Christian, can bring God into a place and people in ways that will transform it and them for the better, in a context where such an assumption has wrought havoc for more than 200 years, it is time to open myself to what has been called "mission-in-reverse."

Mission-in-reverse was a term coined in 1984 by French Huguenot theologian and minister Claude Marie Barbour. It describes an approach opposite to that of an imperialist mindset that brings God to people, and in ways that condescend. This, she claimed, has too often shaped mission and ministry, something that has certainly been the case in Australia.[21] In mission-in-reverse a person practices a "presence to people" in such a way that those others become "the leaders in the relationship." This presence to people is done genuinely and with humility. It involves listening for God in the other person, and for the voice of God speaking through them, submitting to this and joining in. Barbour then observed, based on her own experience, that as the more privileged or more powerful one opens him- or herself up to being led

---

21 Claude Marie Barbour, "Seeking Justice and Shalom in the City," *International Review of Mission* 73, no. 291 (1984): 303–09.

and taught, space is created for a true mutuality in relationship that dignifies all and "shapes the way of announcing the good news," with its offer of Godly transformation to everyone. This is relationship and mission *with* rather than *for*: an act of justice rather than charity, empowerment rather than paternalism. It recognises our mutual need and dignifies all. It opens up the possibility of creating new stories and of doing God's work **together**. Genuinely so.

The remarkable thing is that the precedent for this has been provided by God. God-in-Jesus came not in power on clouds out of the sky knowing what was best for us but as a baby needing physical, emotional, mental and even spiritual nurture and training from human parents and elders (Luke 2:1-52). It was an ultimately submissive, vulnerable, humble and open stance practised not from a distance but in the interests of growing deep relationship. The silence surrounding most of Jesus' first thirty years on earth were for him full of learning and of waiting to be given the right to speak and act. His life, including his three years of public ministry, was full of "practising presence" by listening and responding, learning and growing. Of course, in his story as his community raised him, God-in-Christ, in turn, raised up us all (Eph. 2:6).

Finding my Soul

Mission-in-reverse is something that can begin through seeking opportunities to engage. It may begin by way of a gift. For me my story holds both.

Before I came to South Australia I had spent time learning Maori language and working for a Maori Anglican diocese, the Hui Amorangi ki te Manawa o Te Wheke, in the Waikato and Bay of Plenty of Aotearoa New Zealand. For six months I had lived immersed in Tikanga Maori (Maori culture). This experience was a combination of me pursuing opportunities to learn and a wonderful God-moment invitation from the Hui Amorangi. I could feel myself changing as they took me under their wing.

When it turned out my path was heading to South Australia I was concerned. I was well aware that relationships cannot be forced, the indigenous population here is much smaller proportionately, and invasion is "the primary defining context."[22] I arrived excited about the job I had been offered but grieving my loss of connection to indigenous knowledge and understanding.

In my first week here I met Aunty Denise Champion, an Adnyamathanha woman from the Flinders Ranges of South Australia, a storyteller and leader in the Uniting

---

22 Budden, *Following Jesus*, 17.

Aboriginal and Islander Christian Congress (UAICC). She had been invited by Rev Dr Steve Taylor, the principal of Uniting College for Leadership and Theology, to speak at an intensive taking place at the college, my new place of employment. I also met Uncle Nelson Varcoe, a Ngarinndjeri-Narungga man, and Aunty Denise's daughter Candace. I made sure to talk with Aunty Denise and Uncle Nelson. The opportunity to engage with Candace happened later. Meeting them proved to be a wonderful gift.

Uncle Nelson was the first of the three I spoke with. He showed me a piece of his art and explained it to me. He then showed me a map of Aboriginal nations in Australia and told the grievous story of the coastal peoples of Southern Australia, whose women were taken, raped, and abandoned on Kangaroo Island – the sacred island of the dead, which he warned me not to travel to – or killed by visiting mariners. Listening to him I was offered my first chance to appreciate and to grieve for Aboriginal cultural history.

In the carpark before the week ended I had the opportunity to speak with Aunty Denise. I suspect I was too talkative in my keenness to connect. She was gracious, however, and in the course of conversation mentioned a dream she had to write a book of her reflections around her *Muda*.[23] Something cautioned me to hold back. I listened and I remembered.

Meanwhile Ian Dempster, the Resource Officer for the UAICC in South Australia, who was there that day, recommended I read books by the Australian historian Henry Reynolds. I took his advice and from there began devouring all books I could find, including *Maybe Tomorrow* by Boori Monty Pryor, and *My Place* by Sally Morgan.[24] I found these books moving, shocking, upsetting and deeply challenging.

I met Aunty Denise and Uncle Nelson again through gatherings of the Covenanting Committee of the Synod of the Uniting Church in South Australia, which I joined, and then Aunty Denise agreed to help take a college group Walking on Country.[25] In planning for it there was a meeting in December at my home, which extended into dinner and storytelling over food.

Later I was told that in the Adnyamathanha worldview it is in sitting together over a meal that people become family.

---

23 *Muda* is the Adnyamathanha word for worldview as contained in law, ceremony and stories.
24 Boori Monty Pryor with Meme McDonald, *Maybe Tomorrow* (Sydney: Allen and Unwin, 1998); Sally Morgan, *My Place* (Melbourne, Penguin, 1988).
25 An immersion experience, the idea of Steve Taylor.

Walking on Country happened two months later in February on Ngarrindjeri country at Camp Coorong. Rev Dr Tracy Spencer, a Uniting Church minister who has walked her own soul-finding journey with Aboriginal peoples, facilitated the trip while Uncle Tom Trevorrow, who sadly passed away not long after, and Aunty Denise aided her in teaching us. Uncle Tom was plain about the pain of his people and their country – his brother was Bruce Trevorrow, who was stolen at the age of thirteen months –but he also introduced us to the wonder of Ngarrindjeri culture, their deep love of the land and knowledge of it, their arts, stories and spirituality. Meanwhile Aunty Denise chose to share (for me more) from her own story and culture, again mentioning in passing that she would love to write a book. It seemed appropriate to speak and so I asked if she would be interested to make her dream happen if I could find funding. She said yes but she was wary. A white anthropologist, Dorothy Tunbridge had come to the Adnyamathanha, and recorded their Dreaming Stories.[26] Once done, she published them, claimed copyright and never returned. Today Adnyamathanha have to pay her royalties if they tell their own stories in the version she wrote down. Feeling betrayed they have withdrawn her book from sale.

I went away quietly mulling things over and while sharing what I was learning with another they offered to fund the book via an unconditional loan to be repaid as books were sold.

In May I received a request from Aunty Denise. She had work for a college topic outstanding and was wondering if she could spend time with me to finish it, orally. On the agreed date I brought along the contract for the unconditional loan and at an appropriate moment showed it to her. The material she was sharing with me I felt was profound and worthy of publication. It was certainly opening my eyes to knowledge and ideas I had not encountered before. She decided to sign. I humbly offered to ghost write for her, mindful of her oral fluency but reluctance to write. The project was on.

Over the next months we met as Aunty Denise's timetabled allowed and whenever she was ready. For the next February's Walking on Country we decided to take a pilgrimage to her country in the Flinders. By then I was keen to hear the stories in situ, for I had learned that every Muda is geographically located. There were stories and reflections during the day, late conversations into the night in shared accommodation, lessons in bush tucker cooking, walks on country, and opportunities to take photos.

---

26 Dorothy Tunbridge in association with the Nepabunna Aboriginal School and the Adnyamathanha people of the Flinders Ranges, South Australia, *Flinders Ranges Dreaming* (Canberra: Aboriginal Studies Press for the Australian Institute of Aboriginal Studies, 1988).

The following May we were in the final stages, me reading to her in her own words, checking language together, and confirming the structure I had suggested. Paintings, drawings and photos were created and collated.

I found photographing and painting her country created for me a deeper link to it for now I knew and had walked its stories. Meanwhile it was delightful to read to Aunty Denise her own words and witness her genuine amazement over their insight and wisdom.

The book was launched two and a half years after a conversation in a carpark.

Why do I tell all this?

I feel that in the process of learning to listen, to practice humility and to wait I have been finding my soul.

This relationship, unfolding over time, has opened me to the wonders of an ancient culture and the tears of its history under colonisation. Aunty Denise has told me that Adnyamathanha are more open than most Aboriginal nations about sharing their culture but the elders tell things in pieces, revealing only what they think you are ready to know and respect, giving you more when they judge you are ready for it. This method is an ancient one of testing listening, comprehension, concentration, willingness to learn and grow, memory and patience. The compulsive, rash, foolhardy, disrespectful and napuchi (cheeky) did not survive here. And so I was told the same story many times over, given new detail each time and new interpretation, offered deeper understanding and tested in patience. The process of listening, I have discovered, is not simply about words. There is a form, a different kind of logic from what I have been trained in, in what Aunty Denise was offering me. I had to learn a different way of listening, to hold stories in my head, weave threads of teaching and the relating of connections into my memory, and wait for their grounding until literally I walked on the ground they came from. She spoke of Yarta Wandatha: the land is speaking, the people are speaking. This is not a process of hearing only the words of humans but of learning to listen to the Spirit in the land and its messages for us.

Let anyone with ears, listen! (Matt 11:15)

The academic part of me became excited as I realised that Aunty Denise was doing something with her God-knowledge that is different from standard processes of theology that place God into a culture or stand God against culture. I asked her questions about method. Surprised, she responded and revealed an extremely sophisticated hermeneutic underlying her reflections. Genuine listening holds many gifts: not only does one learn to appreciate another as described in their own words but sometimes as an outsider one can point out riches taken as understood by the insider. This is the point at which mutuality truly becomes possible.

While she has since caught my excitement as she attends conferences and is able to explain what she is doing, at the time the contrast for me was stark: I was excited about method; she was excited because the book would be her legacy for her children. It was a salient reminder to me of the importance of people and culture and memory.

In the end this project has been not so much about ideas as about relationship. And in the process something mutually good and life-giving has been created. Is this what reconciliation looks like?

Why Walk the Journey?

Ross' words have stayed with me because I found the notion of a nation without a soul and the observation that non-indigenous Australians probably do not even realise their lack, disturbing. As one who has made my home here and been told this culture is now my culture it has felt imperative for me to prove him wrong in my own life at least and to join the long journey of reconciliation. With reconciliation central to the biblical narrative and the reason for the incarnation I cannot see how Christians can do anything otherwise, even while I am fully aware that it is easy to end up telling it slant and doing other-ways.

I am incredibly grateful for the gracious and wise tutelage Aboriginal elders here have offered me. Through them and through Aunty Denise in particular in this place, I feel I have been growing a soul. It is my prayer that more Australian Christians might also walk the path of reconciliation so that the church can address its history, rewrite its own metanarrative in this land, and engage well in this its contemporary context.

Denise Champion with Rosemary Dewerse, *Yarta Wandatha* **(Salisbury, SA: Denise Champion, 2014).**

B. A MULTICULTURAL VISION

From around the world,
We're a rainbow church,
And our prayer is one,
For the nations to be healed.

Different cultures, different tongues,
But we gather today.
Different dress and different songs
Sung a different way.
We are a sign of the commonwealth of God
Jew and Gentile, women and men
God's great love through all the world,
Let it grow!

Often thinking we're complete
We just shut out the rest.
God invites us, "Open out –
I'll be there in your guest."
We are a sign of the different in God,
Open table, Jesus is here,
God the stranger, breaking in.
Open out!

So much learning! We still fail,
Yet God's Spirit is near.
So much joy! We're so enriched!
There is nothing to fear.
We are a sign of the colours of God,
Breaking barriers, welcoming all,
So diverse yet one in Christ.
Live it out!

Ross Langmead, "From Around the World" (2006)

4. Finding Communitas in Liminality: Invitations from the Margins in the New Testament and in Contemporary Mission

George Wieland

Migration has brought substantial and rapid demographic change to Aotearoa New Zealand. The most recent national census (2013) reveals that 25.2% of NZ's population, and 39.1% of residents of Auckland, NZ's largest city, were born overseas. For new migrant communities and more established local populations alike this changed landscape is experienced as a liminal space of discomfort, uncertainty and fear of loss, but also of potential for transformation. The narrative of Cornelius and Peter in Acts 10-11 illustrates the role of liminality and communitas in the transformation of the church that was necessary for it to participate in God's mission as it crossed new boundaries. What would be the possibilities of transformation for New Zealand's churches if we were to accept invitations from the new margins of immigration to enter liminal space and embrace the potential for change in communitas with those who are already there?

Migration and Liminality

The anthropologist Victor Turner is credited with taking up and developing the term *liminal* to describe the in-between state experienced by individuals or communities who have left behind one settled condition and have not yet entered into another.[1] This movement from separation through *limen* (Latin: threshold) to aggregation has proved fruitful in explicating processes of learning.[2] Liminality is characterised by disorientation, discomfort and a destabilising of the settled order. It is accordingly rich in potential for new orderings of experience and understanding, the emergence of new relationships and ways of being, indeed for transformation. Pastoral theologian Tim Carson describes it thus:

---

1 See e.g., Alan J. Roxburgh, *The Missionary Congregation, Leadership, and Liminality* (Harrisburg: Trinity, 1997), 23. Whereas the liminal state is usually assumed to be transitional, the experience and conditions of liminality may for some migrants become more permanent. On this see Caroline Wanjiku Kihato, "Migration, Gender and Urbanization in Johannesburg" (DPhil diss. University of South Africa, 2009), 18-19; accessible at http://uir.unisa.ac.za/handle/10500/2693

2 See e.g. Alison Cook-Sather and Zanny Alter, "What Is and What Can Be: How a Liminal Position Can Change Learning and Teaching in Higher Education," *Anthropology and Education Quarterly* 42 (2011), 37-53.

> In the first phase of transition in the rites of passage, that of separation, there is a time of detachment and detaching from the earlier period, place or state in the cultural or social context. In the last phase of this process, the time of aggregation, there is a return to a stable position; one that is socially located but different from the former phase—a transformed, altered condition.[3]

Liminal space, then, is a uniquely fertile place of learning. Discomfort precedes discovery, and the trauma of separation and disorientation is the necessary precondition of re-orientation and transformation.

Liminality is an inescapable dimension of the migration experience. Migrants are, quite literally, "a people in-between."[4] Theirs is the "forced liminality" of those who enter a new context from its margins.[5] The dislocation and disruption of migration creates a degree of emergency but, as Homi K. Bhabha points out, "the state of emergency is also always a state of emergence."[6] This emergency and consequent emergence may be observed across the full range of attitudes, relationships and behaviours of migrant groups, including their religious practices, values and beliefs, and the life shared within their communities of faith.[7]

Gemma Tulud Cruz describes ways in which the structure of religious groups may be impacted, "as traditional leadership, rituals, and myths are challenged, and new types of worship, new sacred places, and new structures emerge when groups are confronted with migration."[8] Although there is a counter tendency to seek security in the new context by preserving forms and practices and looking back to the place of origin for spiritual nurture and the provision of religious leaders, migration inevitably precipitates change. Cruz continues:

---

3   Timothy L. Carson, "Liminal Reality and Transformational Power: Pastoral Interpretation and Method," *Journal of Pastoral Theology* 7 (1997), 99-112, 100-101.

4   Brij V. Lal, "People In-between: Reflections from the Indian Indentured Diaspora," in *Chinese and Indian Diasporas: Comparative Perspectives*, ed. Siu-Lun Wong (Hong Kong: University of Hong Kong, 2004), 69-83.

5   Sang Hyun Lee, "Pilgrimage and Home in the Wilderness of Marginality: Symbols and Context in Asian American Theology," in *Korean Americans and Their Religions: Pilgrims and Missionaries from a Different Shore*, eds. Ho-Youn Kwon, Chung Kim Kwang, and R. Stephen Warner (University Park, PA: Pensylvania State University Press, 2001), 55-69, 57.

6   Homi K. Bhabha, *The Location of Culture* (London: Routledge, 1994), 41.

7   "Virtually every behavior in a person's repertoire is a candidate for change following one's involvement with other cultures." J.W. Berry, "A Psychology of Immigration," *Journal of Social Issues* 57 (2001), 615-31, 621.

8   Gemma Tulud Cruz, "Between Identity and Security: Theological Implications of Migration in the Context of Globalization," *Theological Studies* 69 (2008), 357-75, 365.

Migration ... is also likely to be among the most conspicuous agents of change of religious systems because it exposes migrants to new ideas, challenges the power of control and religion in their places of origin, and raises profound questions of community, personal identity, and affiliation.[9]

Liminality Observed: The Case of a Chinese Church in Auckland

This process may be illustrated from the recent experience of one church in Auckland that was established twenty-five years ago by immigrants from Hong Kong.[10] Tensions were surfacing between its first generation migrant members and some of the church's young people, comprising 1.5 and second generation migrants. Sunday School and Bible Study leaders were reporting difficult behaviour in their classes, and parents and church leaders feared that their young people would be lost to the church as they became more reluctant to participate in its services and activities.[11]

At first, language was assumed to be the problem. While most of the young people speak Chinese with their families at home, many have not learned all the characters necessary to read the Chinese Bible with any fluency, and prefer to use an English translation for Bible study. This creates difficulties when the mode of teaching requires students to report verbatim the words of the text, and accurate memorisation of Bible verses is valued. For a growing number of the young people it is also a struggle to comprehend preaching and teaching that utilises Chinese language above an everyday conversational level. The decision was therefore made to initiate an "English Ministry" specifically for the church's New Zealand educated young people. In parallel to the church's Chinese programs, a Sunday service, Bible study and discipleship classes and cell groups in English were launched.

This bold move was welcomed by many of the young people, but it did not resolve all the issues. In the pastor's words, "We realised that we were just giving them a Chinese service in English!" Teachers were still offended when students asked questions,

---

9   Cruz, "Between Identity and Security," 365-366.

10   Hong Kong is a context, incidentally, that Ross Langmead knew well, having spent much of his childhood there. Such experiences, with their liminal aspects, may well have helped to form the notable empathy that he displayed with migrants, refugees and asylum seekers as well as other people on the margins.

11   The fear expressed was not so much that the young people would abandon Christian faith as that they would leave the Chinese church and join school friends in local English speaking churches. It was deeply important to the Chinese parents and church leaders that families should remain together in the same church. There was also a lack of confidence in the formation that their young people might receive in "Kiwi churches." In several conversations with Chinese pastors in Auckland it has become evident that, from the perspective of Confucian cultures, youth programs that seem to emphasise entertainment at the expense of Bible teaching, and encourage young people to express their own opinions on ethical matters rather than accept clear instruction, appear quite inadequate.

spoke without being invited to, and offered their own ideas; the style of the English worship service, replicating exactly that of the Chinese service, was more formal than the young people seemed to prefer, and the preaching, though in English, retained a manner of authoritative instruction and exhortation that did not align with styles of discourse experienced by the young people in the educational and other contexts of their lives outside the church. The church leaders recognised that there were deeper cultural shifts that had to be taken into account.

Their response was to take steps to reorient their youth program towards a more intentional preparation for Christian life in New Zealand contexts, adapting their practices of formation to align more closely with the modes of learning and relating that the young people were being shaped by in New Zealand's education, leisure and work environments. Training was organised for youth leaders, potential pastors emerging within the church were encouraged to undertake theological and ministry training in New Zealand institutions, and teachers and preachers from outside their Chinese church networks were invited to contribute to the English services and youth training events.

The church's negotiation of this complex liminal terrain is on-going. For the older members, participation in the life of their church might represent a partial relief from the liminality of their everyday lives as migrants in a new context. Their children, however, experience that dual liminality of 1.5 and second generation migrants as they move through the week from the Chinese family home into the non-Chinese world of education and employment and then as they leave that world on Sunday and enter the very different environment of their Hong Kong church. At the same time, changes in the English program bring a new element of liminality into the experience of the majority Chinese congregation, particularly as young adults who have participated in the English program take their place in ministry and leadership in the church as a whole. Conversely, a tendency may be observed in the English service for young people who are given leadership roles to assume the style of dress and deportment nearer to that considered appropriate for leaders in the Chinese service.

And what of those guest speakers and trainers? Majority culture people who have accepted invitations from this Chinese church to participate in their English services and youth programs have also experienced liminality. Passing through the glass doors into the foyer of the custom-built worship centre on the outskirts of an otherwise unremarkable commercial and industrial district, they have found themselves abruptly leaving behind the familiar sights, sounds and atmosphere of their customary Kiwi Sunday to join a self-consciously distinct migrant community in its liminal space at the margins of New Zealand society. They may be unsure how to interpret and receive the deferential treatment they are afforded as honoured guests, teachers or pastors; perhaps they suddenly feel self-conscious about their clothes (probably too casual?), or accent (they don't seem to have been understood), or gestures (should they have bowed their head when greeted? what was that about accepting something with both hands?) It may be disconcerting to find themselves to be the only non-Chinese among several hundred worshippers in the building, and unable to read signs directing members of the congregation to their various groups and activities.

More profoundly, as they enter into conversation, participate in small groups, or even listen to the church notices, they begin to appreciate that this migrant community faces significant challenges that have not been part of their own experience. It might be the financial vulnerability of migrants, or the tensions of living with sensitivity to family members who practice other religions, or pressures on young people who feel burdened by obligations to fulfil what seem impossibly high aspirations for academic and career success. They certainly feel discomfort as they begin to see their New Zealand churches through the eyes of migrants and recognise the validity of at least some of the perceptions of lack of enthusiasm for growth in spiritual understanding and life, indifference to matters of ethical and doctrinal importance, failure to welcome and make space in their churches and ministries for Christian believers who arrive from elsewhere, and unwillingness to adapt in order to enable their participation in local Christian communities.

Intercultural Engagement and Communitas

Even without such intentional relating, migration produces a state of liminality not only among migrant groups but also in the communities into which migrants arrive. In New Zealand the acceleration of immigration resulting from the passing of a new Immigration Act in 1987 has meant that for many New Zealand born people over the age of forty the country they now live in seems dramatically different to the more mono-cultural environments of their formative years.[12] They, too, experience a changed context and are confronted with difference in new ways or to greater degrees, provoking discomfort and a disordering of former norms. Though often resisted,

---

12 See Andrew Butcher and George M. Wieland, "The New Asian Faces of Kiwi Christianity," in *Interrogating Multiculturalism in New Zealand: An Asian Studies Perspective*, eds. Jaqueline Leckie and Gautam Ghosh (Otago: Otago University Press, forthcoming).

that liminality contains within it the potential for development and rejuvenation.[13] For New Zealand's churches, however, this is an opportunity that has scarcely begun to be embraced. Whereas increasing diversity is readily apparent in schools, the labour force and other public spaces, it must be admitted that in church congregations a much greater social and cultural homogeneity generally persists.[14]

What explains this lack of effective integration of new Christian migrants with existing New Zealand churches? It is certainly not due to a paucity of Christians among the migrants. While considerably more diverse in religious identity than those who arrived in New Zealand from the predominantly Christian Pacific Island nations a generation before, the more recent immigrants from Asian source countries include more Christians than adherents of any other religion.[15] It might be viewed as a failure of hospitality, either of host communities to offer it with sufficient generosity or of migrants to be willing to step out of the relative security of their homogenous group in order to receive it. There are problems, however, with the assumptions encoded within the host/guest relationship. As Averil Bell asserts, "[H]ospitality encompasses a complex and power-laden set of relations between people and place."[16] It is the host who holds power, assumes ownership of the place of meeting, sets the conditions on which the guest might enter and be welcomed and any subsequent relationship might proceed, and controls the mode of relating. The structure of such a relationship impedes its development towards fuller mutuality and the emergence of a new reality.

I want to suggest that the most fruitful way forward in relationship between New Zealand's more established, majority culture churches and those Christian groups that have arrived in the country more recently would be for the established churches not to assume a place at the centre into which to invite guests, but to accept invitations from

---

13 Berry, "Psychology of Immigration," 616, affirms that, "immigrant-receiving societies and their native-born populations have been massively transformed in the past decades."

14 There is a need for more research to quantify and nuance the anecdotal reporting that most church congregations are less diverse than the communities in which they meet. A significant step forward in this regard is the research conducted by Rev Tokerau Joseph, Minister of First Presbyterian Church, Dunedin, for his thesis entitled, "Ethnic Flames of the Burning Bush: An Exploration of Ethnic Relations in Congregations of the Presbyterian Church in Aotearoa New Zealand" (PhD diss. Otago, 2014).

15 For fuller comment see George M. Wieland, "Christianity: The Surprising 'Asian Religion,'" opinion piece on the website of the Asia New Zealand Foundation: http://asianz.org.nz/newsroom/insight/christianity-asian-religion. According to the latest New Zealand census (2013), Asians now comprise over 10% of New Zealand's Catholics and Baptists and almost 10% of Pentecostals and those who describe themselves as "Christian not further defined."

16 Averil Bell, "Being 'At Home' in the Nation: Hospitality and Sovereignty in Talk about Immigration," *Ethnicities* 10 (2010), 236-56, 240, drawing on Derrida's deconstruction of hospitality as an exercise of power.

the margins to enter into liminality with those who are already there.[17] With the risk of liminality comes the promise of *communitas*. This is a "community of the inbetween" that develops uniquely among those who share a common liminal experience. In such companionship relationships, practices and leadership are not predetermined by what any of the participants might have been before entering that liminal space. Chester characterises communitas as "a community of anti-structure whose bond continues even after the liminal period is concluded. A significant sharing of the liminal passage creates strong egalitarian ties which level out differences in status and station which have been established by structure."[18]

It is in such communitas with others in risky liminal space rather than by assimilation or integration into the perceived security of settled existing churches that the potential for transformation may be grasped. What it offers is companionship on the journey into a future that is as yet not fully known, and into a becoming that is not wholly conditioned by what either new migrant or receiving communities might have been before. For New Zealand's churches this need not require an abdication of the responsibilities of a host community to those who arrive as guests but it would relativise the role of host, recognising that all communities of Christian faith are called to self-identify as "aliens and exiles" (2 Pet 2:11). Accordingly they relate to other Christian communities as travellers together across a terrain where neither group dare allow itself to become completely at home (Heb 13:12-14). Among fellow travellers roles of host and guest are fluid and may be interchangeable.[19]

Of course liminality, whether entered from the margins or from the centre, may be resisted. As Hyung Sun Lee observes in relation to the experience of Korean Americans:

> The people at the center are reluctant to give up any power and thus are prone to be protective of the existing social structure. The people on the edge have a hard time facing up to their experience of liminal ambiguity and will often cling to the comfort zones of their ethnic enclaves.[20]

---

17 In terms of Anthony Gittins' Four Quadrants (ch. 2) this would involve a deliberate relocation from a claimed or assumed place of power among insider participants to the more vulnerable place of outsider participants.

18 Carson, "Liminal Reality," 101.

19 Bell, "Being 'at home,'" 252, writes: "If the roles of host and guest are to offer guidance to the long term relations of migration it must be in this permanently unsettled and oscillating sense, where no-one is forever granted the role of host or forever relegated to the status of guest, whether that be as friends, parasites or charity cases, where all belonging is understood as conditional."

20 Sang Hyun Lee, "Liminality and Worship in the Korean American Context," in *Religion and Spirituality in Korean America*, eds. David K. Woo and Ruth H. Chung (Urbana: University of Illinois, 2008), 100-115, 113.

For that reason the invitation to liminality may not be welcomed, particularly when it is extended from the margins to a perceived centre. This may be when a new migrant group meeting in the premises of a settled church in the migrant-receiving society envisages more mutuality than is provided for in a tenant/landlord or guest/host relationship. Or it may be when the settled church wishes to embark on a journey towards intercultural community that would ask of the migrant group a willingness to step out of the relative security of structures, patterns and relationships that replicate those of their place of origin. But if liminal space is the place of learning and transformation, and carries the promise of communitas in the journey, then for the sake of that which could emerge and for the possibility of liberation from that which impedes our fullest becoming, we might heed Christine Pohl's suggestion, that it "might prove helpful to value more highly those experiences that disorient us and distance us from status and power."[21]

Transformation through Communitas in Liminality: The Case of Peter and Cornelius

Crucial to the narrative and the message of the Book of Acts is the paradigm shift in the stance adopted by the church in Jerusalem to gentiles who were professing faith in Jesus. At the centre of the book's narrative structure is the Council of Jerusalem where that shift was confirmed (15:1-29). Without such a transformation, the second half of the book, and the continuing story of mission and the church through history, would have been very different. As the narrative unfolds leading up to the Council it becomes clear that an important catalyst for the change in the church as a whole is the transformation experienced by one of its key leaders, the apostle Peter, in an episode whose significance is signalled by its repetition. The story itself is told twice (as a third person narrative in 10:1-48 and as Peter's own testimony in 11:1-18) and alluded to a third time in the report of the council (15:14). It is an account of an invitation from the margins to enter liminal space, to discover communitas with others who have entered liminal space from another direction, and to experience there a re-ordering of beliefs, assumptions and values producing radically changed practice.

The outline of the story is well known. It begins in Caesarea, the provincial capital under Roman administration, where Cornelius, a Roman officer, is told in a vision to send for Simon Peter who is in the town of Joppa, about 60 kilometres away (10:1-8). Before the messengers arrive Peter has his own vision, in which he is invited to

---

21 Christine D. Pohl, "Biblical Issues in Mission and Migration," *Missiology* 31 (2003), 3-15, 10.

eat food that he has always regarded as unclean, protests, and hears the response, "What God has made clean, you must not call profane" (10:9-16). This prepares Peter to receive the messengers from Cornelius, give them hospitality and then return with them, accompanied by other Jewish believers, to Caesarea (10:17-23). After an awkward start Cornelius and Peter go together into the officer's house where, as Peter is telling the assembled group about Jesus, the Holy Spirit is poured out on them. This convinces Peter that these gentiles should be baptised into the community of followers of Jesus, after which he accepts their hospitality and stays with that household for several days (10:24-48).

For both Cornelius and Peter a state of liminality is precipitated by a divine encounter that requires them to open themselves to new understanding and experience. This in turn impels both of them towards a human encounter that, in its extraordinary circumstances and initial discomfort (10:25-29), throws them together in communitas. In shared vulnerability, they step into what becomes a startlingly new and transforming series of experiences and insights. For Peter the insight comprised not new knowledge but fuller appreciation of what he had already thought that he knew. In the Acts account of the day of Pentecost Peter proclaims that "everyone who calls on the name of the Lord will be saved" (2:21). That had been in Jerusalem, at the centre both of Jewish faith and of the early life of the community of believers in Jesus the messiah. Now he is at the margins, geographically at the border of Judean territory, politically at the headquarters of the Roman administration and culturally in a largely gentile environment. It is in this setting, in the company of the gentile Cornelius in whom he is discovering God to be at work, that he exclaims, "I'm really getting it!" (*ep' alētheias katalambanomai*, 10:34).[22]

The learning that takes place in liminal space is theological, experiential and behavioural. The universal scope of God's acceptance (10:34-35), Christ's lordship (10:36) and the offer of forgiveness received by faith (10:43) come into much sharper focus on the margins than they could at the centre of the Jerusalem church's life. The experience of the Spirit in that gentile environment corresponding to the original Pentecost outpouring in Jerusalem (10:44-46) confirms the theological insight and challenges the Jewish believers to enact the truth that they are discerning in baptising their gentile hosts into the name of Jesus Christ and the community of believers (10:47-48). Community is further realised in shared intercultural life as Peter and the

---

22 The NRSV rendering, "I truly understand," does not convey the force of the present tense katalambanomai here. "I now realize" (NIV) and "I most certainly understand now" (NAS) get closer.

Jewish believers are welcomed into that gentile home, an invitation that, prior to the transformation effected through communitas in liminality, they would have found impossible to accept.[23]

Ross Langmead frequently affirmed – and exemplified – the significance of hospitality in the practice of mission, particularly where it connotes reconciliation. He wrote:

> By living out a new set of relationships counter-culturally, roughly in the shape of God's Commonwealth, we proclaim the possibility of a new creation where love and justice rule and those on the edge are welcomed into the centre.[24]

In this case, however, it is those on the edge who offer hospitality to people from the centre. On their return to that centre, the community of believers in Jerusalem, Peter and his companions are challenged (11:1-3), and the clash of old and new perspectives is exposed. The question asked from the centre about those at the margins is, "What must they do in order to belong with us?" (15:1, 5) The question asked by those who have entered liminal space in communitas with people at the margins is rather, "What must we do to align ourselves with what God is evidently doing among them?" (10:47; 11:17; 15:7-11). The return of the newly transformed Peter and his companions generates a new liminality in the centre itself, that in time proves to be a catalyst for the centre's own transformation in its self-understanding as a people of mission and its orientation towards others (15:13-30).

For the Church in New Zealand: An Invitation from the Margins

The arrival in New Zealand of substantial numbers of immigrants certainly presents New Zealand's churches with the challenge to practice hospitality with glad generosity. At the same time, however, the presence of so many Christian migrants and migrant churches on the edges of New Zealand society represents an opportunity for the transformation of more established congregations. At a time when they and their national church bodies are experiencing dislocation from a remembered or assumed

---

23 It is notable that the accusation levelled at Peter and his companions by some at the centre, in Jerusalem, was that they had accepted hospitality from and eaten with uncircumcised men (11:3). On the significance of eating together for community formation see Pohl, "Biblical Issues in Mission," 8: "Shared meals, a centerpiece of hospitality, became a key context in which believers worked through issues of social, ethnic, and economic differences, and provided for the poor in their midst. These meals and the practice of hospitality also provided a context within which a new identity and new relationships could be formed and reinforced; young believers were nurtured into a new community, with its particular beliefs and practices, commitments and connections."

24 Ross Langmead, "Transformed Relationships: Reconciliation as the Central Model for Mission," *Mission Studies* 25 (2008), 5-20, 15.

place near the centre of society, with accompanying demoralisation and decline, there comes an invitation from the margins. To respond will mean discomfort and disorientation, but for those who, from the centre, enter that liminal space there will be the joy of communitas with those who have entered it from the edge. In that communitas there is the potential of liberation for both: on one side, from the social exclusion that restricts fullness of life and participation in the new context; on the other, from entrapment in limiting traditions and the illusion of security that inhibit a more authentic pilgrim existence.

In 2009 Ross Langmead generously travelled to Auckland, to lend his considerable mana and encouragement to meetings of the Aotearoa New Zealand Association of Mission Studies. He presented there a paper entitled, "Contextual Mission: An Australian Perspective," in which he identified the five areas that receive attention in this book. At a number of points, particularly in relation to multicultural realities and what he called "the Asian horizon," Ross invited conversation on how far what he had described resonated with New Zealand contexts. For me there were opportunities, which I deeply valued, to pick up those themes with Ross at a Whitley College conference in 2011 and again at the IAMS conference in Toronto in 2012. In a sense this chapter, presented at the AAMS conference in Adelaide in September, 2014, represents a continuation of that conversation. I am privileged to have the opportunity to offer it here in honour of Ross, and in gratitude for his example of engaged scholarship within an integrated life of faith, community and mission.

5. Growing a Truly Multicultural Australian Catholic Church

Noel Connolly

One of the features of Australia that interested Ross Langmead as a missiologist was our growing multicultural nature. If anything this has become a greater challenge to the Christian Churches. We are now living in an age of unprecedented migration and the Australian Catholic Church is among the most multicultural Churches. There is both pain and possibility in this reality. The Church's mission in Australia today is to break down walls that divide, alienate, exclude, discriminate and dehumanise and to be a sign of the life to be found in unity in diversity. This chapter tries to place our reflections on migration in their historical, theological and anthropological contexts and suggests that migrants and international priests may have a singular role because of special insights and sensitivities they can gain in successfully crossing the boundaries involved in migration.

"Birth Pangs of a New Humanity"

Migration is part of the human DNA. It has been critical to human development. Today we are experiencing the greatest movements of persons of all time, such that the Pontifical Council for the Pastoral Care of Migrants and Itinerant People described us as being in the "birth pangs of a new humanity."[1]

According to the International Organisation for Migration the number of people living outside their country of origin rose from 150 million in 2000 to 214 million in 2010.[2] In addition the United Nations High Commission for Refugees (UNHCR) on 20 June 2014 announced that the number of forcibly displaced people in the world was now 51.2 million (17 million refugees and 33.3 million internally displaced).[3] Such movement of peoples is having a dramatic effect on many nations including Australia.

---

[1] Pastoral Care for Migrants Itinerant People, *Erga Migrantes Caritas Christi* (Vatican City 2004) #12.

[2] Gemma Tulud Cruz, *Toward a Theology of Migration: Social Justice and Religious Experience* (New York: Palgrave Macmillan, 2014), 1.

[3] UNHCR statement, http://www.abc.net.au/news/2014-6-20/number-of-forcibly-displaced-people-hits-51.

Migration to Australia

The 2011 National Census found that 47% of all Australians are either born overseas (27%) or have a parent born overseas (20%)[4] and four million Australians speak a language other than English at home. Australia is the most multicultural country in the western world. Until 1960 the majority of immigrants were from Europe but between 1960 and 1990 non-western migration grew from 12% to 52% of all migrants.[5]

Migration has changed the religious landscape of this country.

> Since World War II, immigration has played a huge role in the development of religious faith in Australia. That role has been evident in the place that many of the world's religions now have in Australia. Since 1971, the number of Australians associated with a religion other than Christianity has risen from just 0.1 million to 1.5 million. However, many millions of the immigrants have been Christian and some denominations would hardly exist today without the enormous influx of members that immigration has brought.[6]

Catholics & Migration

The Australian Catholic Church has been a major beneficiary of migration trends in Australia and graphically illustrates the pain and the possibilities of migration.

Between the 2001 and 2011 Censuses 319,564 of the 1,771,924 migrants who came to Australia were Catholic[7]. Hundreds of international priests also arrived. At present 24.2% of Australian Catholics are migrants, 23.0% are the children of migrants and 53.8% are third generation Australians.[8] According to the 2011 Census, four dioceses, Sydney (35.3%), Perth (34%), Parramatta (29.7%) and Melbourne (29.1%) had around one-third of their Catholics born overseas. The national average for all Dioceses is 23.6%.[9] The top ten countries of birth among Catholics born overseas are: Italy, the Philippines, England, New Zealand, Ireland, India, Vietnam, Malta, Croatia and

---

4   Australian Bureau of Statistics, *Cultural Diversity - Reflecting a Nation: Stories from the 2011 Census*, 2013.

5   Jehu J. Hanciles, "Migration and Mission: The Religious Significance of the North-South Divide," in *Mission in the 21st Century: Exploring the Five Marks of Global Mission*, eds. Andrew Walls & Cathy Ross (Maryknoll: Orbis, 2008), 124.

6   Philip Hughes, "The Impact of Recent Immigration on Religious Groups in Australia," *Pointers* 22:4 (2012), 1.

7   Hughes, "The Impact of Recent Immigration on Religious Groups in Australia," 3.

8   Figures prepared by the Australian Catholic Bishops Conference (ACBC) Pastoral Research Office from the Australian Bureau of Statistics 2011 Censuses of Population and Housing. www.pro.catholic.org.au.

9   Figures prepared by the ACBC Pastoral Research Office from the Australian Bureau of Statistics 2011 Census data.

Poland in descending order.[10] About three-quarters of Australian Catholics born overseas were born in non-English speaking countries.[11]

At the same time hundreds of international priests were invited to take up parishes in Australian dioceses. It is difficult to find accurate statistics, Peter Wilkinson estimates that while in 2003 there were 150 overseas sourced priests working in Australian parishes, today it is between 500-550, or one in every three priests in parish ministry and the percentage is growing. Also one in every two seminarians was born or recruited overseas and the majority of ordinands between 2010 and 2013 were overseas born.[12]

First generation immigrants are significantly better at attending Church. Migrants make up 40% of those under 65 attending religious services. They are more accepting of authority and more traditional in their devotions. They are attracted to devotions that Australian-born Catholics have recently given up. Consequently, "it is hard to provide religious nurture for both groups of people within the same context."[13] So while migration has enriched the Catholic Church it brings with it some challenges.

Much the same can be said of many of the international priests now ministering in Australian parishes. They are mostly younger. They are zealous. But they are often traditional and sometimes authoritarian, finding it difficult to work with parish councils and women pastoral associates. Because of their accents many parishioners find it hard to understand their homilies. A great deal of effort and planning needs to be put into programmes to welcome, enable and support overseas priests. Some dioceses are good at this, others are not. More consultation and preparation of the local priests and parishioners is essential.

The arrival of so many migrants and international priests is a significant change in the Australian Catholic Church bringing with it pain and possibilities which we do not fully appreciate. It demands serious reflection and planning. I would like to limit myself in this chapter to discussing not the challenges but some of the possibilities for all of us, migrant and "local", to living happily and creatively in the new multicultural Church that is developing. The chapter will therefore situate this movement within its historical context and within the theology of migration before highlighting the

---

10   Philip Hughes, Margaret Fraser & Stephen Reid, *Australia's Religious Communities: Facts and Figures from the 2011 Australian Census and other sources* (Nunawading Vic: Christian Research Association, 2012), 35.
11   ACBC Pastoral Research Office, *E-News Bulletin*, 10th August 2012.
12   Peter J Wilkinson, "Who ministers in Australian parishes? *the swag* 22:1 (Autumn 2014), 28-29.
13   Hughes, "Impact of Recent Immigration on Religious Groups in Australia," 8.

possible contribution migrants and especially international priests may make in helping to build a truly multicultural church.

The Historical Context – The Great European Migration

Andrew Walls[14] and Jehu Hanciles[15] trace the massive growth in present day migration back to the great movement of Europeans from Europe into the developing world beginning in the 16th Century and lasting till mid-way through the 20th Century. Between 1800 and 1925 between 50 and 60 million Europeans migrated to other parts of the world. In 1915 21% of Europeans lived outside of Europe.[16] We know this period as the time of colonisation. On this migration was built Europe's economy and hegemony. Because of this migration we have the development of Australia, New Zealand, Canada and the United States and less happily, Latin America, India, slavery and indentured labour.

However, since the 1960s the movement has reversed and now the movement is from "South" to "North," from the developing countries to the developed. This applies also in Australia where the rise in non-European migration has been marked.

A Missiological Interpretation

Although many missionaries may have been critical of colonialism most used its structures.[17] They were very successful in planting the church in Latin America, Africa and to some extent in Asia, with the result being that we now have a thriving Non-Western Christianity and a predominantly "Southern" Church. Philip Jenkins claims that by 2025 approximately 60% of Catholics will live in Latin America and Africa and by 2050 80% of Catholics will live in or trace their origins to the Global South. Also by 2050 there will be three billion Christians of whom somewhere between one in five and one in six will be non-Hispanic whites. We already have a Pope from Latin America. The Church is and will be quite different to the one many of us were brought up in.

---

14 Andrew Walls, "Afterword: Christian Mission in a Five-hundred-year Context" in *Mission in the 21st Century: Exploring the Five Marks of Global Mission*, eds. Andrew Walls and Cathy Ross (Maryknoll: Orbis, 2008), 193-204.

15 Jehu Hanciles, "Migration and Mission: The Religious Significance of the North South Divide" in *Mission in the 21st Century: Exploring the Five Marks of Global Mission*, eds. Andrew Walls and Cathy Ross (Maryknoll: Orbis, 2008), 118-129.

16 Hanciles, "Migration and Mission," 119.

17 Hanciles, "Migration and Mission," 120.

The direction of mission has also changed. Most missionaries, formal and informal, now come from the "South." Many migrants see themselves as missionaries to a secular West in need of revitalisation in the faith. Today some of our most vibrant churches in Australia are ethnic churches. The future of the missionary movement is in the hands of these Southern missionaries.

Walls has written extensively on the serial nature of Christian history.[18] Unlike Islam whose development has been linear, Christianity has always waxed and waned. Countries which have been "jewels in the Christian crown" are no longer. But Christianity has always moved on. This is because Christianity is essentially a religion that has to be incarnated, inculturated and translated. It must speak to the host culture or it wanes. Walls highlights six stages but in this chapter I will concentrate on only three.

The earliest "Church" was Jewish based largely in Jerusalem, but through persecution and the power of the Holy Spirit it spread and disciples from Cyprus took it to Antioch (Acts 11:19-20). It was from there that the Church grew. The movement to Antioch came just in time because if it had not moved out of Jerusalem Christianity might have ended up as a footnote in Jewish history after the Romans destroyed the city in 70 AD. From Antioch Christianity spread throughout the Hellenist and Roman worlds but again might have disappeared with the decay of the Roman Empire except that the Holy Spirit had moved it on to the Irish Celts and the German Goths. They reconverted Europe and developed Christendom. Now, Walls writes, Christianity has moved from Europe and the North to the South. It is in the South that the shape and future of Christianity will be worked out. Migrants and missionaries may be our major contact with this new life for Christianity.[19]

The Theology of Migration

Not only is migration part of the human DNA it is also at the heart of the Judaeo-Christian scriptures. Jehu Hanciles comments that "migrant" or "pilgrim" is a common "metaphor for the life of faith and distinctive feature in the divine plan."[20] In the Old Testament God's call comes frequently through migrants, foreigners and outsiders, including Abraham, Joseph, Moses, Esther, Ruth and Daniel. Moreover, major defining

---

18 See particularly Andrew Walls, *The Cross-Cultural Process in Christian History* (Maryknoll: Orbis, 2002).

19 See "Christianity in the Non-Western World: A Study of the Serial Nature of Christian Expansion," in Walls, *The Cross-Cultural Process in Christian History*, 27-48.

20 Jehu Hanciles, "Migrants as Missionaries, Missionaries as Outsiders: Reflections on African Christian Presence in Western Societies," *Mission Studies* 30:1 (2013), 64-85.

events often occur in the context of migration, notably the Exodus and Babylonian exile. Hanciles writes: "Abraham is celebrated as a model of faith among Christians precisely because he became a migrant.... Moses was migrant refugee when he stood before the 'burning-bush'; and it was to a migrant people that the Law was given."[21] It was during the Exile in Babylon that Israel produced some of its most beautiful poetry and its most sensitive and universal understanding of salvation.

Just as during the Exodus Yahweh became a migratory God, walking with his people and residing in a tent, in the New Testament God reveals himself even more powerfully as a migrant. In the Incarnation, God becomes a man. God empties himself and migrates to the human race. Daniel Groody comments:

The basic premise of a theology of migration is that God, in Jesus, so loved the world that he migrated into a far distant country of our broken human existence and laid down his life on a cross so that we could be reconciled to him and migrate back to our homeland with God and enjoy renewed fellowship at all levels of our relationships.[22]

The New Testament is full of stories of migration. Jesus is born in Bethlehem because of a census. Joseph, Mary and Jesus flee into Egypt. Jesus spends his public ministry as an itinerant preacher who has nowhere to lay his head (Lk 9:58). The Acts of the Apostles portrays the early Christians as being scattered by persecution and spreading from Judea through Samaria, Antioch, and Asia Minor to Rome, so much so that they were known as people of the "way" (Acts 18:25-26; 19:23; 22:4; 24:14, 22).

Contribution of a Theology of Migration

Given that migrants and refugees are such a major part of our political life it is strange that there is so little theological reflection on migration here in Australia. We have a challenging tradition to draw on. Groody argues that the social sciences and theology need each other in discussing migrants and refugees. Social sciences contribute the data and many insights but "theology offers not just more information but a new imagination. It supplies a way of thinking about migration that keeps the human issues at the center of the debate and reminds us that our own existence as a pilgrim people is migratory in nature."[23] The role of theology is to enable us to look at things in a new way and to give hope and energy.[24]

---

21 Hanciles, "Migrants as Missionaries," 67.
22 Daniel Groody, "Theology in the Age of Migration," *National Catholic Reporter* (14 September 2009).
23 Groody, "Theology in the Age of Migration," 2009.
24 Daniel Groody, "The Church on the Move: Mission in an Age of Migration," *Mission Studies* 30:1 (2013), 27-42

The deepest experiences of Israel, Jesus and the early Church were marked by migration. To be human means to be on the way to God. We are pilgrims in search of the Kingdom of God. In the Exodus we learn that the nature of God is to be liberator and lover of the poor and that we should welcome strangers because we too were once strangers (Ex 22:21-27). We come to realise that we, the settled, might have something to learn about God, about ourselves and our needs, vulnerability and spirituality. "The human reality of the migrant challenges the experience of those who falsely assume they have absolute control of their land and their own destiny."[25] We learn that "sovereign rights" are not absolute. They are subject to human rights and we should not limit compassion to our family or our national borders. We lose touch with our own vulnerability and endanger our own salvation when do not welcome the stranger.

The Church and Migration

Part of the mission of the church is to break down the walls that divide, alienate, exclude, discriminate and dehumanise, to be a sign of the Kingdom of God.

> In fact all should find 'their homeland' in the Church, for the Church is the mystery of God among men, the mystery of love shown by the Only-Begotten Son, especially in His death and resurrection, so that all "may have life, and have it to the full" (Jn 10:10), so that all may find strength to overcome every division and act in such a way that differences do not lead to rifts but communion by welcoming others in their legitimate diversity.[26]

The Church is not just, however, a "homeland." It is also an instrument of God's mission in the world. It should model to Australia that "plurality is a treasure, and dialogue is the as yet imperfect and ever evolving realisation of that final unity to which humanity aspires and is called."[27]

Erga Migrantes Caritas Christi believes migrants offer something to the local church:

> Migrations offer individual local Churches the opportunity to verify their catholicity, which consists not only in welcoming different ethnic groups, but above all in creating communion with them and among them. Ethnic and cultural pluralism in the Church is not just something to be tolerated because it is transitory, it is a structural dimension.[28]

---

25 Donald Senior, "Beloved Aliens and Strangers," in *A Promised Land, a Perilous Journey*, eds. Daniel Groody & Gioacchino Campese (Indiana: University of Notre Dame Press, 2008), 28.
26 Pastoral Care for Migrants Itinerant People, *Erga Migrantes Caritas Christi*, #27
27 Pastoral Care for Migrants Itinerant People, *Erga Migrantes Caritas Christi*, #30
28 Pastoral Care for Migrants Itinerant People, *Erga Migrantes Caritas Christi*, #103

Culture as an Essential part of being Human

We cannot fully appreciate the contribution of migrants to the local church unless we have a deeper understanding of what culture is and greater appreciation for what is involved in crossing cultural boundaries.

Culture is largely unconscious. For all of us to live a productive and relaxed life we have to take many things for granted. We could not cope with having to make original, imaginative judgements in every decision we make each day. Culture is the pattern of assumptions that limit our choices, pre-programme us and make life possible precisely because they are largely unconscious. As Edward Hill reminded us in *The Silent Language,* "Culture hides as much as it reveals and strangely enough what it hides, it hides most effectively from its own participants."[29]

Edgar Schein defines culture as,

> the pattern of basic assumptions that a given group has invented, discovered, or developed in learning to cope with its problems of external adaptation and internal integration that has worked well enough to be considered valid, and therefore, to be taught to new members as the correct way to perceive, think and feel in relation to those problems.[30]

Peter Berger and Thomas Luckman once described the process of socialisation as one of externalisation (a group tries to make sense of or put an order on their environment), of objectification (this order then becomes part of reality, "that's just the way things are") and finally of internalisation (it becomes part of us and we will even teach it to others without knowing the reason why).[31] In other words a group puts an order on its environment and then proceeds to take it for granted not appreciating the power it has over their lives.

A Parable[32]

I once heard a parable that illustrates this process well. Many centuries ago a tribe lived in a mountainous region where there were also many lions. Often at night the

---

29 Edward Hill, *The Silent Language* (New York: Anchor Books, 1973), 30.

30 Schein, Edgar. "Coming to a new Awareness of Organizational Culture," *MIT Sloan Management Review*, Winter 1984. Downloaded from http://sloanreview.mit.edu/article/coming-to-a-new-awareness-of-organizational-culture/ 3rd November 2014.

31 P Berger and T Luckman, *The Social Construction of Reality* (Middlesex: Penguin University Book, 1973).

32 Told in greater detail in Noel Connolly, "The Things We Take for Granted," *The Furrow* (October 1986), 639-640.

lions would attack the weak and elderly on the edge of the village. The tribe met to decide how they could cope with this problem. They decided to build a fence around the village with one gate. Because no one in particular was responsible for closing the gate, however, it was often left open and people were still being killed. They met again and decided that the second son of each family would take it in turns to close the gate. This worked well and no more people were killed. About a hundred years later lions had disappeared from the area and two hundred years later no one in the village could remember that there had ever been lions there, but second sons were still closing the gate each evening. When they asked why, their fathers replied, "That is just the way things are." These sons in turn taught their sons. What was an eminently sensible plan persisted long after its *raison d'etre* disappeared. After several more decades the tribe may even have invented a spiritual reason, totally unrelated to lions, as to why they closed the gate.

The Power of Culture

The power of culture is that it is unconsciously absorbed and rarely questioned. It makes society and life possible by limiting our choices. But culture is a partial view of the environment and only *a* way of being human, not *the* way of being human. It is not the best and only way of doing things. Unfortunately most people do not become aware of this until they have to live among people of another culture.

Our culture influences how we feel about God and when, where and how often we relate to God. It influences what we think is holy, what is sin, what is good ritual, and how we think of and feel about family, community, authority, celebration, recreation, body, sexuality, spirit, suffering and death. Culture determines what is important and relevant, what is thinkable or unthinkable. It shapes our questions and determines how satisfactory answers will be.

Culture is the framework within which we will inevitably situate everything we come to know. There is a Latin saying which illustrates this. *Quid quid recipitur ad modum recipientis recipitur*: Whatever is received will be received according to the mode of the receiver. People can only hear, remember and apply what makes sense to them. Unfortunately in our Western and more individual-centred society our emphasis in communication is mostly on the speaker conveying his or her message. In many group-oriented cultures, however, the emphasis is more on the listener and what they can hear.

We can learn much from this listener-centred approach if we want to speak to the hopes and fears of our people because, unless the Gospel is understood, it cannot be meaningful and invite conversion.

The Pain and Gain in crossing Cultural Boundaries – another parable[33]

Imagine again a tribe living in a valley in the mountains. This tribe has a rule, which if you break, you are banished from the village. Fred has been banished for a month, but after a week he becomes bored and he does something no one in his tribe has ever done before. He climbs over the mountains where he meets a previously unknown tribe. They welcome him into their village. At first Fred finds it difficult there. The people are good to him but they have strange and even "immoral" customs. Slowly he comes to like them and he stays about six months. Nevertheless it is not home so eventually he returns back over the mountain to his own people. Now the trouble begins. Fred begins to question the way his village does things. After an initial welcome the tribespeople and elders become angry with him for all his questions. But worse still his experiences and especially his questions have isolated him. He wants to be there, but he feels cut off by his intellectual awakening. He no longer shares the same taken-for-granteds. He has questions that no one appreciates. He wants to talk about the other village and no one wants to listen. Fred becomes lonelier and angrier because no one seems to understand in his home village. It is no use returning to the other village because things may be the same there.

This, of course, is part of reverse culture shock. The only successful resolution is when Fred comes to the realisation that he, his tribe and the other tribe all have limitations, and that while his tribe might not be perfect it does have a valid human way of living and real achievements, issues and needs. If he can successfully manage to cross cultural boundaries he will end up with greater insight and tolerance, increased sensitivities and an expanded humanity. He will be a resource for his tribe.

Birth pangs of a new Australia and new Australian Church

Given the historically unprecedented movement of migrants and the evidence of several Australian Censuses, we are clearly living in a multi-ethnic if not multicultural reality (one where we aspire to unity and a positive acceptance of difference). You only have to catch a capital city train or visit a university campus to realise that our future is going to be vastly different to what it used to be. Most can see this but unfortunately

---

33 Connolly, "The Things We Take for Granted," 641-643

there has been little systematic reflection on how to plan for a happy and satisfying future for the Church.

We all have a vital role to play

We all, Australian and overseas born, have a vital role to play in building a truly multicultural church. We need each other's energies and more importantly visions to correct, enlarge and focus our own and help build a unified community with positive respect for our different cultures and contributions. We all need to change and grow because we can only become fully human together.

International Priests as a Resource

Much can be said about the pros and cons of inviting international priests to work in Australia but instead of entering that debate, I would like to propose a vision that might help us to see these programmes in a new and more enabling light. I believe we can make a breakthrough if we learn to look at these priests in a new way. Normally we regard them as priests to fill gaps in diocesan sacramental programmes. This is important but it sells them and their possible contribution short. If they can successfully negotiate crossing into Australian culture they will have sensitivities and insights for building a truly multicultural church that no local person can have unless they too cross similar boundaries. We should value them for their difference and not make them just like us. That would be impossible, unethical and a wasted resource.[34] "Since culture, although a human product, is so essential to our very humanity, to take away a person's culture is to damage a person grievously. It is a denial of an important aspect of who we are."[35] Our goal should be to help them live happily and minister creatively in Australia without losing their integrity. That is a more valuable missionary role than filling pastoral gaps.

International priests also see themselves primarily as parish priests. So the challenge to them is to also be missionaries in the fullest sense of that word. As we have seen, we are all enculturated beings. We believe that our way of doing things is *the human*, moral and best way of doing things. We tend to carry our Church of origin, with its assumptions, ways of doing things, roles and traditions around with us. We will see, hear and judge our new Church from that framework. Being human we "can do no

---

34 Yang, Seung Ai. Commentary in *International Priests in America: Challenges and Opportunities*. eds. Dean Hoge & Aniedi Okure (Collegeville: Liturgical Press 2006), 131-137
35 Schreiter, R. "Ministry for a Multicultural Church," *Origins* 29:1 (May 1999), page not recorded.

other", until we learn the limitations of our way of doing things and the strengths of the local culture. As missionaries, we are guests and should learn to live on our hosts' terms. We must learn to respond to local needs. We must be conscious that although we may be perfectly logical in making judgements according to our terms we may be wrong because we just don't fully understand what is going on. Sensitive missionaries are slow to judgement and recognise their need for a local mentor. We should be learners constantly searching for meaning in the local's terms.[36]

Acculturation for All

Undoubtedly there will be successes and misunderstandings for the local Church in being a good host. It is not always easy to be welcoming, supportive and understanding especially of people who may be suffering from culture shock, who are not suitable for overseas mission or who have come here unwillingly.

One of the weaknesses in our present programmes for welcoming and enabling international priests is that they are frequently run for the international priests alone. This only makes for resentment among the international priests, who question why they alone need education, and ignores the fact that local priests, parishioners and especially parish staff are also challenged by their arrival. Programmes should be organised to include local clergy and laity so that they can understand culture and what is involved in welcoming international priests. Such programmes should include the basics of cross-cultural communication and encourage structures for friendship, support and dialogue.

Fuller life for us, the hosts

The tendency in migration is for the hosts to think they have little to learn and do not have to change. Exposure to other cultures, however, can be an opportunity for profound personal learning, for a deeper insight into us, for learning greater tolerance and for developing increased freedom and ability to love. Engagement with our migrant brothers and sisters will help us develop the ability to listen to minorities, cultural awareness and the cultural competence we need for mission in Australia today. It will also provide us with a link and exposure to the Majority World church where the Holy Spirit is clearly saying something. Personally, it will expand our humanity and offer us the opportunity for a happy, creative and full Christian life. We must accept Pope

---

36 Cf. Gittins, Anthony. *Ministry at the Margins: Strategy and Spirituality for Mission* especially Chapter 3, "Sense and Nonsense: Understanding Other People" (Maryknoll: Orbis, 2002).

Francis' challenge to become pilgrims, to go out onto the streets. We have a worthy and exciting mission to welcome migrants and model for Australia unity in diversity. It will put us in touch with the poor. We may end up "bruised, hurting and dirty" but we will be happily alive.

6. A Mission of the Second Generation (Australian Born Chinese) in South Australian Migrant Churches: Dealing with Unintentional Marginalisation due to Confucian Values

Samuel Chan with Kim Chan

The presence of Confucian values (such as harmony, filial piety, ritual propriety, respect and honour) in South Australian Chinese Migrant Churches has unintentionally marginalised the Australian Born Chinese (ABCs) who are the minority culture. ABCs are the children of the migrants who started the churches. However, a conflict arises because although ABCs have been raised by Chinese parents, they don't hold as strongly to such Confucian values because of Western influence. This chapter will consider what ABCs in South Australia are, how Confucian values marginalise them, and that one strategy could be for ABCs to have the mindset of a missionary when dealing with migrants.

Introduction

I used to think of mission as going overseas, to a foreign culture or to an unknown group of people. That was until I started to investigate the situation of the Australian Born Chinese (ABCs) in South Australian migrant churches, which have a large population of Chinese (Chinese Migrant Churches). My own journey, which included being an ABC born into a Chinese Migrant Church and then being the first ABC in South Australia to undertake an internship into full time ministry, led me to do this.

ABCs start as children in Chinese Migrant Churches. Their parents were born overseas, but they were born here. That, however, is only one of the many differences. Conflict can arise because ABCs don't hold as strongly to Confucian values (such as harmony, filial piety, ritual propriety, respect and honour) as their parents. Being the minority culture, there is a risk that ABCs can be unintentionally marginalised because of their more Western views. This chapter will consider what ABCs in South Australia are, how Confucian values affect them in this setting, and suggest that one strategy for ABCs could be to have the mindset of a missionary when dealing with migrants.

ABCs in Chinese Migrant Churches in South Australia

While ABCs have been in Australia since the 1800s, ABCs have existed in South Australia for a shorter period of time for a number of reasons such as that Sydney and Melbourne are the main entry points for new migrants, it is more rural and there are more Chinese in other states – like attracts like. If Chinatown is an obvious sign of settlement, it is interesting that Adelaide's Chinatown was only established in the early 1980s, in contrast to that of say Sydney, which was around in 1860.

The first ABC born into a South Australian Chinese Migrant Church (i.e. to parents who were attending a Chinese Church) was my brother in 1977. He was born to migrants, my parents, who arrived in 1969 and 1975. They were university students who converted to Christianity through the Overseas Christian Fellowship and were part of the first Chinese Migrant Church congregation which was formed in 1976. Like other Chinese Migrant Churches in South Australia, it was developed on the basis of not only a spiritual need, but also linguistic, cultural and sociological needs.

Today there are over 30 Asian Migrant Churches, all with different theologies and practices. All have a second generation.

ABCs have their own culture

ABCs are living between two worlds (see Figure 1). They have the ability to move beyond their first generation migrant parents' original language and culture because they are exposed to at least another culture. The first is the Chinese traditional culture which they experience in their family, home and church. Secondly, their education setting, work and the wider society is Western. Both of these cultural backgrounds contribute to their identity formation and the development of their spirituality. Being marginal ethnics, they still have ties to their ethnic roots that they usually have no desire to sever. In fact, many of the core traditional values of their Chinese culture continue to influence their decision making. They are not, however, entirely comfortable in a Chinese setting because of the Western influence. For some, the complexity can result in an identity crisis.

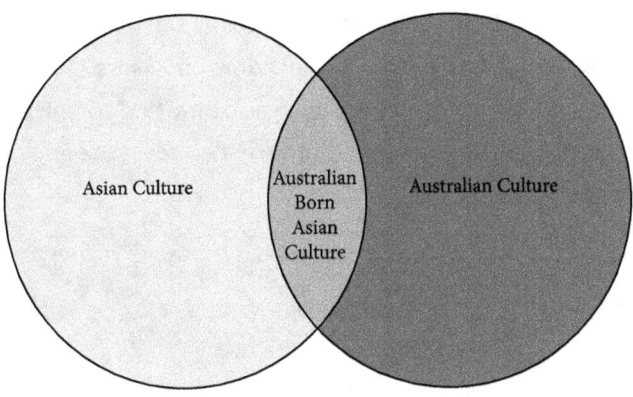

Figure 1

ABCs have distinct qualities, which differ from their Western classmates and colleagues and also their parents. They have their own unique culture (see Figure 2). FACE, an American organisation whose purpose was to address the large numbers of ABCs dropping out of Chinese churches and improve ABC ministries, gives the following example to illustrate:

> For instance, when you eat a nectarine, you never think that you are eating half a peach and half a plum. In fact, you realize that a nectarine has a special texture and flavor of its own. Even though a nectarine is the combination of a peach and a plum, it has its own singular qualities. Another example is the combination of tin and copper resulting in a new metal. Bronze has qualities that neither tin nor copper has; e.g., it has exceptional strength.

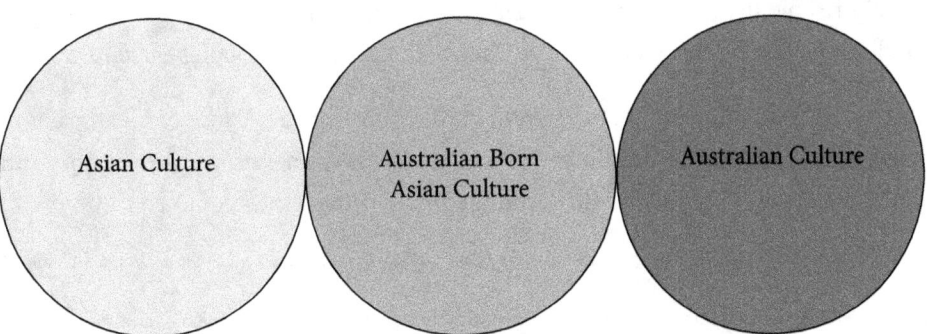

Figure 2

Despite the fact that they have their own culture, this can be on the scale from very Chinese to very Australian (see Figure 3) depending on factors such as their parents, environment, schooling, church and self-image. Given this complex set of factors, "even a sophisticated computer cannot accurately describe how an ABC is likely to turn out in the end."[1]

| Asian Culture | Australian Born Asian Culture | Australian Culture |

Figure 3

Although they are the minority culture in Chinese Migrant Churches (not necessarily in numbers, but in voice), they tend to stay while they are young for a number of reasons, a couple of the main ones, as Chung identifies, being family and community.[2] Another is because they feel most comfortable worshipping and gathering with other ABCS. Sociologists refer to this as the "homophily principle: the idea that similarity breeds connection, that ties between similar individuals are more binding."[3] However, there is a large dropout that can start as early as high school and this is a major problem.[4]

What Confucian Values do People have?

Values are a learned organisation of rules. They dictate how we make choices and resolve conflicts. Values form the basis of social norms. People of a particular society or culture hold their values in high regard.[5] Many values are unconscious to the person holding them, but form who they are. They become visible through behaviours.

Confucius is a total contrast to an ABC but is of relevance because of his impact on migrant and ABC values. Confucius was an ancient Chinese sage who was born in 551BC and died in 479BC.[6] He was arguably the first professional educationist in

1   Fellowship of American Chinese Evangelicals, *Completing the Face of the Chinese Church in America* (Fellowship of American Chinese Evangelicals, California, 2009), 28

2   See Mei Ling Chung, "Chinese Young People and Spirituality" (School of Religious education, Faculty of Education, Australian Catholic University Research Services, 2006), 313.

3   Rebecca Kim, "Second-Generation Korean American Evangelicals: Ethnic, Multiethnic , or White Campus Ministries," *Sociology of Religion* 65:1 (2004), 19, 27.

4   Fellowship of American Chinese Evangelicals, *Completing the Face*, 5.

5   Ann MacNaughton, "Cross-cultural conflict resolution: finding common ground in disputes involving value conflicts," *Willamette Law Review* 33 (1997), 747.

6   Pierre Ryckmans, "An Introduction to Confucius," *Quadrant* (March 1995), 18, 21.

China. He taught anyone who wanted to learn, no matter what sort of person they were.[7] This was revolutionary and broke the ancient custom because previously learning opportunities were only given to people such as aristocrats who had power.[8]

He wanted his disciples to be "round men," useful to state and society but not as followers of a certain school. He took it upon himself to interpret the classics to his disciples. Confucius was a transmitter but not an originator.[9] He theorised and made operational the philosophy of ancient legendary kings like Yao and Shun.[10] The *Analects* is the place that Confucius can be most directly encountered; it contains the disciples' report of Confucius' sayings and his mode of living.[11]

When people from East and South East Asian countries migrate to South Australia they tend to carry with them some level of Confucian values (as well as a number of other values). People with Confucian values in South Australia are far more diverse than people with Confucian values in Asia who are more similar to those in mainland China. Depending on the generation, family type, length of stay and other factors, those people fall along a wide spectrum of very close to Confucian values to integrated into their new society.[12]

The following describes only a few Confucian values which, if held by a party, could potentially impact on their behaviour in a Chinese Migrant Church setting. The focus is on Confucian values that are different or held to a different degree to ABCs.

Harmony

Of all Confucian values, harmony is one of the most important. It is relational and presupposes the coexistence of multiple parties. All parties in a group possess more or less equal importance. Harmony is achieved by coordinating these parties in a cooperative way. It requires each individual to be attentive to the norms of the group, emphasise group achievement and others' contribution to the group, act in accordance with others and deemphasise their own needs and thought. Those out of the group are perceived as separate, unequal, distant or even threatening.[13]

---

7   Yu-lan Fung, "The Place of Confucius in Chinese History," *Chinese Society and Political Science Review* 16:1 (1932), 4.

8   Fung, "The place of Confucius," 3.

9   Fung, "The place of Confucius," 3.

10 Leon Laulusa, "Confucianism and its implications for industrial relations in China," *Journal of Management Spirituality and Religion* 5:4 (2008), 385, 389.

11 Ryckmans, "An Introduction to Confucius," 19; and Fung, "The Place of Confucius," 2.

12 Urs Martin Lauchli, "Cross-cultural negotiations, with a special focus on ADR with the Chinese" *William Mitchell Law Review* 26:4 (2000), 1045, 1045.

13 Xiaohong Wei and Qingyuan Li, "The Confucian value of harmony and its influence on Chinese social interaction," *Cross Cultural Communication* 9:1 (2013), 60, 62-63. Westerners typically value individualism over harmony.

Confucian harmony is not, however, about merely agreeing without difference. Sameness is not necessarily harmony. Instead, harmony is more about respecting different opinions at the same time as working with people in a harmonious way. Such a process may require some tension; "for Confucians, strife between the two individuals or parties serves as an instrumental step toward harmony in the long run and, on a large scale, for the world."[14] While "conflict avoidance, when it is possible, is the motto for keeping [a] harmonious relationship," disharmony (as opposed to conflict) is necessarily present during the process of harmonisation.[15]

Ritual propriety

Of about equal importance to harmony is the value of ritual propriety. Ritual propriety is a "set of rules centred on the order of the clan system."[16] It focuses on five relations: ruler and subject, father and son, husband and wife, elder and younger brother and friend and friend.[17] Ritual propriety does not gain its authority from God, but from positive natural blood relationships.[18] It organises and relates the different parts of society so as to leave no doubt or equivocation as to ones status.[19] So, a person does not have to think about the exact nature of his or her duties. He or she knows exactly how they are to behave towards their grandma, sister-in-law, uncle three times removed, or cousin seven times removed. It is an instrument to "inculcate mutual honesty and promote peaceful relationships [and] to strengthen the important relations in life."[20] It assists in achieving harmony which is its pre-eminent aim.[21]

Confucians favour ritual propriety as a positive means of resolving social problems as it teaches people right from wrong and if everyone follows it, there is no need for more serious measures.[22] Confucius said:

---

14 Wei and Li, "The Confucian value of harmony," 63.

15 Laulusa, "Confucianism and its implications," 388; and Wei and Li, "The Confucian value of harmony," 62.

16 There is not such an emphasis on hierarchy in Western society. Peng He, "The Difference of Chinese Legalism and Western Legalism," *Front Law China* 6:4 (2011) 645, 651.

17 Luke Tee and Whalen Lai, "Chinese Conceptions of Law: Confucian, Legalist, Buddhist," *Hastings Law Journal* (1978), 1307, 1309.

18 He, "The difference of Chinese legalism," 651.

19 Yu-Tang Lin, "Li: The Chinese Principle of Social Control and Organisation," *The Chinese Social and Political Science Review* 2 (1917), 106, 112.

20 Lin, "Li: The Chinese principle," 114, 116.

21 William Devoe, "Commercial Dispute Resolution Between the United States and The People's Republic of China," *Suffolk Transnational Law Journal* 7:2 (1983), 329, 336.

22 Wai Mun Au Yeong, "International Dispute Resolution: Conflict in a Chinese Cultural Context," *Singapore Law Review* 26 (2008), 77, 81.

> Do not look at anything unless it is in accordance with ritual propriety; do not listen to anything unless it is in accordance with ritual propriety; do not speak about anything unless it is in accordance with ritual propriety; do not do anything unless it is in accordance with ritual propriety.[23]

Filial Piety

Filial piety is a set of moral principles including "duty, obligation, and importance of family name, service and self-sacrifice".[24] As Yu Tzu says in the Analects, filial Piety is "being good as a son and obedient as a young man". This is the "root of a man's character."[25] In addition, a filial son should also show his parents reverence.[26] A son's obedience should continue even after the death of the father. "The filial son should not think for himself, but almost live vicariously for his parents." The filial son should not go too far away from his parents. Even if his parents are doing wrong, he should "remain reverent" and "wear himself out of obedience of them".[27]

Respect [28]

The Confucian principle of differentiated statuses between the morally cultivated and petty persons entails that people do not deserve the same level of respect. Morally cultivated people deserve additional respect: "In the Confucian view, respect is a particular form of valuation. To recognise someone (or something) as respectable is to deem her worthy of respect...To respect a person is to recognise human value in the person."[29] People who deserve more respect are often older or more senior in status.

Honour

The Confucian ethic of face is the respect offered by a social group to an individual with moral dignity; it represents public trust in a person's morality. "It is the kind of fame that is deliberately accumulated through effort and achievement with pride during the course of one's life."[30] It is highly valued in a society with Confucian values as it acts as a strong deterrent ensuring fulfilment of obligations.

---

23 Confucius Analects 12.1.
24 Chung, "Chinese Young People," 35. Western culture generally does not expect such loyalty to the family clan.
25 Confucius Analects I, 2.
26 Confucius Analects II, 7.
27 Andrew Hong, "Confucianism – and filial piety" http://andrewhong.net/2008/05/05/confucianism-and-filial-piety/
28 In Western society, respect is earned and not necessarily through moral means. It is not dependant on age.
29 Li, Chenyang, "Equality and Inequality in Confucianism," *Springer Science+Business Media* (2012), 295, 305.
30 Kwang-Kuo Hwang, "Face Dynamism in Confucian Society," *China Media Research* 7:4 (2011), 13, 13. There is not such an emphasis on honour in Western society. It is not used as a penalty for defaulting one's social obligations.

To save face, an individual may try to create a most favourable impression in others' minds by presenting a figure consistent with their own self-image in accordance with the demands of the role in that particular social situation. They may save or give face for others as a way to show respect for them or to boost their self-esteem. The system cares more for formality rather than substance.[31] The penalty for defaulting on one's role and reciprocal obligations is the "loss of face", which causes them to lose the respect of the person they have wronged and also others who are aware of the transgression.[32] Once lost, it is hard for a person to function as usual in the social group.[33]

Examples of Unintentional Marginalisation due to Confucian Values

A recurring problem in Chinese Migrant Churches is the conflict that arises between ABCs and those born overseas.[34]

Church Voting

A first example is that the way voting in Chinese Migrant Churches happens can be different to the expectations of ABCs. Although it may follow the rules in the constitution, the manner in which it occurs is different to Western society because the "real source of authority is different." For people with Confucian values, the leader has the authority because of respect and ritual propriety, but in Western Culture, it is a group decision.[35] Also, people with Confucian values will, in many instances, find out how others are voting and vote with the majority. It will happen this way even though they may be voting contrary to their better judgment.[36] This avoids loss of face and keeps harmony. In order to find out how others are voting, there can be many discussions and meetings prior to the voting day. The "voting comes after decisions have already been made, and is affirmation of support."[37]

People with Confucian values who vote with their conscience and end up among the minority may suffer shame:

> To restore some of the lost honor, they may resort to a variety of strategies. The most common way is to break off from the minority and start a new

---

31 Hwang, "Face Dynamism," 16.
32 Wei and Li, "The Confucian Value of Harmony," 64.
33 Hwang, "Face Dynamism," 13.
34 Fellowship of American Chinese Evangelicals, *Completing the Face*, 7.
35 Andrew Hong, "Voting – East and West" http://andrewhong.net/2010/07/07/voting-east-and-west/
36 Duane Elmer, *Cross-cultural Conflict* (Downers Grove: Intervarsity Press, 1993), 62.
37 Hong, "Voting – East and West."

group with as many of the minority people as possible. Others, rather than break away, will attempt some sort of revenge such as spreading rumours or other subversive activities that make it difficult for the majority to conduct business. Of course, they would deny such activity if ever confronted. In more extreme cases the "loser" may isolate himself or herself and go into exile for a time.[38]

This system can be frustrating for some ABCs for a number of reasons. Firstly, they may be told by their parents to vote (as they may not care about the subject matter and would otherwise choose not to) and who or what to vote for. Parents may expect them to follow because of filial piety and respect. Secondly, they may be disappointed because "although the vote [was] unanimous or virtually so... so many people seem uncommitted to the decisions."[39] They may not be able to understand "how people could vote for something and then not get involved in the implementation process". For ABCs who follow Western thought on this subject, "voting is part of the process of decision making. ... [which] allows the group as a whole to choose."[40] It may result in ABCs beginning to question people's "sincerity, integrity, even maturity, resulting in mistrust."[41]

Running of a meeting

Because of respect and ritual propriety, a committee of people with Confucian values will have a "benevolent dictator":

In this model, the chairman functions much like king of the committee. He decides what will happen, and what will not. He decides who will do what. And other people in the committee merely function to support or obey the direction of the chairman.[42]

You will see from Figure 4 that the chairperson is the prominent person with lines between him and the committee members being strong because it is expected that the chairperson lead and the committee members be led. In this kind of committee the chairperson has a major influence in how the meeting is run and what is decided.

---

38   Elmer, *Cross-cultural Conflict*, 62.
39   Hong, "Voting – East and West."
40   Hong, "Voting – East and West."
41   Elmer, *Cross-cultural Conflict*, 57.
42   Hong, "Committees – East and West" http://andrewhong.net/2009/02/17/committees-east-and-west.

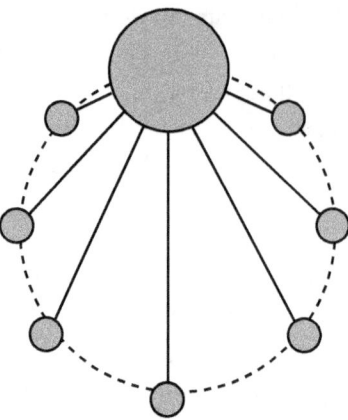

Figure 4[43]

This model may be difficult for ABCs to work within because they want a Western committee where the chairperson is more the facilitator of the committee and more equal to those involved (see Figure 5):

He sees his role as allowing others to say what they want to say, working out the intention and plan of the group, and basically serving the group. What tends to be prominent here is the group, not the chairman. Here you could have a chairman with no plan of his own of what he wants to do, yet the committee can still function well – because he is able to get out of the people what they think should happen.[44]

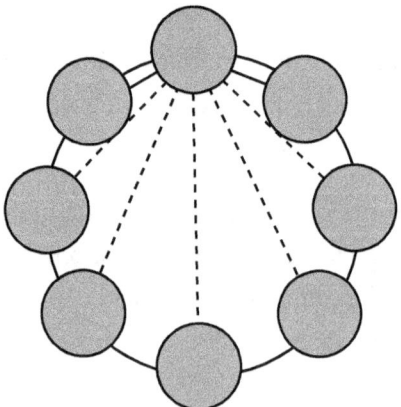

Figure 5

---

43   Figures 4 and 5 come from Hong, "Committees – East and West". Permission has been given to use them.
44   Hong, "Committees – East and West."

ABCs who do not agree with the Chairperson may wish to speak out, but this would show lack of respect and understanding of ritual propriety. It would also disrupt the harmony of the committee. They may wish for a more consultative approach in the meetings and wish for the Chairperson to allow discussion of issues. People in the committee with Confucian values may not wish to do so because it may bring shame and show a lack of respect, depending on who or what the issues are about. The Chairperson may not see it as his role to bring this to fruition.

The Mission

The examples above show that ABCs, by simply being themselves, can create conflict because they operate from a different value base. While the values of individualism and treating people as equals in a Western sense are valued and expected in South Australian Anglo-Celtic culture, to some degree, in Chinese Migrant Churches "these same values, even when demonstrated respectfully, can be considered rude, unrefined, ill-mannered and even contemptuous."[45] Once the difference in values is understood, it is easy to see how conflicts can arise.

The answer to how ABCs should deal with unintentional marginalisation due to Confucian values is complex, if there is a workable solution at all. In fact, Andrew Hong proposes in his blog titled "Second generation strategies that don't work" that all approaches can be difficult.[46] Here I will discuss only one strategy, which could be part of the answer, and that is that ABCs adopt the attitude of a missionary.

There are sound theological reasons for ABCs committing themselves to this. When God finished creating the world, he looked at the "vast array" (Genesis 2:1, New International Version) and announced that "it was very good" (Genesis 1:31). We need to celebrate diversity, including of people. As all people bear the image of God (Genesis 1:27), Elmer observes that "to learn of them with an open mind is to discover how God reveals something of himself through their distinct world and life view."[47]

---

45 Elmer, *Cross-cultural Conflict*, 62.

46 Andrew Hong, "Second Generation Ministries that Don't Work," http://andrewhong.net/2010/12/24/second-generation-strategies-that-dont-work/ . The approaches he talks about are stay and submit, communicate, fight for change, leave for another church and act as a buffer for the next generation. Ying Yee has a contrary view, however. See Ying Yee, "Second Generation Strategies that Do Work?? Maybe!" http://yingyee.wordpress.com/2013/10/19/second-generations-strategies-that-do-work-maybe/

47 Elmer, *Cross-cultural Conflict*, 13.

In Romans 14, "Paul deals with differences that endanger unity, primarily eating preferences and observance of special days."[48] Rather than be divided over these matters, he says "accept him whose faith is weak, without passing judgment on disputable matters" (Romans 14:1). Disputable matters are individual preferences, opinions or debatable points – "issues where there is reasonable doubt as to the absolutely correct interpretation."[49] At verses 19 and 20, Paul says "Let us…make every effort to do what leads to peace and to mutual edification. Do not destroy the work of God for the sake of food". Paul goes on to say "Accept one another, then, as Christ accepted you" (Romans 15:7).

Love cannot be expressed in a vacuum. It can either be expressed "egocentrically (my way) or sociocentrically (as the other person would define an act of love)."[50] If love is expressed in a contextual and incarnational way, "the fewer conflicts we will experience, the more we will be able to build authentic relationships, and the greater will be our ability to communicate God's truth." [51] It could contribute to creating a community of inclusion and embrace.

So, where an ABC does not have Confucian values, but a migrant does, it may be for the ABC to enter the mission field and express love to them in their way. For example, they could choose not to get frustrated following a vote and observe the Confucian hierarchy in a committee meeting. However, if an ABC uses this strategy, there are at least a few things they could be mindful of.

Firstly, this concept can be quite difficult for an ABC to discover. The difficulty arises because the mission field of an ABC is in their home or local church, in a culture that they have grown up in and to a community that more or less raised them. An ABC can have expectations that the Chinese Migrant Church should have the same culture and values as them and not understand that they are in fact the minority culture. They may expect the Chinese Migrant Church that they were born into to understand them.

Secondly, it can be incredibly painful and frustrating for an ABC to do. In fact, an ABC might find it easier go on the mission I described in the first sentence of this chapter - overseas, to a foreign culture or to an unknown group of people. It is more

---

48 Elmer, *Cross-cultural Conflict*, 30.
49 Elmer, *Cross-cultural Conflict*, 30.
50 Elmer, *Cross-cultural Conflict*, 14.
51 Elmer, *Cross-cultural conflict*, 14. See also Ross Langmead, "Mission and Contextualisation," *Journal of Tribal Studies*, Vol II No. 1 (January to June 1998), 45, 49 and Ross Langmead, "Taking Shape: Incarnational Mission," *Verbum SVD* 45 (2004), 173-186.

than an ordinary challenge. For ABCs to set aside their cultural identity can be almost sacrilege.[52] They will have to take the example set by Christ who did not cling to a cultural identity and became not only a Jew but also served among the Jews.[53] With humility, ABCs must consciously release their attachments to their own values. This can produce "emotional stress" and "antagonism". To become incarnate in another culture, particularly one that ABCs sometimes deliberately distinguish themselves from, is a "trial by fire, a test of inner strength, of personal faith, and most of all a test of the veracity of one's love."[54]

Thirdly, an ABC must understand Confucian values in order to be an effective missionary; "engaging contextually involves exploring worldview, language, customs, traditions and what gospel transformation might mean in each context."[55] ABCs can mistakenly believe that they understand these things because they have had a lifetime of close association with people with Confucian values. However, that may not be the case even if they know how to navigate their way around a community who values them. They may know that they exist in vague terms. They may not know them at all. They may deny them. It can take some education, provoking conversations and good thought to truly gain an appreciation of them. ABCs need to "construct....a hypothetical profile of [their] values and then compare [their] own values...to that profile."[56] From that profile, they can identify areas in their value orientation that they must adapt and change.

Fourthly, expressing love in their way does not always mean doing everything their way. Sometimes it will be necessary, but sometimes it will be wise not to if, for example, it is not biblical, lawful, reasonable, is sinful or impacts on health and safety. On some occasions when an ABC is trying to advocate for change (particularly in relation to culture) it may be effective to do things using the values of ABCs, while still loving those born overseas as much as possible. However, an ABC should understand that change is generally slow. It could be generational change. As Ying Yee says:

Real deep seated long lasting change does not happen overnight. It can take a life time. How can we expect a church, that has long standing traditions with all their cultural complexities, [to] change within a matter of a few years. It is totally unrealistic.[57]

---

52 Sherwood Lingenfelter, *Ministering Cross-Culturally* (Grand Rapids, MI: Baker Academic, 2003), 24.
53 Langmead, "Taking Shape: Incarnational Mission," 173.
54 Lingenfelter, *Ministering Cross-Culturally*, 24, 17 and 25.
55 Langmead, "Contextual Mission," 4.
56 Lingenfelter, *Ministering Cross-Culturally*, 118.
57 Ying Yee, "Second Generation Strategies that Do Work?? Maybe!"

Fifthly, given the difficulties, in my experience, it is necessary for ABCs using this approach to have support. I have received much support from ABCs who are older and more experienced in different States, ABCs who are going through the same things as me, and non-ABCs who have a particular interest in these issues such as a Senior Lecturer in Intercultural Studies. I am also involved in supporting younger ABCs who are wrestling with these issues. This is part of what "red," the organisation I founded, does. My support to them in relation to this issue includes providing mentoring, leadership training, linking them with others who can share similar experiences, and assisting them to deal with migrants in their Church context.

Finally, ABCs may be unaware of the strategy of adopting the attitude of a missionary. In order to encourage cultural intelligence amongst ABCs, more education and training is required. The churches, bible colleges and organisations like red could all have a part in this.

Conclusion

With the presence of Confucian values (such as harmony, filial piety, ritual propriety, respect and honour) in Chinese Migrant Churches there is a risk of ABCs being unintentionally marginalised. In situations such as voting and being part of a committee, ABCs are the minority culture so usually the migrants' values are preferred. If an ABC exerts their Western values, there could be no effect. Worse, there could be detrimental consequences. One solution is for ABCs to have the mindset of a missionary and to love the migrants in the way that they understand. This is part of what God calls us to do and can increase communication, result in fewer conflicts, build authentic relationships and contribute to creating a community of inclusion and embrace.

This chapter makes it seem like I am a foreigner in my own land. Sometimes it feels like that. Despite this, the Christian Migrant Church is home to me and perhaps it is also where my heart is.

7. Becoming a Diverse Multicultural Church in Central Adelaide. A Case Study

Elizabeth Vreugdenhil[1]

In 2001 Maughan Uniting Church embarked on a multicultural journey as we welcomed a Chinese congregation and a group of Sudanese desiring to worship in their own languages. As both congregations increased in size our mutual cooperation developed. In 2003 a loan fund was established to help Sudanese refugees come to Australia. Programs were developed to assist with the difficult process of settlement. When people from different cultures began attending the English speaking worship service, communicating the gospel in accessible ways became a priority as many had only limited English and a minimal knowledge of Christianity. Our role as guides and gatekeepers into Australian society entailed walking alongside those from different cultures, as we learned from their faith and courage. This chapter explores the first nine years of our multicultural journey, the methods developed and their theological and conceptual bases.

Introduction

Maughan Uniting Church's journey into a new multicultural mission during the years 2001 to 2010, occurred in response to the changing landscape of multicultural South Australia and led to the development of a complex multi-faceted ministry with people from different ethnic backgrounds. Two congregations, one Chinese and one Sudanese joined the Maughan community who also welcomed many other cultures into their English speaking congregation.

Setting the Scene: Changes in the Landscape

History and Location

In 1864 Maughan Methodist Church (later Maughan Uniting Church) was built close to the very centre of Adelaide's Central Business District albeit on the poorer western side.[2] From its inception the Church was involved with the poorest and most marginalised people.[3]

---

1 With grateful thanks to Judy Shaw, consultant for this chapter, Judy Shaw was the Coordinator of the Multicultural Ministry with the Sudanese Congregation at Maughan Uniting Church from 2003 to 2009.
2 Ivor Bailey, *Mission Story: the Story of Adelaide Central Mission*(Adelaide: Lutheran, 1987), 157.
3 Bailey, *Mission Story*, 106.

Maughan's connection to its surrounding physical and cultural landscapes was underpinned and guided by a theology of caring and hospitality inspired by the sayings of Matthew 25:31-40 ("truly I tell you, just as you did it to one of the least of these who are members of my family, you did it to me"), and biblical stories such as Abraham's hospitality to the three strangers (Genesis 18:1-15).

A Central Mission was established at Maughan Church in 1901.[4] The Minister of the church was also the Superintendent of the Mission, with church staff and members participating actively in the work of helping the poor, the homeless, and alcoholics. In the 1980's the increased professionalisation of the Central Mission led to the appointment of an independent CEO alongside a Minister to the Mission. The Congregation now no longer participated in the day to day running of the Mission. By 2001 Maughan had a greatly reduced role in helping the poor although it still provided the homeless with a free weekly meal, a Christmas day meal, and some emergency financial help. The changed relationship with the Mission, now known as Uniting Care Wesley Adelaide (UCWA), was mourned by some long term members of the congregation.

The Building

In 1964, work commenced on rebuilding the Church and Mission as one complex. The exterior style was designed to blend in with the surrounding offices to increase connections with the secular world. The cross on top of the tall tower signified "the cross over the city." Whilst this innovative approach was appropriate at the time, it later became a liability. As architectural developments enabled taller buildings to be constructed on Adelaide's unstable soil, the church tower and the cross were dwarfed by the surrounding buildings, yet the cross was too high to be visible at street level. Many passersby now did not realise Maughan was a church. Thus the very characteristics that had increased the church's connection to the community, by 2001, were hindering it.

The Congregation

From the church's inception congregational numbers waxed and waned but by the 1970's many hundreds were attending worship.[5] In later years and in keeping with many mainline churches numbers slowly declined, however. During the period of the

---

4   Bailey, *Mission Story*, 157.

5   Bailey, *Mission Story*, 109.

case study new people of all ages joined the church but overall the decline continued. Nevertheless the congregation's passion for helping others was still strong.

Passersby

Inner city churches need to be aware of the flow of passersby who may be interested in what the church has to offer. In the 1800's most passersby were of British background with some Chinese and Aboriginal people. Most were nominally Christian. By 2001 the characteristics of the passersby had changed and now included immigrants and students from all parts of Asia, and refugees from many countries including the Sudan. The very poor and homeless were a continuing presence.

Thus much had changed in the geographical and cultural landscapes surrounding Maughan Church. What remained constant however was a Church at the very centre of the city with a Christian congregation who wanted to bring the gospel to those most in need, through Christian hospitality, caring and service.

Multicultural Ministry Arrives at Maughan

In 2001 a profound change of missional direction occurred for the church as it moved from being a mono-cultural to a multicultural community.

Two groups approached the then minister of Maughan, Rev Dr Brian Phillips, asking to worship in the church in their own language – a group of about fifty Cantonese and Mandarin speaking Chinese and a small group of Dinka speaking Sudanese. Maughan church suited both groups because its central location made it accessible by public transport from all parts of the city. In the years that followed, increasing numbers of people from other countries joined the English speaking Uniting Church service.

The Uniting Church congregation embraced the consequent missional and evangelical challenges and sought to create a multicultural community. Despite many cultural differences we were united by the gospel of Jesus Christ and empowered by the Holy Spirit. Eric Law writes that:

> We are called to engage in intercultural dialogue through which we can see God more clearly apart from our own culture. We are called again and again to discern what the 'essentials' of the gospel are as we share and compare our faith and culture with others who are different.[6]

---

6   Eric H F Law, *The Bush was Blazing but not Consumed* (St Louis Missouri: Chalice, 1996), 40.

This chapter discusses: (A.) working together with the Sudanese; (B.) reaching out to immigrants in the Uniting Church congregation; and (C.) the combined multicultural ministry and mission of the three congregations.

A. Working With The Sudanese

The Loan Fund

By 2003 the Sudanese group had increased in numbers with incoming refugees, mostly from Kakuma refugee camp in Kenya. They asked the Uniting Church congregation for financial help in bringing their relatives and friends to Adelaide. Although the International Organisation of Migration paid half the fare they needed help to provide the rest of the money. The Sudanese leaders decided they would like an interest free loan fund which the recipients could pay back thus making the money available for others. Twenty thousand dollars was raised. The Sudanese selected the recipients and the Uniting Church congregation administered the finance. There was a strong sense of personal responsibility in the Sudanese community regarding the repayments as discharging your debt meant that others could come to Australia. Eventually the loan fund assisted over 100 people with only one bad debt.

The New Arrivals

There was great excitement when, in 2003, the first Sudanese family arrived in Adelaide. However it was quickly apparent that providing an airfare was only the beginning and they needed a great deal more help. Life in Australia was very different from life in Sudan let alone a refugee camp, where they had spent the last 12 years. Later two Social Work students from Flinders University were commissioned to develop a resource pack to help other churches assist Sudanese New Arrivals.[7] The pack was devised with the help of a group of Sudanese and included advice about money, banking, Centrelink, housing, clothing, use of bedding, household appliances, the cold winter weather, schooling, public transport and so on. In a rural society where cattle rather than money represented wealth, and where a strict hierarchy of family relationships existed, these issues and more had to be addressed and this must have felt overwhelming.[8] One person said that it was wonderful to be in Australia and to be safe at last without guns in the streets. However after a few months a great grief took hold of her as she adjusted to a very different way of life.

---

[7] Simone Pal and Ross Bouchier, eds. *Information for Churches Supporting New Arrivals* (Adelaide 2004); Judy Shaw, ed. *Information for Churches* (Adelaide 2006).

[8] Pal and Bouchier, eds., *Information for Churches*.

The Uniting Church members took God's call to be a good neighbour seriously and were anxious to help the New Arrivals settle into their new land. Judy Shaw, who felt a strong sense of vocation for this work, became the Coordinator. She recruited volunteers from the Uniting Church congregation and beyond. Non church volunteers were welcome provided their values were congruent with Christianity.

The task of providing practical help and advice soon proved to be more difficult than originally thought. Cultural differences impeded understanding one another with regard to such things as attitudes to property, gender roles, conflict resolution, child rearing practices, concepts of time, and attitudes to helping and hospitality to name but a few. This last issue had to be addressed promptly as differences in the way each group understood the helping relationship was a serious hindrance.

The Helping Relationship: Issues

Limitations and Boundaries

When someone is helped within a particular culture both helper and recipient understand their respective roles. The recipient usually knows the amount and type of help that can be reasonably expected and the helper knows approximately how much will be expected of them. At first, it must have seemed to the New Arrivals that we were extraordinarily wealthy and could meet their every need. This meant that too much was asked of the volunteers who felt inadequate and guilty when they could not satisfy the needs of people who had suffered so much. Some volunteers were tempted to rescue people and try to do everything for them. While rescuing may be necessary in an immediate crisis and can feel wonderful, if continued it creates unhelpful dependency and impedes a person's adjustment to a new way of life.

Formal and Informal Systems of help[9]

In Sudanese culture people rely on informal systems of help. Members of a family group or clan must give help and hospitality if asked, but would never seek advice from a professional person outside of their clan.[10] In Australia, some informal help from family and friends is considered appropriate, but when in serious difficulty, Anglo Australians rely on formal systems of welfare from government and non-government welfare agencies. This cultural difference caused difficulties. While the

---

9   Elizabeth Vreugdenhil, "Power and Influence in Social Work Practice: the Organizational Context" (Ph.D Thesis 1990, University of NSW), 4.9.

10 Pal et al., *Information for Churches*.

New Arrivals trusted the church people and would accept help directly from them, they were reluctant to approach welfare agencies.

Expectations of gratitude

Expressing formal gratitude for help is culturally determined. While saying "please" and "thank you" is very important in Anglo Australian culture, many cultures, including the Sudanese do not use these expressions to the same extent. This can lead to hurt feelings and the incorrect assumption that the recipient is ungrateful.

Power in Helping Relationships

In Australian culture the helping relationship, by its very nature, bestows more power on the helper than the recipient.[11] Knowledge is a source of power, and so knowledge of the mainstream culture and its resources gives power to the helper.[12] It was important to minimise the power differential between the New Arrivals and ourselves. Law writes "(In the scriptures) the powerful in society are challenged to achieve equality among the people of God."[13]

The Helping Relationship: A way ahead

The Sudanese Support Group

Both Sudanese and Anglo Australians needed to find a way through the complexities of the helping relationship and the many cultural differences between us. To address these issues Judy Shaw proposed that we set up a Sudanese Support Group as a forum for our two communities to listen to one another and work together.

The terms of reference of the Support Group stated there were to be equal numbers of Sudanese and Anglo-Australians and equal numbers of men and women with Judy as Coordinator. The Aim was to assist Sudanese people sponsored by members of the Sudanese Maughan Church community to settle into life in South Australia.

The main objectives were:

- to support the Maughan Sudanese community as they help their own people;

---

11 Dora Peyser, *The Strong and the Weak: A Sociological Study* (Sydney: Currawong, 1951), 8.
12 JRP French and B Raven, "The Bases of Social Power" in *Group Dynamics,* eds., D Cartwright and A Zander (New York: Harper and Row 1959), 118-129.
13 Eric HF Law, *The Wolf Shall Dwell with the Lamb: a Spirituality for Leadership in a Multicultural Community* (St Louis Missouri: Chalice, 1993) 41.

- to act as guides and gatekeepers into Australian society until the Sudanese people could cope on their own;
- to enhance the ability of the Sudanese people to make the best possible adjustment to Australian life.

This was a strengths based model of helping based on an equal partnership between the two groups who each brought their knowledge and expertise to the situation. It differed radically from the previous charity model, which was based on meeting the recipient's needs, where the helper had all the knowledge and expertise and the recipient brought nothing beyond their needs to the relationship.[14]

The atmosphere of the support group meetings was open, friendly and non-judgmental. The Uniting Church members were soon able to explain the limitations of our help. When this was understood unreasonable requests could be curtailed. For example people were taught how to use a bus timetable rather than continually being given lifts to appointments. This approach helped people to develop skills that would aid independence.

As mutual understanding grew we learned to accommodate one another's cultural attitudes. For example, given the reluctance of the New Arrivals to use formal welfare systems, the volunteers brokered such help for them when necessary, while understanding that gratitude may not be expressed as expected.

When cultural practices clashed each group was faced with the difficult task of discerning their own culture (which is usually taken as given and is rarely articulated), and then explaining how it worked. For example, when arrangements went awry the Australians expected the Sudanese to approach them and explain what had happened. However in Sudanese culture it is polite to avoid the person you may have offended if they are of high status, until they approach you and initiate some form of resolution and reconciliation. The direct approach is seen by Sudanese as arrogant, and avoidance is seen by Australians as shifty, whereas both approaches were meant to be polite. Discussing these issues openly and without judgement enabled a way forward to be found.

The strengths based model enabled the power differences between the two groups to be minimised. No longer were the Anglo Australian helpers one up and the Sudanese

---

14 Susan Rans and Hilary Altman, *Asset-based Strategies for Faith Communities* (Chicago, IL: ACTA, 2002), 2.

recipients one down.[15] The Sudanese understood their own culture and could judge which needs were the most pressing and which options would be best for their people. They could explain cultural practices and were also able to identify behaviour that was unreasonable rather than culturally determined. The Anglo Australians understood the complexities of Australian society and had networks that could be used. Thus they could act as guides and gatekeepers to Australian society and so enable the Sudanese to find their own way of making a successful adjustment. This model was appreciated by the Sudanese who were keen for other groups to adopt this method of working together.

Guided by the Sudanese Support Group the volunteers worked tirelessly to aid the New Arrivals and also to help with longer-term settlement issues. It is not possible in this chapter to cover the many areas of assistance given. Some examples are as follows:

Finding housing

Landlords were nervous about offering leases to Sudanese and needed persuasion and reassurance from the volunteers. This was followed up with instruction in housework and gardening, especially for the young men as gender roles in Africa are strictly defined and they lacked these skills. In one suburb drug dealers pushed drugs under the New Arrivals' doors in an attempt to get them addicted. Other accommodation in better areas had to be found quickly. Support in using the legal system was provided when landlords tried to take financial advantage of their Sudanese tenants.

Settling into the neighbourhood

New Arrivals were assisted in making connections to their new communities by linking them to local organisations such as the church, kindergarten etc. Other help was provided, e.g. school enrolments, using public transport, coping with the health system and finding employment. A different cultural understanding of time impacted on much of this work. For example, opportunities for employment are lost if the applicant turns up for the interview a day late. This is also disappointing for the volunteer who may have spent considerable time setting up the interview. However, with patience and explanation the new sense of time was gradually learnt.

Schooling

Some scholarships at private schools were negotiated for Sudanese secondary school students.

15 Peyser, *Strong and the Weak*, 8.

Projects

Government funding was obtained for two projects, "Living in Harmony"[16] and "Aussie Mates"[17] to further improve understanding between different cultures and to help New Arrivals make their adjustment to Australian life.

Living in Harmony

Several multicultural days on such topics as food, building relationships, recreation, the place of the law, the place of humour, and ceremonies, rituals and symbols, were planned by a multicultural steering committee comprising Nuer and Dinka Sudanese, Chinese and Anglo Australians. Most wanted to celebrate the differences between the cultures but the Sudanese wanted to emphasise the things each had in common. Their experiences in Africa had taught them that differences cause dissension. Thus Nuer and Dinka cooks looked for things in common to share, but all were delighted to learn how to cook a Chinese stirfry as this could be done quickly after a tiring working day.

Some cultural mistakes included inviting a journalist and photographer from a daily paper to the cooking day. A published photograph of a young Sudanese man and several women, standing, eating together in the outside atrium, greatly upset the Sudanese community. In traditional Sudanese culture men and women eat separately, sitting down, inside. Their culture was changing in their new land but at different rates and in differing ways.

When sharing ceremonies and rituals, weddings were discussed. After a young Indian woman and her mother in law described her wedding day for her arranged marriage, the Sudanese group relaxed and gained the confidence needed to share their customs. It is difficult to do this if you are afraid that people will judge you for being different. The day helped to alleviate fears and build bridges between the cultures.

Aussie Mates

A group of Australian families were trained to mentor Sudanese families. The project included a homework club, and various group outings to encourage participation in community activities.

---

16 Judy Shaw, "Living in Harmony Grant Activity Report, 2006," Program funded by Department of Immigration and Multicultural and Indigenous Affairs.

17 Judy Shaw, "Aussie Mates Project Evaluation report 2008," Program funded by Community Benefit SA.

Sudanese Welfare Workers

In 2009 the Sudanese Support Group expressed concern that the Sudanese were still not accessing appropriate UCWA services. Meetings were facilitated between UCWA senior managers and Sudanese community leaders which resulted in the employment of two Sudanese workers, one male and one female, to assist the Sudanese community in this regard. Thus a transition could be made from an informal to a formal system of care. The project was a success and brought to a close the need for the Sudanese Support Group.

B. Reaching Out To Immigrants In The Uniting Church Congregation

The Signs

When the Maughan Uniting Church congregation realised that passersby were mistaking the church for an office building we knew that we had to make better connections with the community. A graphic designer, Bronwyn Drew, was employed to design suitable signs to make our invisible life, visible. Following extensive consultation, Bronwyn created signs with large photographs of people of varying cultures and life stages, with accompanying questions which reflected the congregation's vision and mission. These were positioned on the outside walls to catch the eye of pedestrians and passing motorists. They included photos of a child with a grandparent and the question "Do you want to know the joy of the generations?", an Asian man with the question "Do you want to support those in need?", another of a young woman asking "Do you want to just be still and reflect?"; and so on. The photos clearly proclaimed "the ideals upon which the Kingdom of God is founded."[18] Underneath the photos was the invitation to "Visit us at Maughan." Two large signs advertising worship times, office hours etc were placed on the tower walls at eye level with photos of our intergenerational congregation engaged in various activities. Crosses were placed on three of the tower walls at an easily noticeable height. Maughan Uniting Church was now clearly seen to be a welcoming church for all ages and backgrounds.

People of differing nationalities were observed studying the signs and soon the number of visitors increased thus bringing multicultural ministry into the Uniting Church congregation. Some were Christian, some had no previous faith background, and a few were from other faiths. Some had settled in Australia and others were students in Adelaide for a limited time. We made no overt attempt to convert anyone but we were

---

18   Anne Morisy, *Beyond the Good Samaritan: Community Ministry and Mission* (London: Continuum, 1997), 110.

ready and willing to discuss our faith if asked. All were met with hospitality, kindness, and practical help if needed.

Worship Services

As many of the newcomers had limited English some changes were made to the worship to make the gospel accessible to all. The content remained the same but plain language was used and a short sermon summary and directions about when to sit or stand were provided. Being able to understand what was happening was greatly appreciated by the newcomers. A young Chinese woman wrote to us after her very first church service to say she felt "cleaned in mind and body by the noble words." Teaching the faith to individuals with limited English and no previous knowledge of the Christian story was a challenging task but children's bible story books proved helpful.

The newcomers were included in the life of the church wherever possible, e.g. in the choir, reading scripture, and contributing ideas from their cultures. They attended bible study groups and baptism and membership classes. Two were elected to Church Council.

The Centre of Welcome

To help new immigrants feel at home in Adelaide, Rev Liellie McLaughlin and Judy Shaw initiated and developed the Centre of Welcome.[19] It comprised a multicultural playgroup and an English class with a pastoral focus.

C. Combined Multicultural Ministry and Mission of the Three Congregations

In order to coexist peacefully in such a confined space the three congregations needed to exercise great hospitality toward one another. We acknowledged our common faith and began to develop a multicultural identity which in turn enabled an optimum expression of individual mission. Our mutual cooperation was in itself a witness to the values of the Kingdom of God.[20] As one of the Chinese leaders remarked, "We are brothers and sisters in Christ."

---

19 Rev Liellie McLaughlin joined the ministry team in 2008. The Centre of Welcome was funded by Uniting Foundation Seed Funding Innovative Project Grants.

20 Morisy, *Beyond the Good Samaritan*, 110.

Two important elements of our mutual ministry and mission were *sharing the property* and *combined multilingual worship*.

Sharing the Property

The Chinese and Sudanese congregations quickly grew to some hundreds. With three congregations and up to 700 people sharing the building each Sunday, the likelihood of chaos and conflict was high. Nevertheless we got along well, with many cross cultural friendships being formed; but there were some problems. For example, there were large numbers of children which led to inevitable breakages, damage to the courtyard garden, and so on. The internal layout of the building further complicated matters. The interior of the church had been designed to connect to the UCWA offices to signify the permanent union of Church and Mission. However this provided open access from the church to the UCWA area. For example frequent opening the fire doors, which were alarmed at the weekend, led to the Uniting Church congregation being fined as we were responsible to UCWA for the care of the property.

As one of the Uniting Church ministers I had the unpleasant duty of constantly asking the other leaders to control their respective children. In order to avoid much mutual embarrassment we formed a joint property committee to deal with these issues. This proved to be an important step in maintaining harmonious relations.

Joint Property Committee

In my doctoral thesis I observe that setting up a formal committee within an organisation to coordinate the work of several departments (or in this case congregations), prevents disorganisation in day to day operations.[21] It enables separate groups to form a common group where everyone can work together. In addition, the wider organisations/congregations recognise the legitimacy of decisions made in a formal meeting. Thus the joint property committee enabled us, with much prayer and discussion, to understand each other's point of view and reach mutually satisfactory solutions which would be respected and owned by the congregations. For example, the committee decided that all damage and alarm fines would be paid for by the congregation of the offending children and the problems ceased.

---

21 Vreugdenhil, "Power and Influence," 10,19.

Multi-lingual Worship

On Good Friday and Pentecost each year the three communities worshipped together. These combined multilingual Services were an important statement of the unity of faith in the diversity of culture. They represented an integrated approach to cultural differences as each group brought aspects of their own culture to the common experience.[22]

The Good Friday Service began with the Sudanese choir processing into the church with a large rough hewn cross, followed by the three ministers, with the sound of African drums and chanting filling the church. Then the Easter story was reflected upon in short segments, each worship leader speaking in their mother tongue with translations provided, either on screen or in paper form. We sang the hymns we knew in common, e.g. "There is a green hill far away," each one in their own language, creating a glorious cacophony of sound. The various choirs, accompanied by traditional instruments added to the richness of the worship. The Service moved swiftly, to minimise the potential boredom that comes from not understanding the words.

The children were involved in the Pentecost Service – a Uniting Church practice not usually shared by the other congregations. We worshipped together with much colour and movement which included singing and dancing from the Sudanese children's choir. At the conclusion of the Service we shared a communal meal with food from our respective cultures.

While a substantial number of people attended these services, not everyone came as some preferred to worship in their own language. These people had adjusted to life in Australia by keeping separate their expression of faith.[23] However as the years progressed more people came to appreciate worshipping together. A Chinese woman remarked on how much she had enjoyed the Pentecost celebrations that year saying, "At first I didn't see the point of these Multicultural Services, but now I do. The Holy Spirit is here today." After one Good Friday Service an elderly Chinese woman, clothed in traditional dress, clasped my hands and said with joy, "We are one. We are one."

---

22 John W Berry, "Immigration, Acculturation and Adaptation," *Applied Psychology* Vol 46 (1997), 10.
23 Berry, "Immigration, Acculturation and Adaptation," 10.

Conclusion

As the physical and cultural landscapes altered, Maughan Uniting Church congregation, with its long history of a loving and caring connection to its surroundings, and its practice of radical hospitality, took up the new challenge of multicultural mission which had arrived on its doorstep. This was a complex and difficult mission that required the congregation to take up the cross of discipleship as they cared for those in need.[24] Along with the difficulties there were rich rewards as we came to know Christians from other cultures whose depth of love and faith despite adversity, was astounding. We were also fortunate to be given the great privilege of sharing the faith with people who had never before heard the Christian story. In the words of the writer of Hebrews, "Do not neglect to show hospitality to strangers, for by doing that some have entertained angels without knowing it." (Hebrews 13:2, NRSV).

---

24 Morisy, *Beyond the Good Samaritan*, 109.

C. Mission in a Post-Christian Society

Hear the voice of God our future calling.
We can walk the path of change.
With Jesus as our guide, move on.

Though we long for safety, God disturbs us
Out into the marketplace.
In the Spirit, struggling pilgrims
Can be the future church.

Ross Langmead, "Future Church"(1996)

8. But is it Church?
Karyl Davison

Genuinely fresh expressions of church rarely look like church as we understand it. So much so that I am often asked "But how is that any different from a social club?" In an attempt to answer that question, I will briefly explore some claims about the essence of church in scripture and tradition, but I will also challenge some common understandings of church. Underlying these challenges is the assumption that the church needs to undergo a "corrective shift," a "radical rethink about the actual mode of the church's engagement"[1] in order to be relevant and able to share the gospel in our vastly changed context.

It is a beautiful autumn day in the South West of Western Australia and the community has come out to a local park to enjoy the day! Games are played. There are even a few races echoing Sunday school picnics of a past era and children concentrate on various craft activities. As well as coffee, parents and grandparents enjoy the cupcakes on offer. Then comes the time for the Easter Egg Hunt, except that the big kids have already been around and grabbed more than their share. There is no need for concern though, as the volunteers from the Eaton/Millbridge Community Project (EMCP) make sure that everyone gets their fair share of the eggs.

This annual Easter Egg Hunt is just one of the events the EMCP organises for, and with, the community. It is offered as a gift and there is no expectation beyond the hope that participants enjoy being outdoors as a family, and perhaps meet their neighbours.

Such events are emblematic of the life of the EMCP in its first 2 ½ years. The response from the community has been amazingly positive and significantly some people, initially suspicious of any connection with the church, are now strongly supportive. However, in the church, I find myself located at its very margins. When explaining the EMCP to people in the church, the most common response is, "But is it really church?"

I will try to answer this question by drawing on scripture and tradition as well as more recent developments in theology and the particular context in which the Project is located. I will argue that this context requires "a new imagination that expands

---

1   Alan Hirsch, *The Forgotten Ways: Reactivating the Missional Church* (Grand Rapids, Michigan: Brazos, 2006), 51.

beyond our current concept of church."[2] It also requires, as Ross Langmead identified in "Contextual Mission: An Australian Perspective" in 2009, "incarnational mission, integrating word and deed as we live into the kingdom, in the hope that in God's power the story will be heard freshly by an ignorant generation."[3]

The Eaton/Millbridge Community Project is one example of this new imagination. It is a fresh expression of church which enacts simple acts of radical hospitality in and with the community, thus providing a tangible expression of God's love in the real life of the neighbourhood.

What is "church"?

One of the challenges we face whenever we try to explore what is essential to our understanding of the church is the multiplicity of meanings attached to the word "church." At times in the church's history "church" has been equated with clergy, with people speaking of "entering the church", with a building, an institution or its organisation, and doctrine.[4] "Going to church" most often means attending a Sunday morning service of worship. All of these meanings carry some truth about what we understand by church and undoubtedly church exists in relation to them all.[5] However they also convey something of the challenge faced in ascertaining what church really is. As much as possible I will concentrate on what theologians have asserted the essence of church as being, and how that might be expressed in the context of the Eaton/Millbridge community.

As we begin to explore what might constitute the essence of the church, it is crucial to remember that "the church never exists in a vacuum" but is always "developed within a particular cultural context."[6] As Kung noted:

> There is not and never was an essence of the Church by itself, separate, chemically pure, distilled from the stream of historical forms, and no form of the church, not even that in the New Testament, mirrors the Church's essence perfectly and exhaustively.[7]

---

2 Paul Sparks, Tim Soerens and Dwight Friesen, *The New Parish: How Neighbourhood Churches are Transforming Mission, Discipleship and Community* (Downers Grove: Intervarsity Press, 2014), 30.

3 Ross Langmead, "Contextual Mission: An Australian Perspective," Paper presented to ANZAMS mini-conference, Auckland (30-31 October, 2009).

4 Harvey Cox, *The Future of Faith* (New York: HarperCollins, 2009), 97.

5 Craig Van Gelder, *The Essence of the Church: A Community Created by the Spirit* (Grand Rapids: Baker Books, 2000), 14.

6 Van Gelder, *Essence of the Church*, 41.

7 Hans Kung, *The Church* (London: Search, 1968).

With this important proviso in mind, it can be said that theologians have long disagreed on what comprises the essence of the church.[8] Resulting from efforts to apply biblical understandings about the church to specific historical settings, different churches have stressed different issues or come to different conclusions about the same issue, with the result that there exists a wide range of ecclesiologies.[9] A full critique of these ecclesiologies would require a book in itself, so I will focus briefly on some of the most significant.

Within decades of the birth of Christianity, church leaders began formulating orientation programs for new recruits who had not known Jesus or his disciples personally, replacing faith *in* him with tenets *about* him. Prior to this, to be a Christian meant to live in Jesus' spirit, embrace his hope and to follow him in the world that he had begun.[10]

After the legitimising of the church, and as a result of the Councils of Nicea and Constantinople, the bishops named four attributes as representing what they believed to be the essential characteristics of the church in the world: one, holy, catholic, and apostolic. When the Apostles Creed came into final form in the eighth century a fifth characteristic was added: the communion of saints. These five attributes came to be the common way of describing the church for many centuries. Echoing biblical language, the church is to be one and holy as it displays the presence of God in the world. The characteristic of catholic, or universal, was therefore self-evident. Describing the church as apostolic meant that the church was founded on the work of the apostles and prophets and it confirmed that the church's authority and teaching were based on the work of the original founders of the church.[11] The communion of saints alludes to the church being a community of people across the ages.

A significant shift occurred in the late medieval period, when the Protestant Reformation began to see these characteristics as exclusive properties which the Roman Catholic Church alone possessed, and no longer seen as characteristics that were to be consistently demonstrated. While not actually rejecting the Nicene attributes, the reformers downplayed them in favour of two or three marks of the church to ensure that pure preaching of the Word and the proper administration of the sacraments were maintained. With this focus on preaching and the sacraments,

---

8   Michael Moynagh, *Church for Every Context: An Introduction to Theology and Practice* (Norwich: SCM, 2012), 104.
9   Van Gelder, *Essence of the Church*, 47.
10 Cox, *The Future of Faith*, 5.
11 Van Gelder, *Essence of the Church*, 50.

worship came to be viewed as the primary ministry of the church the legacy of which remains in Protestant churches today.[12] While it was not intended, the church came to be conceived as "the place where certain things happen" rather than the people or presence.[13] It also became essential to establish who would be authorised to carry out these tasks, which led to an emphasis on defining, developing, organising and governing the *work* of the church. Any notion of a ministry of believers was overshadowed by the rise of a professional clergy[14] and the main task of many small congregations became understood as "keeping the doors open on Sunday morning."[15]

In his important work on the foundational document of the Uniting Church in Australia, the *Basis of Union*, Dutney answers the question "How do we know (the church) is the church?" by outlining the classic Reformation marks of the church: the word truly preached, the sacraments rightly administered, and godly discipline.[16] But, he says that these marks are used in such a way (in the *Basis*) that a fourth mark, "mission" underlies the others.[17] The writers "suggested that the measure of preaching, sacramental celebration, and disciple-making is the extent to which these activities equip the participants for mission in the world."[18]

The emphasis on mission in the *Basis of Union* coincided with the articulation of a new vision of mission. At a missionary conference in Germany in 1932 Barth commented that in the early church, the term *missio Dei* did not have to do with sending missionaries to other countries but was an expression of the divine sending forth of self.[19] In other words mission was not a human activity but the action of God. In practical terms this resulted in a shift from understanding missions as just one of the tasks of the church, a marginal task at that, to an understanding of mission as an inherent aspect of the nature of the church.[20] In this re-emerging ecclesiology, the church is seen as essentially missionary – it is not the sender but the one sent. Mission,

---

12 Van Gelder, *Essence of the Church*, 52-53, 57.

13 Darrell L Guder (ed), *Missional Church: A Vision for the Sending of the Church in North America* (Grand Rapids: Eerdmans, 1998), 79-80.

14 Van Gelder, *Essence of the Church*, 58

15 From conversations with small rural congregations in the Presbyteries of Central Queensland and Mary Burnett while the writer was Rural Ministry Coordinator 2008-2012.

16 Andrew Dutney, *Where Did the Joy Come From? Revisiting the Basis of Union* (Melbourne: Uniting Church Press, 2001), 21.

17 Andrew Dutney, *Manifesto for Renewal* (Melbourne: Joint Board of Christian Education, 1986), 32-35.

18 Dutney, *Where did the joy come from?*, 21.

19 Alan Kreider & Eleanor Kreider, *Worship & Mission after Christendom* (Harrisonburg: Herald, 2011), 44.

20 Kreider & Kreider, *Worship & Mission*, 44.

therefore, is not secondary to the church's being. Instead the church exists in being sent and building itself up for the sake of mission.[21] Put bluntly, "mission is the most basic reason for the existence of the church."[22]

The task of the Joint Commission on Church Union, initiated in 1957 to work towards the union of the Congregational, Methodist and Presbyterian Churches in Australia was not simply concerned with the mechanical problems of how to merge three denominational institutions "but with the existential question of what it means to be the church" in the new, post war Australia. The question of "the Faith of the Church" had already been on the agenda of the international ecumenical movement for at least thirty years. But with the new impetus and hope brought on by the 1952 Lund World Conference on Faith and Order, the Joint Commission went beyond confessionalism and comparative ecclesiology as it listened for God's contemporary call: "There was no question of dispensing with the traditional creeds and confessions, but the Commission sought to emphasise that their true value could only be appreciated when due consideration was paid to their limitations."[23] Firstly, a confession only has authority in so far as it points to, and 'puts itself under' the witness of Scripture.[24] Secondly, a confession made in a certain time and place is always subject to "eschatological correction", speaking as it does of something of which it knows wholly but not in its particularity, and always remaining open to the possibility of correction by the Word of God.[25] To the surprise of "many European observers" the Commission took two lessons from the Barmen Declaration[26]: first, the affirmation of the centrality of Jesus Christ as the Word of God, and second, the call to go beyond confessionalism to enunciate the faith appropriate to the historical occasion.[27] In his preface to the 1978 edition of the Commission's first report Davis McCaughey reminded members of the three Churches that "Faith comes by hearing, and we asked men and women to listen again."

---

21 David J Bosch, *Transforming Mission: Paradigm Shifts in Theology of Mission* (New York: Orbis Books, 2008), 372-373.
22 Douglas John Hall, *Why Christian: For Those on the Edges of Faith* (Minneapolis: Fortress, 1998), 138.
23 Dutney, *Manifesto for Renewal*, 13-15, 17.
24 O S Tomkins (Ed), *The Third World Conference on Faith and Order* in Dutney, *Manifesto for Renewal*, 11.
25 "The Faith of the Church" The First Report of the Joint Commission on Church Union (1959) (Melbourne, 1978) 19.
26 The 1934 Theological Declaration of Barmen emerged out of an effort by the German confessing churches to mount ecumenical opposition to the totalising claims of Nazism, and the Declaration is now considered an important step forward in the history of the European ecumenical movement. Theological Declaration of Barmen, Cited May 31, 2001, http://berkleycenter.georgetown.edu/.
27 Dutney, *Manifesto for Renewal*, 17-20.

Church as an expression of the gospel of Jesus

Echoing words in the Commission's first report, I believe "the present to be an occasion important enough to justify us in speaking afresh of the faith."[28] I agree with Hirsch: "I do not think that the inherited formulas (for being church) will work anymore."[29] We are past time for "tinkering around the edges," leaving the prevailing assumptions of church and mission intact. Those tools and techniques fitted previous eras of Western history but do not work any longer.[30] The evidence is all around us. The results of a 2013 Uniting Church Census showed that there has been a 31% decline in the number of congregations since 1990, and a decline of 40% in the number of people attending church in the same time.[31] "A fresh hearing of the gospel" and contemplation of its vision of church in the light of recent social and cultural trends is required.[32]

Kung contends that the essence of the church is in the good news told in the New Testament that is continually spawning the church in every time and place, and always embodied in some tangible, visible form that is shaped by its particular time in history and its place in some specific human society.[33] "But what explains the church – what makes it the church – is that its life is birthed by the Holy Spirit as the Spirit gives hearing and response to the gospel."[34]

The gospel is both Jesus himself *and* it is the gospel that he preached and lived out.[35] In giving testimony about Jesus, the gospel writers select stories and sayings about Jesus' deeds, about bearing fruit, doing God's will, keeping the commandments, being perfect and about practicing justice. This points to a very specific understanding of the church's purpose and mission: neither right doctrine nor any claims to being spirit led,[36] nor "ordered liberty" in services of worship serve any purpose if not corroborated by the bearing of fruit.[37] For those who choose to follow Jesus' way, who collectively represent the church, it means turning both to God and neighbour, and living out the

---

28 "The Faith of the Church," The First Report of the Joint Commission on Church Union (1959) in Rob Bos & Geoff Thompson (eds), *Theology for Pilgrims: Selected Theological Documents of the Uniting Church in Australia* (Sydney: Uniting Church Press, 2008) 41.

29 Hirsch, *Forgotten Ways*, 16.

30 Hirsch, *Forgotten Ways*, 17.

31 NCLS Research, *2013 Uniting Church Census of Congregations and Ministers* (Sydney: NCLS Research, 2014).

32 Guder (ed), *Missional Church*, 86.

33 Guder (ed), *Missional Church*, 86.

34 Kung, *The Church*, 22-24.

35 Guder (ed), *Missional Church*, 87-88.

36 "Ordered Liberty" refers to Uniting Church in Australia Assembly "Guidelines for the leadership of worship for those ordained or commissioned to such a role in the Uniting Church in Australia" at http://assembly.uca.org.au/cudw/worship-resources-and-publications/item/862-guidelines-for-worship.

37 Bosch, *Transforming Mission*, 81.

teaching of Jesus.[38] The absence of the gospel Jesus preached, in the gospel the church has preached, has woefully impoverished the church's sense of missional identity.[39]

Guder also reminds us that the foundational and formative event of the Christian movement is the incarnation of Jesus himself, as the self-revelation of God.[40] Jesus is God's presence in the world. In spite of divergent interpretations, Christians acknowledge that in Jesus of Nazareth, God was present, and that he moved into our neighbourhood in an act of humble love the likes of which the world has never known.[41] In turn, God's sovereign love accomplishes its saving purpose through the people of God, called to serve and witness to God-self.

In the incarnational event, God's presence in the world was once again defined as the "people of God." No longer was God to be seen as confined to sacred places such as the burning bush, the tabernacle or the Holy of Holies, nor to holy people, for example the high priest. God's presence was everywhere, experienced in and amongst the people who were made in God's own image. The prophet Jeremiah foreshadows this when he tells the people of Israel that God will make a new covenant with them: "I will put my law within them, and I will write it on their hearts; and I will be their God, and they shall be my people" (Jeremiah 31:33). In the gospels, Matthew 26 in particular, Jesus made clear that his life ministry was the establishment of the new covenant which would give access both to God's grace and participation in the new community created by the spirit to all people.[42] This new community was expected to carry the gospel message to the ends of the earth.

Unfortunately, while those in the missional movement have taken up their identity as the people of God,[43] far too many church members, including many church leaders, still struggle to accept concepts of church as a communal entity or presence, or the community as the bearer of missional responsibility.[44] For these people, church is still conceived as the place where Christians gather for worship and to manage the business of the church. Much of the church continues to be "a prisoner of its own theories and prejudices its own forms and laws rather than being a prisoner of its Lord."[45]

---

38 Bosch, *Transforming Mission*, 81.
39 Guder (ed), *Missional Church*, 87.
40 Darrell L Guder, *The Incarnation and the Church's Witness* (Eugene: Wipf and Stock, 1999), 1.
41 Hirsch, *Forgotten Ways*, 131.
42 Van Gelder, *Essence of the Church*, 139.
43 Sparks et.al. *The New Parish*, 45.
44 Guder (ed), *Missional Church*, 80.
45 Kung, *The Church*, 4.

However if we, like the early church, take the incarnation seriously, we must also take seriously the call to *live* incarnationally. Jesus identified two commandments as those that lie at the very heart of his way: to love God and to love our neighbour as one's self. We are told in Acts that the early followers of Jesus lived among the people of a particular place while practicing the way of Jesus together; they distinguished themselves by loving and serving the neighbours.[46] Jesus' call on the church is to understand mission locally. "We cannot negotiate around the fact that neighbourliness and neighbourhood are intimately tied in with the call of God, making the neighbourhood one of the most obvious and immediate contexts for Christian mission, and the place to which we are called."[47]

When we understand church as being the people of God rather than the church as building or institution, or even worship, we are able to acknowledge that God is present in the community *before* we attempt to engage the community in mission. Frost develops this concept, arguing for a belief in prevenient grace which assumes that God goes before us even into the most irreligious situations, and creates environments in which our Christlike example can be received.[48] Mission then, is about seeing what God is up to in our neighbourhoods and joining in. In our contemporary context, and contrary to what churchgoers might think, there are many followers of Jesus in the community who are not members of any Church and who "are loving their neighbours as an expression of their love for God."[49]

When we envisage the church as the people of God we also understand that the church is present when people are practicing the presence of God in their own lives, and the lives of their neighbours.[50] Instead of being content in our buildings "we need to get close enough to people that our lives rub up against their lives – so close that they can see the incarnated Christ in our values, beliefs and practices as expressed in cultural forms that make sense and convey impact."[51]

Moving into the neighbourhood: hospitality as missional church

Like a growing number of writers on mission, Sparks *et.al.* urge followers of Jesus to follow him into the neighbourhood with fellow followers of Jesus, allowing the

---

46 Sparks et.al. *The New Parish*, 39.
47 Simon Carey Holt, *God Next Door: Spirituality & Mission in the Neighbourhood* (Brunswick East: Acorn, 2007), 59.
48 Michael Frost, *Exiles: Living Missionally in a Post-Christian Culture* (Peabody: Hendrickson, 2006), 141.
49 Sparks et.al. *The New Parish*, 29.
50 Holt, *God Next Door,* 92.
51 Frost, *Exiles*, 55.

incarnation of God to form our imagination for faithful presence.[52] Just as Jesus "became flesh and blood, and moved into the neighbourhood" so also the people of God are meant to be a tangible expression of God's love in the real life of the neighbourhood.[53] Paul's words in the first letter to the Corinthians "let all that you do be done in love" calls us to live out our faith as a community in such a way that the world can see in your life together the transforming power of God's love.[54]

One way of being that tangible expression of God's love in the neighbourhood is through hospitality. There is probably no greater admonition to the people of Israel than the frequently repeated law of hospitality.[55] Again and again the prophets and lawgivers, including Jesus, exhorted their people to exercise hospitality toward the stranger. Paul seemed to regard hospitality as a qualification for leadership in early Christian communities.[56]

Whilst many people today might regard hospitality as entertaining family and friends, hospitality as practiced by ancient civilisations was about welcoming strangers into a home and offering them food, shelter and protection. For most of the Christian church's history, hospitality required not only responding to the stranger's physical need, but also a recognition of their worth and common humanity.[57] In our individualised and privatised world, this fuller expression of hospitality is subversive and counter cultural. Because of that, the practice of hospitality in our neighbourhoods can transform lives, not by imposing a false religiosity, not by demanding that certain rules be kept, but by allowing love experienced to flow through their lives and the lives of those around them, in the ordinariness of life.

Like all key biblical concepts, hospitality is relational. It is about relating to the other, not in an attempt to "get them to come to church", nor "in order to absorb them into one's own pre-determined worldview, but in order to achieve a real relationship with them."[58]

---

52 Sparks et.al., *The New Parish*, 46.
53 Sparks et.al., *The New Parish*, 26.
54 Guder, *The Incarnation and the Church's Witness*, 43.
55 Hall, *Why Christian?*, 148.
56 Christine D Pohl, *Making Room: Recovering Hospitality as a Christian Tradition* (Grand Rapids: Eerdmans, 1999), 5.
57 Pohl, *Making Room*, 6.
58 Hall, *Why Christian?*, 148.

This is the way the Eaton/Millbridge Community Project expresses itself as the people of God in its neighbourhood. In these suburbs where it is common for people not to know their neighbours at all, creating events where people gather as community is subversive and counter cultural. These events create opportunities for neighbours to meet, and for us all to make connections with people in our neighbourhood. Over time, some of these connections have become relationships of trust.

That we offer these community events as a gift is also counter cultural in our overwhelmingly consumer culture. It is our practice to always provide food and drink at our events because, as Frost reminds us, within the practice of hospitality is potential for transformation – sharing a table can be a sacred act.[59] Jesus' many meals, shared with friends and strangers alike, are never just symbolic: they represent friendship, community and welcome.[60] They represent a new world, a new outlook, and they point to God's new realm.

Not only does the EMCP offer events to people in the neighbourhood at low or no cost, it offers them without strings attached. As Hall notes Christian mission is not about serving in order to lure others into the church. Instead, real hospitality, worked out in ways that are demanded by our changing context, and imaginatively and faithfully lived out is a sufficient implementation of mission. What is important, he argues, is that the people of God should live and teach real hospitality toward others: a hospitality that loves and serves others, a stewardly hospitality, that does not have strings attached and does not offer itself only on the condition that the others acknowledge the Christian sources of this hospitality.[61]

In addition to running events, the Project provides breakfast to students at the local primary school. We were thrilled recently to receive a State Foodbank award recognising this work - thrilled because the citation, composed by the school, reads in part:

> The Eaton/Millbridge Project have (sic) worked tirelessly over the last couple of years to remind us and teach us all about community. (Breakfast Club) is a time for all our children to meet together as equals. Thankyou for teaching and nurturing our students.

---

59 Michael Frost, *Exiles*, 158-176.

60 Tim Chester, *A Meal with Jesus: Discovering Grace, Community & Mission around the Table* (Nottingham: Inter-Varsity Press, 2011), 15.

61 Hall, *Why Christian?*, 150.

Already, intentionally living out of the gospel has made a noticeable difference. The principal of the primary school was initially if not hostile, certainly wary and suspicious. But simply as a result of being an incarnational presence in the school community over a period of almost two years, that principal not only welcomes the EMCP into the school but has twice requested our assistance when a school family has faced a crisis.

In everything the EMCP does, whether it is running an event, providing breakfast, holding a BBQ or meeting people in their everyday lives, the aim is to proclaim the gospel: not *verbally* but through incarnational presence and acts of loving service.

Conclusion

Returning to the original question "But is it church?" the answer must be "yes"! The EMCP may not gather in a church building for worship, or dispense God's presence through a particular form of words or acts. It may not celebrate communion in a form deemed acceptable by traditionalists, but it is most certainly church! It is a visible sacrament through which it offers a glimpse of God's realm.[62] It understands worship as being to do with all of life, taking "your everyday ordinary life and (placing) it before God as an offering" (Romans 12:1, *The Message*). This holistic understanding of worship is enacted in an everyday posture of faithful presence. Finally, the EMCP is most certainly missional. It has been established for our changing culture and for the benefit of people who are not yet, and may never be, members of any traditional church.

Bosch reminds us that, "a church without mission or a mission without church are both contradictions."[63] Perhaps instead of keeping the EMCP and other new expressions of church at the margins of the church, and questioning their veracity as church, it is time for the inherited church to ask that question of itself. Why is it that the inherited church, so often focused inwardly, where many churchgoers seem to be content with the status quo and are uncomfortable with their much loved practices being challenged, is held up as the measure of what constitutes the church?[64]

---

62 Bosch, *Transforming Mission*, 374.

63 Bosch, *Transforming Mission*, 372.

64 Diana Butler Bass, *Christianity after Religion: The End of Church and the Birth of a New Spiritual Awakening* (New York: HarperOne, 2012) 22. Other books that I have found especially helpful on the themes of this chapter include: Guder (ed.), *Missional Church*; Eddie Gibbs, *Churchmorph: How Megatrends are Reshaping Christian Communities* (Grand Rapids: Baker Academic, 2009); Holt, *God Next Door*; Ann Morisy, *Journeying Out: A New Approach to Christian Mission* (London: Morehouse, 2004); Alan J Roxburgh, *Missional: Joining God in the Neighbourhood* (Grand Rapids: Baker Books, 2011); Sparks, et. al., *New Parish*.

9. Where the Margins Meet: An Exploration of the Prophetic Dimensions of a Church Willing to Embrace

Jasmine Dow

The early church had a strong sense of identity; it cared for the marginal, practiced hospitality, and prayed together. In Christendom the church's privilege afforded it the power to define the margins. This power has led to a contemporary church that has little credibility. The contemporary church in the West is in a liminal space between periphery and power. This chapter argues that the church will rediscover its identity as the body of Christ insofar as it embraces the margins, otherness. In this meeting of the margins ecclesiology will be realigned with its prophetic dimensions. The Eucharist is a key resource in schooling this move toward the other and has the potential to play a central role in realigning the church with its prophetic identity and the missiological engagement that flows from this identity.[1]

Introduction

In his appearance on ABC's QandA, Miroslav Volf claimed that it is not such a bad thing that the church finds itself on the margins in the 21st Century.[2] From the margins the church will learn again who it is, particularly in relation to God's mission. At its conception the church was a marginal entity. It was persecuted and yet it had a strong sense of identity. In Christendom the church became the custodian of power, the definer of societal margins. Today the church in the West has no such authority and finds itself floundering, particularly the institutional church, with an opaque sense of identity. The church in the West is residing in liminal space, between the poles of power and periphery.[3] This context provides a challenge for the church: does it clutch at its last remnants of power? Or, does it embrace as an integral part, or even as the foundation of its identity, its move to the margins? The further the church moves to the margins, toward the other, the further it will move toward God and God's mission in the world.

---

1   This chapter will form part of my PhD thesis.
2   *QandA*, ABC, Episode 07, aired 17 March 2014, Video: http://www.abc.net.au/tv/qanda/vodcast.htm.
3   The focus of this chapter is the church in the "West," particularly the Australian church. For the remainder of the chapter when I refer to the church I will be referring to the church in the "West" unless otherwise stated.

The sacrament of the Eucharist, central to the identity of the majority of the Christian tradition, provides a resource for the discussion of ecclesial identity and otherness. In the Eucharist the worshipper takes into herself the person of Christ, the Other, and in so doing invites God's transformation. The Eucharist is a habitual practice of moving to the margins, embracing the Other (Christ) and being sent as the body of Christ to embrace the other (reconcile) in the world. In the church's attempt to connect with society, to undertake mission, and to evangelise, the Eucharist has often been ignored as a resource for or at the centre of mission, or relegated to the status of *insiders only*. This further perpetuates the us/them, inside/outside binaries that stifle the church's missiological identity.[4] Given the liminal space in which the church finds itself, it is integral to rediscover the importance of the Eucharist for its formative and corrective function in the ecclesial life.

In this chapter I argue that the further the Church moves toward the other, the margins, the more it will grow into its identity as the body of Christ. Worship, in particular the liturgy of the Eucharist, is one of the key resources schooling this move toward the other. The Eucharist has the potential to play a central role in realigning the Church with its prophetic identity and in shaping the missiological engagement that flows from this identity.

Mistaken Identity?

A discussion of the identity of the Church, particularly in relation to embrace of other, requires that we turn first to the incarnation – the ultimate turning toward and embrace of the other. In the incarnation God gives of God's self in becoming human in the person of Jesus of Nazareth. Jesus was a boundary dweller, embracing the marginalised and not only embracing but also becoming marginalised. This boundary dwelling was not an act of charity, rather it was an expression of identity. In the incarnation the Word of God, who was God, became what was other – human – and in so becoming humanity found its imprint in the heart of God (cf. John 1. 1-5). The disposition toward embracing otherness, which was present in the birth of God-made-flesh, continued in the life and work of Jesus. This is affirmed in the gospel of Luke when Jesus stands in the temple to read from the prophet Isaiah:

> The Spirit of the Lord is upon me,
> because he has anointed me

---

4 Stanley Hauerwas, *A Better Hope: Resources For a Church Confronting Capitalism, Democracy, and Postmodernity* (Grand Rapids, MI: Brazos, 2000), 159.

> to bring good news to the poor.
>
> He has sent me to proclaim release to the captives
>
> and recovery of sight to the blind,
>
> to let the oppressed go free,
>
> to proclaim the year of the Lord's favour.
>
> (Isa 61:1-2a; cf. Lk 4.18-19)

He proclaims that this scripture has been fulfilled in their hearing; Jesus embodied the fulfilment of the prophets.

As with Israel's prophets, the life and work of Jesus placed him on the societal outer where the powerful condemned him. Jesus' radical life and embodiment of the alternate kingdom led him to the cross where death was absorbed into, and transfigured within, the heart of God. The cross was the expression of God's ultimate embrace of otherness. In the cross absolute Life took into itself what was ultimately other to life – death. In the resurrection death was transfigured, the margins were realigned and the peripheral became central, as Jesus proclaimed to the criminals (outsiders) at his side, "today you will be with me in paradise" (cf. Lk 23.43). In this move to embrace the ultimate other – death – reconciliation was realised, as embodied in the resurrection. Jesus invited his disciples to join him in his ministry of liberation to the marginal (as well as the powerful) and called them to continue proclaiming the good news when he departed (cf. Matt 4. 18-22; Lk 5. 1-11; Matt 28. 16-20; Lk 24. 44-53).

The early church continued this boundary dwelling existence as it lived in intentional community, caring for the marginalised (cf. Acts 4. 32-37; Acts 6. 1-2). This community was residing on the margins, in ominous circumstances, in fear of the Roman Empire and facing threat of the same fate as its Messiah. It hovered in the shadows, dodging the officials with the constant threat of persecution. The question arises how the identity of the church moved so quickly from the periphery to the centre of power. With the conversion of Emperor Constantine in 312AD the tide turned, the name of Christ became a symbol of conquer and imperialism.[5] The more that the church became embroiled in power the more privilege it gained in defining social boundaries. The community once gathered on the edge now found itself defining the margins from its place at the centre. After the Reformation, Christianity's links with the State continued as "denominationally unified states were established according to the motto

---

5   Diarmaid MacCulloch, *A History of Christianity: The First Three Thousand Years* (New York: Penguin, 2010), 189.

curius regio eius religio".⁶ This sustained Christianity's close relationship with power and imperialism. The church was at the centre. However, through the Enlightenment, Modernity, and Postmodernity the church has been subject to a process of decentring. Today, in the West, the church resides in liminal space plagued by self-consciousness and anxiety regarding its future.

Jürgen Moltmann, in his book *God for a Secular Society*, echoes this changing landscape of the church and its relationship with society in mission and evangelism. He questions the church's missional trajectory over history and the dangers that have arisen because of the church's entanglement in empire, and discusses the complexities that are present for the contemporary church because of this long held connection with the centre of power.⁷ The church moved from living within the mission of God, opening its tables to the poor and sharing its purse with the widow, to dining at the banquets of empire, controlling the economy, and defining its own mission (as the expansion of the Christian Empire) and, dare it be said, its own god. It is no wonder that the church in the contemporary West finds itself perplexed in the area of missiology. The New World Council of Churches Affirmation on Mission and Evangelism also acknowledges that the church in the West has seen itself as the centre of mission, that mission was something done by the centre toward the periphery, the margins of which were defined by geographical location and wealth; the wealthy undertook mission to the poor. This methodology of mission assumed superiority and that those outside the centre lacked significantly. The Affirmation acknowledges the shift in missiological understanding that is taking place in Christian theology. No longer can the church of the West claim power over the so called unchristian 'heathens' in the rest of the world, particularly given the superior health of the church in those once-called unchristian places. Missiological understanding is quickly moving from "mission *to* the margins" toward "mission *from* the margins."⁸

The reality of history is that for many people, and certainly also for the environment, the church has been the bearer of authority, and often not God's authority but human authority. It has been the violent "truth" bearer. The question must be asked: Whose truth has it confessed? To what extent can God's truth of justice and peace be communicated and embodied by violent and exclusive hands? Volf, in his book *Exclusion and Embrace*, wrestles with the danger of power in the quest for truth and justice:

---

6   Jürgen Moltmann, *God For a Secular Society* (Minneapolis: Fortress, 1996), 231.

7   Moltmann, *God for a Secular Society*, 227.

8   "Together Towards Life: Mission and Evangelism in Changing Landscapes", The New World Council of Churches Affirmation on Mission and Evangelism (2012), 5-6.

> But as we long for Caesar's sword, we should not forget to ask whether truth and justice will reign with Caesar's sword. How can truth and justice be anything but deception and oppression to those who have been brought to insight by violence?[9]

The church has been the culprit of much violence in history. It has placed itself at the centre and as such its missiological identity has been marred. The church has used its own power in its search for justice and peace and in so doing has travelled far from the power of God's justice and peace. The violence that the church has committed in its attempt to make *God's way* known has not only been physical, it has also been the violence of judgement, exclusion, and arrogance. The church is seen with suspicion in society as it faces the consequence of its violent exclusion and ivory tower residence throughout history and into the present. Its treatment of women, relationships, the environment, sexuality, war and ethics has led it deeper into the status of irrelevance and hypocrisy. While the church has been preoccupied with being at the centre of power, society has sought its moral and spiritual compass from new places.

"If we hope for the reign of truth and justice, must we not hope for the day when the power of Caesar will be no more, when swords will be beaten into ploughshares?"[10] Further to this, if we hope for the reign of justice must we not also hope for the day when the power of the church will be no more? The church has become so preoccupied with itself, its ego, and now with survival, that we reside in a church with a mistaken identity. In the ecclesial move from the centre of power toward the other it will come closer to its identity as the body of Christ, and the mission of God, which it is called to serve in the world.

Moving Toward the Other

The Latin *Missio Dei* provides a significant aid in conversing about mission and embrace of other. Translated as "mission" or "sending" of God, it relates to a movement. To be sent is to move; you cannot be sent and remain in the same place. As in the incarnation God moved toward humanity and the created world, mission requires a movement toward another. While for Moltmann *Missio Dei* refers to God's sending of the Holy Sprit, it does support the discussion of moving toward the other.[11] In mission we move toward God and therefore move toward the other. It is in this movement, in communion, that the church learns its identity.

---

9 Miroslav Volf, *Exclusion and Embrace: A Theological Exploration of Identity, Otherness, and Reconciliation* (Nashville, TN: Abingdon, 1996), 277.
10 Volf, *Exclusion and Embrace*, 277.
11 Moltmann, *God for a Secular Society*, 240.

William Temple claims that no human "is fitted for an isolated life." It is with our neighbour that we become who we are. Identity is realised in "social fellowship."[12] Echoing this understanding of identity, Volf speaks of the importance of an embrace of otherness for a deeper understanding of the self.[13] He draws from Paul Ricoeur's work *Oneself as Another*: "the selfhood of oneself implies otherness to such an intimate degree that one cannot be thought of without the other."[14] Volf argues for the widening of theological and social understanding:

> The narrative of Abraham's call underlines that stepping out of enmeshment in the network of inherited cultural traditions is a correlate of faith in the one God. ... The ultimate allegiance of those whose father is Abraham can be only to the God of "all families of the earth," not to any particular country, culture, or family with their local deities.[15]

Volf's theology of embrace requires a breakdown of the binary opposite *us/them*, as he argues that God's generous and self-giving embrace of humanity into the "divine community" should be a model for how humanity is to live with each other: reconciled.[16] Theology's task is to facilitate the "non-final reconciliation."[17] Theology's task in word and deed is to serve God in God's making known God's reign on earth as it is in heaven. The concept of reconciliation, both in reconciling with the other, and in facilitation of the non-final reconciliation, is central to understanding mission.

Ross Langmead argues that reconciliation is central to a theology of mission. He claims that we have moved beyond the 19th Century "expansionist" model of mission, through the 20th Century "accompaniment" model of mission, and that the model that is needed most in the 21st Century is "reconciliation."[18] One of the central, if not the central, characteristic of God's mission is the "renewing of relationships so that humanity may live fully in relationship to God, each other and creation."[19] Central to this model of reconciliation is the relationship between *selves*; reconciliation is a life lived toward others and in love for others.[20] This movement toward the other

---

12   William Temple, *Christianity and Social Order* (Southampton: Camelot, 1976), 69-70.
13   Volf, *Exclusion and Embrace*, 65-67.
14   Paul Ricoeur, *Oneself as Another* (Chicago: University of Chicago Press, 1992), 3.
15   Volf, *Exclusion and Embrace*, 39.
16   Volf, *Exclusion and Embrace*, 99-101.
17   Volf, *Exclusion and Embrace*, 109-110.
18   Ross Langmead, "Transformed Relationships: Reconciliation as the Central Model for Mission," *Mission Studies* 25 (2008), 7.
19   Langmead, "Transformed Relationships," 10.
20   Langmead, "Transformed Relationships," 11.

requires vulnerability.[21] In order to move in the missional direction of reconciliation the church will need to let go of being the centre of power and embrace vulnerability in order to truly embrace its identity as the body of Christ serving the mission of God. The church has the cross as its ultimate example of vulnerability – the cross is central to this movement toward vulnerability.

"People who just stay in their own little circles and stew in their own juice become stupefied, because wherever they are they always hear only the same thing, the thing which endorses them."[22] Here, Moltmann states the danger of remaining insular and self-centred. The contemporary church is self-conscious and ever seeking to endorse itself as worthy and meaningful. The more it steps away from this anxiety, which finds its basis in the self, and moves toward God and therefore the other, the more it will grow into its true identity as the body of Christ.

Eucharistic Identity as Missiological Identity

Together Towards Life, the recent statement on mission from the World Council of Churches, acknowledges the importance of seeing mission as an approach not only to *what* the church does, but *who* the church is, arguing for a spirituality of mission.[23] The Eucharist offers a complex and radical spirituality of mission. Christian worship in the form of the Eucharistic liturgy is a ritual that shapes those who wilfully participate in it to live in the world in an alternate way, a way of reconciliation.[24] Active participation in worship requires "that our bodies submit to training" so that tools are acquired to recognise the "false gods" whose powers are present and active in the church and the world.[25] In the habitual performance of the Eucharistic liturgy, however ordinary, subjects are open to transformation. In the continuous reconciling of the ordinary and the holy the "Eucharistic self" is born.[26] The "Eucharistic self" is a self schooled in beatitude "blessed and blesses," and in dynamic relationship with the Creator and the created. This self is characterised by "being for" others, in joy and for "human flourishing."[27] This self is a self-in-community whose identity is inextricably linked with other selves-in-community.

21 Langmead, "Transformed Relationships," 12.
22 Moltmann, *God for a Secular Society*, 227.
23 *Together Towards Life*, 4-5.
24 Don Saliers, "Pastoral Liturgy and Character Ethics: As we Worship so Shall We Be," in *Source and Summit: Commemorating Josef A. Jungmann, SJ*, ed. Joanne M. Pierce and Michael Downey (Minnesota: Liturgical Press, 1999), 183.
25 Hauerwas, *A Better Hope*, 159.
26 David Ford, "What Happens in the Eucharist?," *Scottish Journal of Theology* 48:3 (1948): 359-382.
27 Ford, "What Happens in the Eucharist?," 378-381.

Before turning to an examination of the Eucharistic liturgy and its potential to form the church as the body of Christ, it is necessary to visit the scriptural precedent for the Eucharist or table fellowship and its missional dimensions. Jesus was named by his opposition as a "glutton and a drunkard" (cf. Luke 7. 34) because his public ministry so frequently involved eating and drinking. The tables that Jesus sat at gave honour to all and were characterised by inclusion rather than exclusion, characterised by embrace. This radical inclusion was characteristic of God's reign, which Jesus lived on earth and the church is called to proclaim in word and deed.[28] In scripture it is often in the context of hospitality that revelation takes place and Jesus is recognised as the Christ. In the midst of pain and grief the disciples in the Emmaus Road narrative recognised the resurrected Christ in the breaking of the bread and went from the table into the world to proclaim Christ risen from the dead (cf. Luke 23).

Jesus' table ministry was offensive, his radical inclusion of society's outcasts was an unsettling reversal of society's norms and held grave consequences. On the night before Jesus was killed he gathered with his disciples for a meal where he performed acts of service and redefined power. It is therefore important to consider the missional dimensions of any ritual that is performed in remembrance of this event.[29]

The communal nature of the Eucharist runs counter to the individualistic, self-oriented paradigm of the contemporary West, in which the church is deeply implicated. After a Sunday Eucharistic service it is not uncommon to hear, "that service did nothing for me." Implicit in statements such as this is the rampant individualism evident not only in society but in the church. If the liturgy is based on the Jesus revealed in the gospels, it could, perhaps should, cause offense.[30] It is not the role of liturgy to placate the individual and perpetuate apathy. The Eucharistic liturgy, which some may label dated, archaic, and ritualistic, holds within it resources which are invaluable to the contemporary context of the church. Not only is this context characterised by individualism but also privatisation and commodification.[31] The worship of the church has become a commodity to be consumed. The link between the church's prophetic identity and its worship has been diluted by the relegation of the Eucharist to commodity status.[32]

---

28 Stephen Burns, *SCM Studyguide: Liturgy* (London: SCM, 2006), 3.

29 Edward Capuchin, "Engaging the Liturgy of the World: Worship as Public Theology," *Studia Liturgica* 38:1 (2008), 43.

30 Capuchin, "Engaging the Liturgy," 41.

31 Capuchin, "Engaging the Liturgy," 38-41.

32 There are a number of individuals and individual churches that are faithful to the prophetic dimensions of the Eucharist. Here I am referring, in generalised terms, to the institutional church.

In order to recover the Eucharist as central to the missional or prophetic identity of the church, it will require the church to take seriously this radical and powerful ritual so central to its being. The power for ritual to engage the human imagination is profound and has the potential to make real some of those imaginings, or at least expand the world that is possible.[33] Don Saliers claims that the Eucharist "is the most radical meal, the most revolutionary symbolic action in which human beings can partake."[34] The four-fold Eucharistic liturgy has the potential to form the community of the church to live in such a way that gathers and values all peoples in their diversity, listens to the stories of the other, recognises the centrality of the table at which a vision of justice and peace is glimpsed, and proclaims peace in the world. I will turn now to a brief examination of each section of the liturgy.[35]

Gathering

The first section of the Eucharistic liturgy is Gathering. Given the context of individualism the church lives within, the "communal enterprise" of gathering is by its nature counter cultural.[36] People gather around the altar to focus their attention on the Other, God, and in so doing open themselves to the world, their neighbour, and themselves as a Eucharistic *self-in-community*. Individuals within the community do not choose who will gather, rather a community of diverse peoples gather, potentially from varying social demographics. Timothy Radcliffe argues, "no community of the like-minded is a sign of the kingdom of God."[37] This gathering of diversity is integral for the church to be the Church, fully human – "we become fully human in interdependence with others."[38]

Storytelling/Story-hearing

> Moral awareness requires a community that gathers together to tell its founding memories, to rehearse its fundamental attitudes, and to symbolically enact overtime the root images and narratives, by which it lives and understands how to become human, and live worthily.[39]

---

33 Stephen Burns, "Liturgy and Justice," *International Journal of Public Theology* 3:3 (2009): 376.

34 Saliers, "Pastoral Liturgy," 191.

35 I acknowledge that there will be differences in the order of the liturgy across Christian traditions. My focus is the order of Anglican liturgy but recognise that this order is shared by many traditions.

36 Stephen Burns, "Worship, Mission and the Public Square" (Paper presented at Christian Mission in the Public Square Conference, Australian Centre for Christianity and Culture Canberra, October 2008).

37 Timothy Radcliffe, *Why go to Church? The Drama of the Eucharist* (London: Continuum, 2008), 60.

38 Anne Loades, "Table," in *Renewing the Eucharist, Volume 1: Journey,* ed. Stephen Burns (Norwich: Canterbury Press, 2008), 69.

39 Saliers, "Pastoral Liturgy," 187.

Following the gathering around the altar comes the sharing of stories. This act of storytelling is another process of decentring the self and moving toward the other. Scripture is read and the worshipper is invited into the story of the "scriptural other".[40] The sermon is preached and prayers are offered. The sermon and prayers invite the worshipper to make space within herself for the other, particularly the marginalised other.[41] Listening to the other is a counter intuitive practice in a culture that demands that we move at great speed to succeed. There is very little space in daily life to really make space to hear another. Individually and corporately (as the church) we are self-obsessed.

> Listening to Moses cry and Miriam sing, to Jesus' silence as well as his words, and becoming immersed in the nuances of scriptural narratives, we may become 'mythically more' than narrowly self-reflective narratives may allow.[42]

This section of the liturgy reminds the worshipping community that their identities are interwoven.

The Sacrament/Communion

At the Eucharist the whole Christian story is told. The people hear the story of God creating the world, speaking through the prophets, working in Jesus to bring about God's reign on earth, experiencing the suffering of humanity and offering a pathway to healing and resurrection. After the retelling, the scene shifts and the community is re-membered around the table of Jesus' last supper, that ominous night charged with grave violence. The bread is taken, blessed, broken and given. The communicant takes within herself the body and blood of Christ, requiring her to make space within her being for the other.

> The Eucharist: if the body and blood were assimilated into our bodies, they would become what we are. But the Eucharist is the reversal of normality: we eat and drink the bread and wine, but it is the bread and wine which eat us. We are to become what they are: the body and blood of Christ.[43]

---

40 Burns, "Liturgy and Justice," 378.
41 Burns, "Liturgy and Justice," 378.
42 Burns, "Liturgy and Justice," 379.
43 Rubem Alves, *The Poet, The Warrior, The Prophet* (London: SCM, 1990), 15.

In the eating and drinking of bread and wine the communicant is drawn into the life of the other, the crucified and risen Christ. The Eucharist takes the worshipper to the margins, to the cross, and makes space within the worshipper for the other. The community is invited to become bread for the world – the body of Christ, as Augustine explicates. [44]

Sending

Having gathered in the name of God, listened to the stories of the scriptural and worldly other, and received the sacrament of the Eucharist the worshipper is sent into the world in peace and with God's blessing. This enactment of sending mirrors the sending of the disciples. In the Eucharistic liturgy the story of the incarnation is heard, a story of the embodiment of God's reign, the consequence of which is betrayal, torture, and ultimately death on the cross. On the third day death is transfigured by life in the resurrection. Jesus, upon rising from the dead, does not proclaim vengeance but peace, even making breakfast for his disciples who abandoned him in his need.[45] The *glutton and drunkard* rises with a message of peace. In the sending section of the liturgy, after having experienced the story, after entering the deep suffering and resurrection of Christ in the Eucharist, it is now time to *make breakfast for the world*, to go and live toward (embrace) the other. In so doing the community of the church claims its identity as the body of Christ, the *real presence* of the boundary dwelling Christ in the world.

While having formative potential in ecclesial life, the Eucharist has been affected by the Church's relationship to power. The priority has been placed on personal salvation at the expense of liberation for the other and the world.[46] Generally speaking, the church has become complacent and has lost sight of the valuable resources within its tradition. The Eucharist has suffered for this complacency. Partaking in the Eucharist is risky because there is potential for transformation. In it we are taken to the margins, into communion with the other. It seems the church carries on blasé to the power of the Eucharist, putting the sacrament into an institutional box and holding it captive to the chosen few. More often than not worship dilutes challenge into platitudes,

---

44 Maria Boulding, *The Confessions,* Saint Augustine of Hippo, Ignatius Critical Editions, ed. D.V Meconi (Villanova, Pennsylvania: Augustinian Heritage Institute, 1997), 180. "I am the food of the mature; grow then, and you will eat me. You will not change me into yourself like bodily food: you will be changed into me."

45 John Dear, "Resurrection," *Australian E-Journal of Theology,* Pentecost 2007 special edition, issue 10, http://dlibrary.acu.edu.au/research/theology/ejournal/aejt_10/Dear.htm accessed 13 June 2009. Now accessible here: http://www.fatherjohndear.org/articles/resurrection.html accessed 31 October 2014.

46 Tom Driver, *The Magic of Ritual: Our Need for Rites that Transform Our Lives and Our Communities* (San Francisco: Harper Collins, 1991), 208.

comfort, and convenience.[47] The Eucharist sits in a liminal zone, offering the world and the church a challenge.[48]

Conclusion

The institutional church in the West finds itself between the poles of periphery and power: the peripheral nature of the early church and the powerful identity of the church in Christendom. The identity of the church as the body of Christ will be revealed as it moves from the seat of power toward the margins, the other. This move to embrace otherness is modelled on the incarnation, cross and resurrection, as God moved toward the world in Jesus Christ, who dwelt on the edges and spoke truth to power. This movement of God revealed the nature of God's reign and God's desire to reconcile the world to God.

In this chapter I have argued that worship, in particular the liturgy of the Eucharist, performs an identity-forming function in the life of the church. It opens the worshipper to the Other, Christ, and in so doing opens the community of worshippers to the other in the world as they are transformed into and sent as the body of Christ. This body of Christ should be, through its embrace of otherness, a prophetic witness to the reign of God realised now and not yet. The church's preoccupation with power stifles this identity-forming function of the Eucharist, although, its potential remains.

In moving to the margins the Church will have no choice but to make space for those who live on the *margins*: the poor, the dispossessed, the occupied, the nameless, the Christ. In this reconciling of the margins ecclesiology will be realigned with its prophetic/missional dimensions as the body of Christ.

---

47 Don Saliers, *Worship as Theology: Foretaste of Glory Divine* (Nashville: Abingdon, 1994), 23-24.
48 Saliers, "Pastoral Liturgy," 186.

10. Grappling for Christ: Incarnational Mission at the Margins of the Church

Mick Pope

Incarnational mission is a mode of missionary engagement that takes as its model the incarnation of Jesus. It emphasises the sentness of mission as an activity done among a particular group of people, as opposed to the attractional model of church that insists people come into the Christian community. Incarnational mission in the martial arts occurs at the margins of the church. The martial arts are often viewed with suspicion by the church, due to concerns over eastern mysticism and the apparent violence. The art of Brazilian Jiu Jitsu is an adaptation of Japanese Judo for self-defence and sport. This sport attracts a diversity of people looking to develop physical prowess, overcome physical and mental health issues, and find personal meaning. This chapter examines the diversity of incarnational mission approaches within the Brazilian Jiu Jitsu community looking at three gyms, their head coaches, and the different ways in which the gospel is contextualised.

Brazilian Jiu Jitsu (BJJ) is a self defence system and a combat sport. It consists of submission holds, which involve the hyperextension or rotation of limbs, or the constriction of blood flow to the brain. Throws may also be taught. Rules for permissible submissions are set so that only more experienced practitioners may use certain techniques deemed too potentially dangerous for the novice. Safety is of paramount importance, including proper hygiene and the use of padded mats on the floor, and "tapping out" (tapping the opponent, self or mat with an open hand or verbally) when discomfort is experienced due to the application of a submission.

BJJ was developed in about 1916, when a Judo black belt settled in Brazil and taught the now famous Gracie family the art.[1] Carlos Gracie developed it into an effective self-defence system. BJJ is often associated with mixed martial arts, incorrectly referred to as cage fighting. The Ultimate Fighting Championship (UFC) was begun with the sole intention of proving the effectiveness of BJJ as a combat system.[2]

---

1 "International Brazilian Jiu Jitsu Federation," http://ibjjf.org/info/history/
2 "Ultimate Fighting Championship," http://www.ufc.com.

It is the contention of this chapter, through examining three BJJ gyms that I am associated with, that incarnational mission is possible in such an environment.

Missional Ministry

I have been involved in the martial arts on and off for nearly 30 years, with the last twelve in the sport of BJJ. BJJ gym Renegade MMA (Mixed Martial Arts) began in 2010 in Kensington, Victoria.[3] Having known Jamie Murray, a co-owner and founder, for nearly eight years I joined the gym as an assistant coach and spiritual support as he was keen to develop it as a Christian ministry. The club now has about 200 students.

One of the Renegade MAA coaches is Ninos Dammo, also the head coach of Australian Elite Team (AET) in Tullamarine, Victoria. Begun in 2005, AET has over 180 grappling students and 19 affiliate clubs with over 1200 grapplers around the country.

Grapplers for Christ (G4C) Geelong started in June 2013 under Woon Ooi and Grady Lewis in the hall of Barrabool Hills Baptist Church in Geelong, Victoria. A small gym with about 20 students, G4C is an outgrowth of the organisation Grapplers for Christ Australia, and is a Renegade affiliate gym.[4]

Incarnational rather than attractional

Michael Frost and Alan Hirsch identify three principles of the missional church or ministry.[5] The first is that it is incarnational and not attractional. The attractional model creates a sanctified space into which the not-yet Christian is invited to enter. Even seeker sensitive services still require the seeker to cross cultural boundaries. By contrast, incarnational mission can operate in the market place, often in commercial enterprise, outside of the bounds of the church.[6] This model emphasises the sentness of the church. In this case, for coaches Dammo, Murray and Ooi, this sentness is being sent to stay in a community they love.[7] Because all three come from the BJJ community they are able to engage in mission in the BJJ community.

All three coaches have had conversion experiences that fit a classic evangelical conversion narrative, coming from Christian homes but having their own crisis of

---

3   "Renegade MMA," http://www.renegademma.com.au.
4   "Grapplers for Christ – Oz," http://g4c-oz.com.
5   Michael Frost and Alan Hirsch, *The Shaping of Things to Come: Innovation and Mission for the 21st-Century Church* (Peabody: Hendrickson Publishers, 2004), 12.
6   Frost and Hirsch, *Shaping of Things*, 26.
7   Kim Hammond and Darren Cronshaw, *Sentness: Six Postures of Missional Christianity* (Downers Grove, IL: InterVarsity Press, 2014), 54.

faith. Ninos comes from a Syrian Orthodox background. Jamie was baptised in the Anglican Church, and received his first bible there. Woon's father is a Methodist minister. All three have also had a long term association with the martial arts. After being attacked at age 13, Ninos took up karate to defend himself, and was involved in many street fights. When he was 20, he saw the UFC and immediately began the study of Brazilian Jiu Jitsu. As an emigrant from Malaysia as a five year old, Woon was the subject of bullying. He enrolled in a local karate school to learn self-defence, but the school's culture was such that it taught Woon himself to become a bully. This now inspires him to teach a much better martial arts culture. Jamie got into the martial arts for the fitness aspect. He found it a helpful outlet for his aggression, which he identified as the flip side of his anxiety. Over time, grappling taught him other ways to deal with his anxiety and that he did not need to roll aggressively.

Two of the gyms (Renegade and AET) are operated as for-profit businesses in former factories. Ninos however, acknowledges that his Christian faith makes him a poor business owner, since the goal is not profit but ministry. Students come with the explicit aim of learning martial arts, for self-defence, fitness, weight loss, etc. It is also clear that students come to train for a number of implicit goals, including a sense of community and belonging, and unspoken spiritual needs.

G4C Geelong operates in a church hall, explicitly as a Christian community. Unlike the other gyms, prayer often begins and ends the session. Bible reflections, sometimes linking concepts of BJJ to the bible and life in general are conducted. Woon Ooi suggests that being in the church hall places it at arm's length from the church proper. Furthermore, the laying down of the mats and the wearing of uniforms marks out the space as being other than a sanctified space. Woon likens the attendance of non-Christians (including a Muslim who also trains elsewhere) like parents sending their children to a Christian school. There is an expectation and acceptance of certain marks of Christian culture as being beneficial. Regardless of the exact physical setting, the practice of BJJ marks them out as physical spaces different from the attractional church. Instead, they function as proximity spaces, places where the not yet Christian and Christians can interact meaningfully.[8]

Although only G4C is explicitly Christian in its name, AET includes a cross and a lion (Jesus) in its team patches for uniforms and clothing, making the club identifiable as reflecting Christian culture. Ninos has observed that most people who do not know or

---

8   Frost and Hirsch, *Shaping of Things*, 24.

understand AET think that it is a cult. Such people he believes have a misunderstanding about Christianity, seeing it as weird and followed by people who are unintelligent. Such an understanding is transformed by experiencing the AET culture (see more below).

Finally, while Renegade is run as a business, Jamie is a well-known Christian in the BJJ community, and often wears Grapplers for Christ clothing at large competitions. He sees the name Renegade as standing for the club's different culture and status in the BJJ community, and Grapplers for Christ as chaplains within it.

A Messianic nature

Frost and Hirsch's second characteristic of a missional movement is its Messianic rather than dualistic nature.[9] The world is not divided into sacred and secular, spiritual and profane. The Christian gospel is holistic in essence.

This is expressed in the very nature of mission in the martial arts, i.e. it deals with the body and fitness. Given the Australian obsession with sport and fitness, the martial arts are a good candidate for incarnational mission. Students come with a variety of goals: looking for weight loss; self-defence; but also struggling with a variety of issues, including depression, anxiety, substance abuse, self-esteem issues and financial difficulties. It is not unusual for example, for Ninos to deal with students who are suicidal, and many have had life changing conversion experiences.

Although AET and Renegade are businesses, students in financial difficulty are often shown generosity in the form of cheaper fees, periods of free training, payment plans for uniforms, etc. Staff and senior students have raised money to buy uniforms for children from the commission housing in Kensington. Scholarships are also offered. Students are given work experience opportunities at Renegade, and Jamie writes references for his students when asked. All of these acts of generosity are accompanied with the gospel as his reason for doing so and so the gospel is communicated in word and deed. Ninos is a firm believer in the supposed dictum of St Francis "preach the gospel, if necessary, use words."

---

9   Frost and Hirsch, *Shaping of Things*, 12.

An apostolic movement

Frost and Hirsch's third mark of a missional movement is that it is apostolic, with a flat hierarchy.[10] Leadership is based on giftedness in BJJ, and then on Christian spiritual gifts.

Ninos believes that he has opportunities that priests and pastors do not. He identifies engagement with ordained clergy as overwhelming for some. In contrast, he sees himself as "just a martial artist." Instead of a relationship with professional limits, he says "I'm their friend," and people can share everything with their friends.

Jamie sees his particular calling to minister through BJJ as an example of the "difference between training the called and calling the trained." He felt called to preach the gospel through a sport he had been training in and coaching for several years, which provides a genuineness to what he does. He opines "it would be foolish to call someone who was theologically trained to do what I do." Already being in the culture he is called to reach provides greater authenticity to the mission because the activity itself is clearly valued. It is not simply a veil for evangelism. As "the called," Jamie is being trained at Ridley Theological College. Woon also believes he has found one of his missional pathways in BJJ and have found that "common ground" in which God wants him to minister from.

Contextualisation to BJJ culture

A key feature of any mission is the need for contextualisation. Ross Langmead defines contextualisation as "the ongoing and multi-layered process of allowing the gospel to take shape in a particular context."[11] This act of contextualisation involves "cracking the cultural code" of the particular culture.[12] To do so involves understanding the cultural narrative of a culture and its associated symbols, myths and rituals. Langmead recognised that "people move between cultures and assume hybrid identities."[13] Tim Foster identifies this as multi-layered narratives.[14] There are three layers, which may be illustrated as three tiers of a triangle. The first is national culture, which in this case is Australian.

---

10 Frost and Hirch, *Shaping of Things*, 12.

11 Ross Langmead, "Contextual Mission: An Australian Perspective" (paper presented at Christian Communities in Contemporary Contexts ANZAMS mini-conference, Auckland, 30-31 October 2009).

12 Tim Foster, *The Suburban Captivity of the Church: Contextualising the Gospel for Post-Christian Australia* (Melbourne: Acorn, 2014), chapter 2.

13 Langmead, "Contextual Mission".

14 Foster, *Suburban Captivity*, 37.

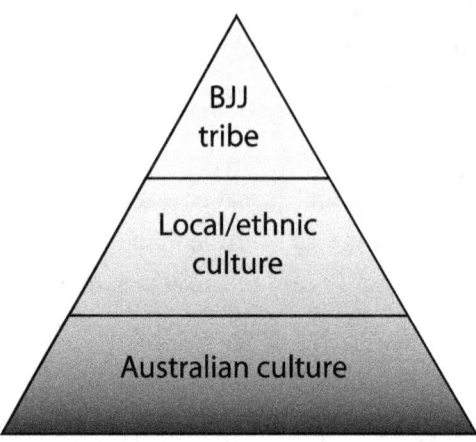

Figure 1: Multi-layered narratives as applied to mission in BJJ in Australia, following Foster's categories.

The second is local, and refers not only to the local context, but also the broad cultural backgrounds of the students. This is particularly the case for AET, which has a large number of European and Middle Eastern students from Catholic and Orthodox backgrounds. Ninos' Syrian heritage enables him to relate a variety of people from those contexts, including Muslims. Ninos believes that many churches in the Catholic and Orthodox traditions are not doing their duty in discipling their flocks and sees what he does as essential to serve the people who come to him.

The top tier of the cultural narrative is tribal.[15] Western culture is profoundly tribal, and BJJ is an exemplar of this.[16] This cultural narrative is of key importance for incarnational mission since it encompasses the shared narrative for BJJ practitioners in their particular gym, lineage of BJJ, and BJJ community in general. Those best able to understand this cultural narrative are those who operate within it. The BJJ cultural narrative is displayed in BJJs myths, symbols and rituals. The mythos includes the origin of BJJ, its effectives against other martial arts, its lineage back to the Gracie family, and the competition successes of its head coach. The symbols include the uniforms and patches, belts of the practitioners (a club with a lot of coloured belts has a higher status), the rank of the instructor, and the trophies the club has earned. Finally, there are a number or rituals that are practiced. These include the way in which gradings (the awarding of new ranks) are conducted, i.e. the amount of rounds

---

15 Foster, *Suburban Captivity*, 37.
16 Frost and Hirsch, *Shaping of Things*, 37.

students do, and belt whipping ceremonies. BJJ students, instead of the traditional oriental bow, typically slap each other's hands and bump fists before engaging in rolling. The Japanese exclamation or acknowledgement *osu* (sometimes spelled oss) is also used by some.

These aspects of BJJ culture are not studied without but learned from within. And so it is, for example, much easier to understand the purpose of doing of hard rounds of grappling, followed by walking a gauntlet of belt whipping, by going through it. This tribal initiation rite is one best experienced. Only then can it not be dismissed as some primal masculine sadomasochism.

As Foster notes, however, an understanding of tribal culture is not enough for contextualisation. What is also required is a critique of the cultural norms from within, and a subversive fulfilment of them.[17] The first critique is of the business aspect of running a club, as exhibited by financial generosity. Ninos recognises that his generosity is painful in that it makes him a poor businessman, but believes he gets back in loyalty far more than he gives away in money. A poor box is available for anyone in need and the culture of generosity bred at AET means it is never empty.

Likewise, Jamie provides financial assistance in the form of reduced fees etc, as a way to promote a "culture that embodies generosity," which can foster a sense of loyalty. Jamie sees this generosity as a way to "live out a genuine Christian faith in acts of love and service." The motivation for his financial generosity is a simple description of his Christian faith and desire to serve others and seek their good.

The second critique is also a subversion in the formation of a Christian based culture of hospitality.[18] As noted above, Ninos believes that people often see his gym as a cult, but what transforms people's understanding is not logical argument, although this plays a role. What is felt first by people is the atmosphere or culture of the gym. A good, welcoming culture is of utmost importance at the gym. This is manifest both in the way in which new students are welcome, but also in the treatment of grapplers from other gyms with respect.

Renegade allows Jamie to do mission because it is a community where he gets to set the boundaries, culture, and values, as well as the spiritual temperature. This includes a code of conduct, and emphasising respect and appropriate behaviour, which has

---

17 Foster, *Suburban Captivity*, 45.
18 Frost and Hirsch, *Shaping of Things*, 12.

sometimes led to having to ask students to leave. The welcoming, hospitable nature of Renegade means that an increasing number of women feel comfortable to train in BJJ, which can otherwise be a claustrophobic and confronting sport.

At G4C Geelong, the mantra is "raise up, not rise up." This focuses on the improvement of others. In a sport that can encourage competitive egos, Woon maintains that "a rising tide lifts all boats," and constantly reminds coaches of their responsibility. G4C also encourages openness in a very non-judgemental environment. Everyone is free to respectfully discuss their thoughts and beliefs.

Another critique from within is about the nature and status of BJJ coaches. In Brazilian culture lower ranks may not ask black belts to roll. Coaches like Jamie and Ninos, however, are very approachable and are not "belt snobs". While some coaches are very proud and hide aspects of their technique, the coaches from all three of these gyms have a culture of no secrets. They are not afraid of being submitted or tapped out by their students; it is an expectation that it will occur at some point. The principle of "leave your ego at the door" is always adopted. Hence, none of the coaches is proud or fearful, but freely shares their knowledge.

Finally, in other communities student poaching is not unusual, with Brazilians being particularly notorious for this. A student who switches clubs is referred to as a *creonte*, a derogative term.[19] Each of these gyms has a no poaching rule and students who leave a club to join another are told to speak to their instructors first. Christian coaches maintain the highest possible integrity in all of their dealings. Jamie believes that people naturally turn to a person on the highest moral ground in a crisis and sees 1 Timothy 3 and its exhortation to be above reproach as his ideal to live by. This has provided many opportunities to share his faith.

Ministry at the margins

The weekly bible study at AET regularly attracts over 70 people. It is not unusual for people to have life changing faith experiences after great hardships and studies are often tailored to the needs of those who come seeking prayer. The study includes ex-Muslims and those with Catholic or Orthodox backgrounds. Ninos' Syrian heritage enables him to relate to both groups. In relating to Muslims, Ninos emphasises the need to demonstrate lots of love. He finds that Muslims are generally keen to discuss religion and he always takes the time to engage them in conversation. The emphasis is

19 "Gracie Academy," http://www.gracieacademia.com/article_002.html.

not on argument but engagement and he advises never to "clash heads" with them but let God do the work. While Ninos is a capable apologist, he does not lose sight of the spiritual nature of evangelism. Ninos is a 24/7 evangelist and often leaves his phone on for students to speak to him. He spends most of his time at the gym and sees his presence there as truly incarnational, taking seriously Paul's attitude of becoming a Greek to the Greeks (1 Corinthians 9:19-23).

Jamie has had many opportunities to share his faith. He draws an analogy with Jiu Jitsu to make the point: "Jiu Jitsu is like evangelism. You have to put the right pressure on at the right time or you'll end up flat on your face." He is very able to introduce his faith naturally into any conversation. Jamie has been involved in various schemes of community outreach both formally and informally. Students from the local flats have been provided with full or partial scholarships for training fees and uniforms in collaboration with church and government organisations. After the very public murder of ABC journalist Jill Maher, Jamie provided self-defence training for various organisations. He has also been involved in trying to help asylum seekers, recently providing a full scholarship to a child from Africa who had fled persecution with his two younger siblings after losing his parents. The opportunity to help people motivates Jamie, without pushing the faith on people, opportunities to share it arise.

Wednesday night bible study is one of the mainstays of the ministry and outreach at Renegade. Although much smaller than the study group at AET, it is no less important in providing an atmosphere where those on the edge of faith, particularly those with experience of Catholicism, are able to sit. Its diversity also includes theology graduates and students. Bible studies focus on the person of Jesus, the need to respond in faith, and life issues. Illustrations are often drawn from BJJ, as many of those who participate are grapplers.

Jamie believes BJJ and Christianity form part of the same journey. Repentance or *metanoia* represents a change of mind. In BJJ, tapping out occurs when a technique is applied. This provides a safe environment in which the practitioner can stop, reassess and turnaround from an incorrect technique. The parallel with Christianity is that we make mistakes in life and in the living out of our faith, resulting not from bad technique but sinful attitudes and behaviours.

G4C Geelong has been praying and fasting for a young girl who was diagnosed with a terminal illness. A non-Christian student wanted to fast the three days as a sign of his support. This student was able to share the story of this young girl and why he was fasting with work colleagues as they saw him picking through his salad and throwing out all the meat that was in it. A few weeks later, he started asking a few questions about God and asked for a bible, which was given to him.

While there is much ministry happening at all three gyms, this ministry happens at the margins of the church. There are critiques of martial arts and their adoption by Christians. Sporting ministry is nothing new, with boxing having a long pedigree in mission.[20] Neither is mission through BJJ anything new.[21]

Ninos sees a good deal of Christian critique of martial arts as superficial, made by people unable to understand the motivations and benefits of its practice. Most practitioners want to have fun, get fit and enjoy a competitive sport. In this sense it is no less violent that many contact balls sports. Critiques of the breeding of ego carry some weight but a gym dominated by a Christian culture means that ego can be contained.

The spiritual aspect is also much less of a concern for BJJ than other martial arts. Over the years I have struggled to reconcile various creeds from martial arts organisations. However, BJJ is more an expression of Brazilian culture, which is broadly Catholic, than Asian culture. At a seminar many years ago, Carlos Machado, one of the founders of Machado school and in direct lineage with the Gracie family explained why people shake hands in BJJ instead of bowing (which is often understood by westerners to have religious overtones) by saying that we only bow to God.

Likewise, the concern over violence is also overstated. As a physical activity, BJJ is tightly controlled and when properly supervised, quite safe. The goal is not to hurt your partner, for whom else would you train with? Rather, the training is as much about self-improvement and the development of technique. As with many other activities, the goal is to achieve a mental state known as "flow." It is therefore the activity itself, rather than the potential for harm that is attractive to many.

A final critique of BJJ is its supposed masculine focus. Well known church planter Mark Driscoll has defended BJJ in general and Mixed Martial Arts in particular.[22]

---

20 Rev George W Rutland, "The Christian Boxer" *Crisis Magazine* (April 8 2013), http://www.crisismagazine.com/2013/the-christian-boxer.
21 Frost and Hirsch, *Shaping of Things*, 29.
22 Mark Driscoll, "A Christian Evaluation of Mixed Martial Arts," http://pastormark.tv/2011/11/09/a-christian-evaluation-of-mixed-martial-arts.

Driscoll's view that martial arts are an essentially masculine occupation is reflected in his macho view of Jesus when he states that "I cannot worship a guy I can beat up."[23] This is not an attitude shared by the coaches discussed here, and all three gyms have a growing number of female students. Their success not only attests to the gender-neutral nature of the activity, or the effective nature of the principles of weight and leverage in BJJ, but also to the value of a culture that does not view women as weak or the targets of sexual objectification. There is also a growing number of lesbian women at Renegade.

Another expression of BJJ mission being at the margins of the church is that none of the gyms were initiated as formal church outreach activities. Each was initiated by practitioners. Ninos is not interested in promoting the cause of his own denomination and strongly encourages people to go back to their church when they come to faith if they have a Christian heritage. Renegade has a close relationship with Jamie's home church. As well as formal activities, like training days for the church, Jamie has a personal relationship with the pastors as sources of personal support and spiritual authority and accountability. G4C Geelong operates out of a church building but has "an arm's length relationship and operates as an independent ministry separate from the church." Being autonomous has removed those political hurdles that can often cause issues for ministries.

While Jamie believes in the idea of incarnational mission, he does not see Renegade as a replacement for formal church attendance. Renegade provides bible studies, prayer, one on one mentoring and the occasional bible talk, as well as prayer and one-on-one discipleship occur as part of the gym. However, Jamie sees Renegade as a gateway to formal church attendance.

Diversity in Mission

As has been highlighted, there is a great diversity in the people who are being reached through these gyms. There is also a wide diversity within the broader umbrella of Grappler for Christ in terms of denominations: Syrian Orthodox, Catholic, Anglican, Presbyterian and Baptist. Not only does this variety exist between the gyms, but also within them. This has meant that issues of disagreement between Christians have been set aside. Ninos is not judgemental towards those who come to him, but has a knack of being able to gently move people forward. Despite his own theological

---

23 Quoted in Craig M. Watts, "Mark Driscoll's Bad Ass Jesus," Red Letter Christians, http://www.redletterchristians.org/mark-driscolls-badass-jesus/.

tradition, Ninos maintains that he follows Christ and not Orthodoxy. His faith is not about banners but the heart. Avoiding ecclesial politics, he finds such talk turns people off the faith but that the love of Jesus Christ guides people.

As mentioned earlier, Woon promotes a culture at G4C Geelong which encourages openness in a very non-judgemental environment, where everyone is free to respectfully discuss their thoughts and beliefs. Likewise at Renegade, Jamie stresses tolerance but also a style of Christianity that is readily accessible to the unchurched or the over-churched (e.g. those with negative experiences of the Catholic school system).

This non-dogmatic approach reflects a centred set approach rather than bounded set approach to mission. People are seen and respected as seekers of the truth (no one is dragged into bible studies or attendance of after class reflections) or as not-yet Christians.[24] Membership of the gyms is a financial arrangement, while membership of bible studies is a voluntary mix of Christian and not-yet Christians. Only a simple encounter with Jesus is encouraged and more sophisticated theological arguments or statements of faith are only used when the occasion warrants them, or only when Christians are in attendance.

Lessons for ministry

The lessons learned from the experience of the three BJJ gyms discussed above are more broadly applicable to incarnation mission at the margins of what the church might consider "kosher".

Firstly, being a martial arts based ministry, it pushes the boundaries of what is deemed acceptable to some Christians. Each coach seeks to redeem the best of BJJ and subvert aspects of its cultural narrative in order to reach people for Christ. This subversion happens by creating a counter-cultural (or renegade) narrative shaped by the gospel that opposes some of the natural tendencies towards ego, profit motive and behaviours that destroy community. The church needs to demonstrate more imagination and moral courage and challenge preconceived ideas on what could be redeemed for mission.

Secondly, while G4C Geelong began with the permission of its host church, all three gyms were birthed in the minds of practitioners of BJJ, not those engaged in full time Christian ministry as traditionally conceived. In this sense, they have demonstrated an entrepreneurial spirit that needs to be encouraged and blessed by the church.

24 Frost and Hirsch, *Shaping of Things*, 47-49.

Blessing does not imply the giving of permission, for these ministries would still exist without church permission. Instead, a formal blessing is the recognition that God is acting outside of and ahead of the church in what is known as prevenient grace.[25] Churches need to make a regular habit of doing this for all their members in their places of work, study or recreation. It is an activity in my own church that members are sometimes interviewed about their work. Many consumer churches need to shake the idea that only full time minsters do "gospel work" and that the "laity" simply earn money to finance their ministry. Instead, the church gathered should focus on how it can support the church scattered. Those engaged in incarnational mission in the margins of the church can speak prophetically back to the centre of ministry to call the church beyond consumerism to sentness.[26]

Thirdly, sentness comes at a price. The serious practice of BJJ takes a lot of time to improve one's skills. Add to that the sacrifices a coach makes in time and their own training. Finally, add the time invested into the lives of others. Bible studies at Renegade are aimed at a very basic level and continually focus on Jesus in a way which Paul would describe as milk and not solid food (1 Corinthians 3:2). But Christians who attend the study are expected to not only study Brazilian Jiu Jitsu but also to seek to contribute for the sake of others. Such studies are not often deep theological reflections and may at times offer little for the mature believer. Many Christians have come and gone through the group; the calling is a tough one. The example of BJJ incarnational mission illustrates the costliness of sentness.

In summary, it is clear that not everyone is sent into the martial arts community to witness at the margins of the church. However, that God is active in these communities is undeniable and such mission provides a useful example to all those willing to move from the centre to the margins to seek the lost for Christ

---

25 Hammond and Cronshaw, *Sentness*, 60.
26 Hammond and Cronshaw, *Sentness*, 27-43.

11. On the Journey to New Creation: Mission with People with Disabilities

Immanuel Koks

This chapter claims missional ministries with all marginalised people, especially those with disabilities, need to be confident that God is breaking into this world and that he is bringing new creation through the Holy Spirit. Yet, at the same time, the church needs to come alongside those of us who experience the disappointing reality that God often does not transform our lives in the way we desire or according to our timing. This chapter draws disability theology into conversation with the theology of missional church and a pneumatology that is both deeply sympathetic and questioning of a charismatic perspective. It argues that the church cares best when it has a broad view of the Spirit's work that extends far beyond any limits we place on God's work. (Not least the limiting charismatic inclination to claim that God is not at work when he does not meet expectations of cure.) This broad view allows the church to ask: how can we celebrate where God is at work? In doing this, the church can hold the disappointed with care and compassion, while leading them further in faithful journey with God and into mutual ministry with their fellow pilgrims.

New Zealander Margie Willers has Cerebral Palsy (CP) which affects her entire body.[1] In her mid-twenties she sought physical cure at a Katherine Kuhlman miracle service in Los Angeles.[2] Despite seeing a young boy with CP get cured, she left disappointed. Willers fell into a daze of depression and doubt. For the next few months she wrestled with God. Her anger with God spilled out into anger with others. Their well-intentioned words of encouragement and graceful, yet firm challenges, confirmed her suspicions; nobody understood. Thankfully, pastoral friends journeyed with her towards surrendering the belief that God would cure her in this life.

Like Willers, I have wrestled with God to cure my CP. About seven years ago I began using an electric wheelchair due to increasing fatigue – which is common for those with moderate CP. Because I had walked independently until then, this was a painful journey. During this time, I attended a Benny Hinn miracle crusade. I left the service surrounded by others with disabilities and angry. I was angry because of what I had

---

1   Margie Willers, *Awaiting the Healer* (Eastbournem, E Sussex: Kingsway, 1991), 20-21.
2   Willers, *Awaiting the Healer*, 61-81.

heard, not because I was not cured. Was God unable to heal? People were told to expect their healing. Did we simply lack sufficient faith? The crowd was urged to "push" into their healing in faith. Or did we poor people simply not put enough money in the offering bucket?[3] We were assured we would reap a healing if we sowed – gave money – in faith.

While the dominant narrative of the West has morphed from the Christian story to capitalist secularism, what we name as "disabled" has not changed much. As Sharon Belcher says, her disabled body is still "marked as fallen" by society and the church even though she believes that "modern theology" claims to have "outgrown such purportedly archaic notions of sin, evil, and the fall."[4] Society now labels as "not normal," those whose bodies do not conform to generally agreed upon standards of what is productive and beautiful.[5] We only need to consider the way the media is flooded with "miracle" stories of the way disabled people "overcome their disabilities" to recognise that usually the hope for people with disabilities is that they be changed to meet norms defined by the dominant society.[6]

Within the context of religious and societal negativity regarding disability, Willers' experience, as well as my own, shows the vexed nature of hoping that the Holy Spirit will heal or cure us now. If he does not heal, life remains hard. Just claiming that the believer needs more "faith" simply exacerbates the hurt, anger, and confusion.

After defining disability and flourishing, I will propose another approach to the question of faith.

Understanding "Disability"

Cornelius Plantinga argues that shalom is a state of "universal flourishing, wholeness and delight."[7] A person *flourishes* when they can grow into the person that God created them to be. Though we all have moments of flourishing and joy, other aspects of our lives are characterised by brokenness and disappointment. In order for us to experience shalom – the full expression of flourishing – we need to experience holistic restoration.

---

3   I use "poor" here, not in a pejorative sense, but in reference to the fact that poverty often accompanies disability.

4   Sharon V Betcher, *Spirit and the Politics of Disablement* (Minneapolis: Fortress, 2007), viii. Her point is valid, even though thankfully, not all contemporary theology has "outgrown" these "archaic notions".

5   Thomas E Reynolds, *Vulnerable Communion: A Theology of Disability and Hospitality Text* (Grand Rapids: Brazos, 2008), 56-68.

6   Rosemarie Garland-Thomson, "The Politics of Staring: Visual Rhetorics of Disability in Popular Photography," *Disability Studies: Enabling the Humanities* (2002), 193.

7   Cornelius Plantinga, *Not the Way It's Supposed to Be: A Breviary of Sin* (Grand Rapids: Eerdmans, 1995), 10.

Though all humans are limited in their ability to flourish, *disability* represents this limitation at a greater magnitude on the scale. Disability stems from an embodiment which fails to function physically, cognitively or emotionally in the way God desires. It is experienced when people with disabilities (PWDs) or our loved ones become aware of pronounced barriers to flourishing as we desire. Such barriers are intrinsic – e.g. impairment, personal attitudes, self-doubt and so on – or extrinsic – caused by the sinful erection of barriers to participation, e.g. societal barriers, economic barriers, employment barriers etc.

God's mission of Restoration

To ensure that Christian discourse does not create barriers, Thomas Reynolds, Amos Yong, and other disability theologians ask how we can re-work our theology to make it less problematic for those with disabilities. This innovative work begins by framing disability as a marginalising social construct which is reinforced by the stereotype of "normalcy," that is, an autonomous, beautiful, rational consumer, who participates fully in western liberal society.[8] According to these theologians, we can further marginalise PWDs by insisting that it is God's will to change their embodiment, so they become "normal." Instead, these theologians claim that disability should be understood as part of the diversity of creation and therefore part of God's will.[9] Christians must not insist that God desires to cure disability but that he accepts PWDs as they are.

Disability theology correctly shows that God is not partial. Therefore, my goal is to use Trinitarian theology to construct a theology of mission for all, including PWDs. I will argue that missional church does mission with PWDs best when they are at the centre of the ministry of universal flourishing in the personal powerful presence of the Holy Spirit. Since our salvation stands on Christ's completed work alone, no ability or disability can stop God's work of bringing new creation. All, therefore, can participate in God's mission.

Ross Hastings sums up this mission: "the Trinity is open to human relationships," in Christ and by the ongoing work of the Spirit. Ross Hastings continues, "*mission is God's mission first*, and we participate by grace in who he is and what he is doing."[10] Therefore, a robust pneumatological theology of mission must first be Trinitarian.

---

8   Reynolds, *Vulnerable Communion*, 15, 88-97.
9   Reynolds, *Vulnerable Communion*, 186-187.
10 Ross Hastings, *Missional God, Missional Church: Hope for Re-Evangelizing the West* (Downers Grove, IL: InterVarsity Press, 2012), 81. Original emphasis.

The saving work of one God in three persons is primary. Only then can we seek to understand the work of the third person. The first time we encounter the Spirit, is when the sovereign creator is at work.

Created in Diversity

While God created the entire cosmos, Abraham Kuyper's famous words hold true for all eternity, "There is not a square inch in the whole domain of our human existence over which Christ, who is Sovereign over all, does not cry: 'Mine!'"[11]

Note carefully though, God rules this good world *in* its diversity. The fourteen instances in Genesis 1 of God creating each "according to their/its kind" celebrates this difference. Because of this good diversity, Hans Reinders seeks to ground his anthropology "in God's Loving Kindness" for all – not our ability to relate to him. This excludes no one – not even those with most profound disabilities.[12] Our differences and disabilities do not minimise the fact that we are each God's good creation.

However, for reasons we cannot explain, the good, sovereign God allowed "things to take their course" and the good creation became corrupt.[13] Genesis 3 is as much a reality as Genesis 1. Yet, the foresight of the proto-gospel (Gen 3:15) confirms John's hind-sight: Christ indeed is, "the Lamb who was slain from the creation of the world." (Rev 13:8) The sovereign creator God, is the compassionate restoring saviour God who is still working through the Spirit.

By participating in this work, the church's difficult task is to parse good diversity, which we celebrate, from broken diversity, for which we are to seek God's restoration. Nevertheless, the goodness within diversity must entice us towards hospitality in many different ways. In this we must follow Ross Langmead's call to mission in whatever context we find ourselves – not least the context of disability.[14]

Breaking Down Barriers

Yet passages such as Leviticus 21:16-23, appear to show God excluding, not celebrating, those who are different (i.e. PWDs). Yong points out that we late moderns detest

---

11 James E. McGoldrick, *God's Renaissance Man : The Life and Work of Abraham Kuyper* (Darlington, England: Evangelical Press, 2000), 62.

12 H S Reinders, *Receiving the Gift of Friendship: Profound Disability, Theological Anthropology, and Ethics* (Grand Rapids: Eerdmans, 2008), 273.

13 J I Packer, *Concise Theology: A Guide to Historic Christian Beliefs* (Wheaton, IL: Tyndale House 1993), 33, Logos.

14 Ross Langmead, "Contestual Mission: An Australian Perspective," in ANZAMS Mini-Conference (Auckland: 2009), 4-7.

what we perceive as God's "discrimination against" PWDs in Israelite purity code.[15] However, in order to affirm God's holiness, Israelite purity laws excluded *many other* people, not just PWDs, through no fault of their own (Gentiles, women, especially those with their period, men who buried the dead etc.)

If holy God's exclusion of us was the end of the story then we should be afraid. However, in contrast to this awful picture, our loving God made a way for PWDs, non-Levite Hebrews, Gentiles, women – indeed *all* of us to enter into his presence. In his death and resurrection, God, in Christ, "broke down the dividing wall of hostility" (Eph 2:14). Nothing, neither ethnicity, gender, social status, nor even disability can prevent our "access to the Father by one Spirit" (Eph 2:18).

Trinitarian theology of the cross explains God's barrier wrecking work. The Father's burning wrath is not assuaged by the involuntary sacrifice of a *completely distinct* Son.[16] Rather, the three in one God chose to give of himself, in the person of the Son, for the redemption of the world. The Father's wrath manifests the triune God's injured love for excluded victim and dominating perpetrator alike.[17] Christ's unique sacrifice discloses the compassionate self-giving of the triune God which releases and fully restores all of us who lie ensnared by sin. Even when we feel utterly excluded and alone, the Triune God never leaves us. This is revealed in the Father's presence with Jesus to receive his spirit (c.f. Mat: 27:50; Lk 23:46) *after* Jesus' gut-wrenching lament while feeling utterly alone, "my God, my God, why have you forsaken me" (Mat 27:46).[18]

Restoration in Christ

Because of the cross, God restores us all. The universal scope of a theology of restoration in Christ alone, and for *all*, challenges PWDs and those without disabilities, to deconstruct all theological marginalisation. PWDs must ask God to open up vulnerable spaces of welcoming, within ourselves, even though true vulnerability does expose us to possible hurt. It is only then that we can request hospitality from others. Conversely, God's promise of universal restoration means those who do not identify

---

15 Amos Yong, *Theology and Down Syndrome: Reimagining Disability in Late Modernity* (Waco, TX: Baylor University Press, 2007), 23.

16 I affirm traditional models of expiation have their place among the many metaphors of atonement, but not *tritheistic* retellings of expiation; where the Father's wrath is set over against the Son's sacrifice.

17 Jürgen Moltmann, *The Spirit of Life: A Universal Affirmation* (Minneapolis: Fortress, 1992), 134..

18 Stein recognises Jesus's words "Father, into your hands I commit my spirit" as a voluntary surrender of life. See Robert H. Stein, *Luke* (Nashville: Broadman & Holman Publishers, 1992), 596, Logos.

as disabled cannot claim God will "heal" those with disabilities, while denying their own need for "healing."

This does not remove the particularity of God's work in individual lives. Recently I was talking to a Christian friend who acquired a spinal impairment in a vehicle accident a few years ago. He is thoroughly aware of the debates around healing ministry and disability, through both his work in disability mission and theological studies. In the past I remember him expressing a desire to be "healed," but in this conversation he said, "recently I have been thinking about prayer and reflected that although my prayer life has grown, I haven't been praying for healing as much as I did after the accident. I wonder if maybe I should." He, like me, still wonders if God's work for us includes "healing" of our physical impairments.

Biblical Perspectives

The prophet Isaiah wrote of a time when God will set the tumultuous world right.[19] God will make creation flourish and will redeem and repatriate the displaced. For the prophet however, the hallmark of a world set right will be universal healing (Isa 35:3-6).

Writing about the suffering servant, Isaiah says, "Surely he took up our pain and bore our suffering, ... the punishment that brought us peace was on him, and by his wounds we are healed." (Isa 53:4-5). The word translated as "pain" could better be translated "sicknesses."[20] "Suffering" could be expanded to include mental and physical suffering.[21] Finally "peace" is the Hebrew *"shalom,"* meaning fullness, completeness, or as mentioned earlier, a state of flourishing. Thus, another rendering could be "Surely he carried our sicknesses and bore our mental and physical suffering ... on him was the punishment that enables us to flourish, and by his wounds we are healed." Isaiah's suffering servant will *holistically restore* God's people. His work will facilitate new creation.

By recording that he would make the blind see, Luke's Jesus picked up the Septuagint's record of Isaiah's hope of curing (Lk 4:18, c.f. Isa 61:1-4 (Septuagint)). Yong helpfully argues that Luke's frequent reports of Jesus curing functioned as signposts towards

---

19 William Sanford La Sor et al., *Old Testament Survey: The Message, Form, and Background of the Old Testament* (Grand Rapids, MI: Eerdmans, 1996), 279-281.

20 *Theological Wordbook of the Old Testament*, s.v. "Ḥālâ."

21 *Theological Wordbook of the Old Testament*, s.v. "Kā᾿ab."

"the saving work of God in Christ."[22] Cure itself was not the main goal. In Zacchaeus' case, cure was not even in the story. God saved him, and began to restore him, even while he remained inconveniently short.[23]

Some 30 years after Christ's ascension, Peter still applied Isaiah 53:4-5 to Christ's ongoing work through the Spirit (1 Pet 2:24). Through Christ our sins can be forgiven and we can be healed. For Peter, what Christ did to restore and redeem our moral corruption goes hand in hand with what he does to restore our embodiment. Whether the person we minster to has a disability or not, a theology of restoration for all must hold *both* forgiveness of sins and bodily restoration. Yet, it must not give false hope of normalisation.

New Creation not Normalisation

By claiming we all, including PWDs, need God to restore us, I can easily be read as saying God will "normalise" PWDs, making us like everyone else. But we fail to love others in their uniqueness when we desire that God make us all alike. Society is rich and people flourish precisely because people are unique. We have also seen that God created diversity, not uniformity. Importantly, normalisation disempowers the marginalised PWDs by placing the power to improve their life in hands of the normal "healer."[24] This illustrates the ever-present corruption of sin, and shows the theological problems of hope that God will make a person "normal" because *our* normal is corrupt.

In contrast to normalisation, *flourishing within new creation is the Christian hope for those with disabilities and those without disabilities, alike.* We all look to Jesus as the foretaste of our new creation. Jesus' resurrected body was a new creation, even though he retained his identity – formed in part by the scars of crucifixion. In his resurrected body, we see the tension of continuity and discontinuity.

New creation life both confirms and challenges this desire for God to changes us all. Whenever God does new things – from the resurrection of Christ, to the smallest signs of the Holy Spirit at work now – he endorses our hopes for change. Nevertheless, we are challenged in those new creation moments, by the continuity of what remains

---

22 Amos Yong, *The Bible, Disability, and the Church: A New Vision of the People of God* (Grand Rapids, MI: Eerdmans, 2011), 66.

23 Yong, *Bible, Disability, and the Church*, 77.

24 This ugly and distorted view of healing ministry occurs when the "healer" is neither fully surrendered to God, nor articulates this to the one they are ministering to. This power dynamic can quickly spiral into control and manipulation.

from before they took place. If our hope for those with disabilities is new creation, not normalisation, then, a tangible "memory" of life with disability must continue for them to be the same person.

Nevertheless, because restoration of the *whole* of life is at the core of what God will do for us, Joni Eareckson-Tada correctly writes, "Restoration to physical wholeness [cure] will only be tiniest fraction of [God's] good plan and purpose for me."[25] Ultimate healing, according to Eareckson-Tada, happens when we reach our home with God.[26] Because new creation bodies are a gift bestowed on us at the resurrection, it is in this context alone that we are assured of full and complete "cure" of our disabilities, as he also restores the myriad other ways we fail to flourish.

Even so, while the fullness of cure, is a "not yet" hope, some experience some bodily restoration "now." This should draw us into celebration and worship, not surprise us, as God's Spirit breaks in with signs of the new creation.

Yet, paradoxically these moments should also draw us into the hopeful worship of lament with those who still wait for restoration. This is the rich lament of saying, "God we know you work, we've seen you work, but the lives of those who await your work are not right Lord." In patience perseverance we will wait and plead with them. In the tension of celebration and heartache, we must hear God say, "*See, I am making* all things new." (Rev 21:5)

Roderick Leupp articulates this sort of hopeful lament for his daughter, on the first Pentecost after a car accident that left her with major head injuries. He calls upon the "healing Spirit":

> Her smouldering brain
> So battered, so emaciated
> So riven
> Is ignitable
> Is combustible
> Is waiting
> For You, Holy Spirit
> You Who are
> Where Father and Son

---

25 Joni Eareckson Tada, *A Place of Healing: Wrestling with the Mysteries of Suffering, Pain, and God's Sovereignty* (Colorado Springs, CO: David C. Cook, 2010), 153.

26 Tada, *A Place of Healing*, 157-159.

Meet in ecstasy
Can You not also
Wake our sleeping babe.[27]

Some people do experience grief over disability. Whatever our perspective on the goodness of a life with disability, we cannot minister with them if we do not share their hope, and share their anguished lament to some degree. Somehow we need to be able to pray for healing. The only way to do this with authenticity is to allow the universal hope of new creation to undo the theological marginalisation of saying God must change the other. Neither PWDs nor those without disabilities can say life would be better "if God only changed *them.*" Instead, in the mutuality of longing for new creation we can say "God is changing *us.*"

The Spirit as God at Work

My argument so far has intentionally focused on the work of the triune God, not the Spirit in particular. It is through the Spirit that the sovereign, creator, redeeming triune God works in the church age. The Spirit has always been revealed as the one true God (Ps 106:32-33; Act 5:3-4; Heb 10:15-17). He is described as the "*ruach*," wind, breath of God, or as James Dunn suggests an "experience of a mysterious awesome power."[28] Whether he gifted the temple artisans or enables those who minister in the church, he is God gifting those who work in his mission (Ex 31:3; 1 Cor 12:4). The Spirit is God empowering his people to live ethical lives (Ez 36:24-27; Rom 8:1-13). The triune God is at work, through the powerful personal presence of the Spirit. We cannot divorce our hope in the Spirit's powerful restoring work from the fact that he is triune God, personally involved in our lives.

Mature Ministry of Mutuality

Through the Spirit, Trinitarian mission of restoration for all captivates the church. This happens when the community of God matures by exercising the gifts of the Spirit alongside each other (Eph 4:13). Then the Spirit gifts them to reach beyond themselves (1 Corinthians 14). 1 Corinthians 12 demonstrates the utterly egalitarian nature of the Spirit's gifts. Writing to the whole church at Corinth, not just the elite, Paul says, "To

---

27 Roderick T. Leupp, *The Renewal of Trinitarian Theology: Themes, Patterns, & Explorations* (Downers Grove, IL: IVP Academic, 2008), 87-88.
28 James D. G. Dunn, "Towards the Spirit of Christ: The Emergence of the Distinctive Fectures of Christian Pnumatology," in *The Work of the Spirit: Pneumatology and Pentecostalism*, ed. Michael Welker (Grand Rapids, MI: Eerdmans, 2006), 7.

each one the manifestation of the Spirit is given for the common good." The Spirit graciously gifts all and sundry in Christ's body. Even the most unseemly members are gifted and should be treated "with special honour" (v23).

This is true for all ministry across the boundaries – not just in the context of disability. Marginalising barriers remain whenever the other is seen as, or sees themselves as, the unequal recipient of charity. The church smashes through divisions, however, when it leads the mind-shift away from the autonomous, self-sufficiency endemic in the "cult of normalcy." We need to move from believing independence is the goal of "growing up," to embracing that fact that mutuality creates the conditions for maturing.

As we grow up, the gifts are no longer ends in themselves. Rather, we embrace love (1 Corinthians 13). The immaturity of clutching our spiritual toys (v11) gives way to holding them loosely as tools to help others grow in the eternal gifts of faith, hope and love (v13). Then, we are propelled outward in mission with the gifts which have been at work in the body. The gifts are not just for those in the church, but are evangelistic tools as well (1 Cor 14:24-25). Thus we turn towards the world in the maturing strength of ministering together.

So, God begins to transform us into new creation now, when mutuality is embedded deep in our missional churches. New creation begins because our ministry with others becomes the context of God's work in each other's lives, not simply because we are the passive recipients of "healing prayer." Nevertheless, as we share and pray with each other, we will also share each other's disappointments, since in our mixed up world, the Spirit sometimes moves contrary to our mixed up desires.

Ministering in the Tension

> In Christ we are invited to participate in the reality of God and the reality of the world at the same time, the one not without the other.[29]

Especially in prayer, this participation is not reaching up to an absent God, pleading for him to act where he is not active. Rather, as Paul Fiddes insightfully argues, when we intercede for each other, we participate in what God is already doing in each other's lives.[30]

---

29 Dietrich Bonhoeffer, *Ethics*, Dietrich Bonhoeffer Works, vol. 6 (Minneapolis: Fortress, 2005), 55.
30 Paul S Fiddes, *Participating in God: A Pastoral Doctrine of the Trinity* (London: Darton, Longman and Todd, 2000), 123.

Nevertheless we find ourselves ministering in a tension. God is sovereignly acting now. But in this confusing, painful world in which we live, he has far from the completed his new creation work. We feel the strain when we can only say, "I don't know why God does not work as we desire now," when faced with the red, tear-stained, disappointment in the face of one we love. In the midst of the tension, full of competing desires for what is best, it takes faith, not to resign, but to surrender to God.

Surrendered faith is a stronger faith than faith for healing. Despite often being repeated as a platitude, surrender is trusting the real truth of 1 Cor 2:9, "What no eye has seen, what no ear has heard, and what no human mind has conceived— these things God has prepared for those who love him." As we let go of our desire for God to work in a particular way, and trust that he will work for our flourishing, then we begin to embrace faith in a God who still works in imperceptible ways; even through the hard road of suffering.

Surrender is not the opposite of faith for healing. Rather, surrender is faith for the restoration of new creation. Because God is at work, we can faithfully lay down our desire for short-term fixes, in confidence that he *is bringing* new creation life now, even while we experience disappointment. This might explain some of the countless testimonies of people who see new creation life *after* they surrender their desires.

Henri Nouwen is right, "when we befriend our pain – or, in the words of Jesus 'take up our cross' – we discover that the resurrection is, indeed, close at hand."[31] Far from being a trite slogan, this is deep truth. It is there from the betrayal of Joseph – through which God saved Egypt – to Moses leading Israel out of Egypt – in the midst of the wail and stench of death. From the rise of David – while a fugitive from Saul – to Jeremiah's prophecy of a new covenant – while lamenting the dying state of Israel – God brings new life in the midst of death.[32] Jesus himself went to the cross, so that new life may come. Suffering was part of following Jesus for Paul and the rest of the apostles, as was faithfully proclaiming the joyful hope of resurrection.

Paul learned that the "thorn in the flesh," was to stop him from getting conceited, and thus hamper the spread of the gospel and his relationship with God (1 Cor 12:7-9). In our seasons of disability and brokenness, the Spirit can still work through us to move

---

31 Henri J M Nouwen, *Here and Now: Living in the Spirit* (New York: Crossroad, 1994), 40.
32 Walter Brueggemann, *The Prophetic Imagination* (Minneapolis: Fortress, 2001), 46-57.

others towards greater wholeness.[33] One only needs to consider the thriving ministry of Elevate: Christian Disabilities Trust – that touches the lives of hundreds, if not thousands of people with genuine love, care, and gospel truth. Most likely this would not have happened if Margie Willers had been healed in that auditorium in LA.[34]

This is not hopeless resignation, but a life of constant and repeated surrender that embraces the melody of hope. Music, according to Jeremy Begbie, offers a metaphor for hope. Music is often waves of intensification and resolution.[35] The waves overlay each other (like a whole song that overlays verses which overlay lines of a verse.) So in a similar way, we hope for new creation's ultimate fulfilment when God renews all of humanity and the cosmos. We experience glimmers of new creation fulfilled hope today, as well as the occasional life-altering miracle. Yet these are often followed by the intensification of another problem, for which we hopefully await resolution. Each problem has simply driven us forward towards the arrival of a still greater hope. Therefore we continue to be driven toward the completion of new creation.

It is in this rhythm that we experience overflow of the Trinity's work in our life. Through the powerful personal presence of the Spirit, missional church is *partially restored people walking alongside other partially restored people and inviting others to journey with them on the path of new creation life.* It is in these communities where PWDs can participate as fellow sojourners. Together we can love and accept who we are now and be strengthened in life's struggles. On this basis, together we can find the deep faith to surrender, but not resign ourselves to our disability and suffering. We can gently yet persistently challenge and encourage each other to keep seeking the restoration of new creation.

---

[33] Please do not read this as my reason for the absence of cure. But rather read it as a plea to turn our focus from the lack of cure to the question: "What does God want me to do now, even though I retain my disability?"

[34] Margie went on to become the co-founder of this ministry.

[35] Jeremy Begbie, *Theology, Music, and Time*, Cambridge Studies in Christian Doctrine 4 (Cambridge: Cambridge University Press, 2000), 106-110.

D. Engaging the postmodern mind

*It's not easy to walk in the rain
And I walk with my eyes to the ground
I often ignore the rainbow above
at the coming of the sun*

Ross Langmead, "Pilgrim Song" (1985)

If the church is to listen to the younger generations we will need to appreciate what world it is they live in…Not only are they the future of our society, they may be bearing aspects of the gospel message *to* the church.

Ross Langmead, "The Best of Times, The Worst of Times: The Australian Context," (Lecture series, 2009), 5.

12. A Mutual Understanding, Emerging Spirituality and the Christian Church

Christy Capper

An emerging postmodern spirituality is identified by social research as growing within the culture of Australian young adults. Neither the research nor the reality of this new spirituality has been heeded and the church struggles to engage these young adults. If the church is to take seriously this emerging generation and their spirituality they will need to engage in a cross cultural dialogue with careful listening. Rather than an aberration of youth, this emerging spirituality may be a harbinger of a new and holistic spirituality. This chapter considers the role of the church in this new spirituality and the need for engagement and dialogue between both parties. Only then might the church hear the prophetic voice of this spiritual wave, only then might the church engage missiologically.

Introduction

"Well, I am interested in spirituality" she said, "but I am just surprised that religious people are too."

This was the response I received from a young women fitting my reading glasses for me after she heard that I was a theology student interested in spirituality, in particular the spirituality of young adults who aren't religious. How is it that this young woman thought of spirituality as so separated from religion? Why would she be surprised to find a religious person interested in spirituality?

Over the past two decades there has been a buzz around the area of spirituality in Australia. Writers such as Gideon Goosen and David Tacey have reflected upon the new importance held by spirituality within the lives of Australians and have considered the new wave of spirituality in Australia. A spirituality which is not New Age, is not marketable and that denies the "death of God" pronounced by modernity.[1] This new spirituality, interestingly, does not translate into religious affiliation or activity, but is cultivated in different ways such as political activity, ancient practices and popular

---

1   David Tacey, "Youth Spirituality as a Response to Cultural Crisis," in *Spiritual Education: Cultural, Religious and Social Differences*, ed. Jane Erricker, Cathy Ota and Clive Erricker (Brighton: Sussex Academic Press, 2001), 91.

culture.² As demonstrated for us by the young woman mentioned above, there is a vast gulf separating religion and spirituality in Australia. It continues to widen.³ This chapter seeks to understand why this gulf exists; why it is growing and how the church might stop the gulf widening further; to build a bridge to allow for mutual discovery of both sides.⁴

How can the church bridge this gap between organised religion and young adult spirituality? To answer this question we first ask what the spirituality of young Australians is. Where did this interest in spirituality come from? How does spirituality express itself in these young adults? What is the spirituality of Christians in the church in Australia? When did this gulf begin to separate spirituality and religion? What can Christians do if they are to connect with Australian society, if they are to be relevant, to speak God's good news into the world? How can the church nurture and develop this spiritual interest if indeed it is a work of God?

Characteristics of emerging spirituality

The characteristics of emerging spirituality are expressions of the worldview of Generation Y, those born from 1980-1994 inclusively. This is a group of postmodern young Australians reacting to perceived modernist limitations such as objective truth and progress.⁵ They see claims of truth as claims to power.⁶ They do not trust science as the purveyor of truth.⁷ Through technology they are influenced by events occurring both locally and globally.

These factors have played a major role in the emergence of this new spirituality, a spirituality having no common forms, and no central governance or holy places.⁸ It is a spirituality in its early stages. It is deeply contextual, deeply felt and deeply actionable: a spirituality of action; which notices problems in the world; and seeks

---

2   See Philip Hughes, *Shaping Australia's Spirituality: A Review of Christian Ministry in the Australian Context* (Mulgrave: Mosaic, 2010), 42; also, James Gollnick, *Religion and Spirituality in the Life Cycle* (New York: Peter Lang, 2005), 2.

3   David Tacey, "Spirituality in Australia Today," in *Sacred Australia: Post-Secular Considerations*, ed. Makarand Paranjape (Melbourne: Clouds of Magellan, 2009), 46.

4   When "the church" is referred to what is meant is the work of Christians within the institutional church. As a whole the church is a large and unwieldy institution, action and change must be promoted and engaged with by the Christians within the institution.

5   Heath White, *Postmodernism 101* (Grand Rapids: Brazos, 2001), 42.

6   White, *Postmodernism*, 55.

7   Paul Hiebert, *Transforming Worldviews: And Anthropological Understanding of How People Change* (Grand Rapids: Baker Academic, 2008), 216.

8   Tacey, "Spirituality in Australia Today," 60.

to address them.⁹ The theology of youth spirituality is creation centred, politically engaged, and holistic.

Creation centred

The environmental crisis is one of the great issues of our time. Generation Y identify the state of the environment as the greatest threat to the world's future.10 Australia is, and has always been, "a land of drought and flooding rains" but with each *La Niña* and *El Niño* cycle the droughts and floods worsen. The spirituality of young adults urges urgent action to prevent the strengthening of these cycles.[11]

The care of the planet is not only a pragmatic, moral or economic concern but a deeply spiritual concern for today's young adults.[12] There may still be time to fix this problem if people work together, in desperation, not only as nations but as a planet. Young Australians desire to change the way in which people live. Yet they know that this is a difficult task.

Concern for the environment is indicative of the creation spirituality of young adults. For the emerging spirituality, God is found in creation, making creation sacred. This is not mere pantheism. Tacey describes this view as panentheism: "all things having their essential being and groundedness in God."[13] The emerging spirituality holds the sacredness of all things and is influenced by Aboriginal ideas of land and space.[14] The creation is sacred. It shows us who God is. It represents God.[15] In creation we experience God in new ways. We see a web of relationships which makes life possible. Everything is interrelated: no person, no species, can exist alone. It is this creation centred theology which drives and shapes the environmentalism of emerging generations.[16]

---

9   Rebecca Huntley, *The World According to Y: Inside the New Adult Generation* (Crows Nest: Allen & Unwin, 2006), 104.
10 Hughes, *Shaping Australia's Spirituality*, 27.
11 David Tacey, *The Spirituality Revolution: The Emergence of Contemporary Spirituality* (Sydney: Harper Collins, 2003), 182.
12 David Tacey, *ReEnchantment: The New Australian Spirituality* (Sydney: Harper Collins, 2000), 162.
13 Tacey, "Spirituality in Australia Today," 56.
14 Tacey, "Spirituality in Australia Today," 60.
15 Wendy Chew. "Cosmology and Ecology: The Way Ahead" in *Developing an Australian Theology*, ed. Peter Malone (Strathfield: St Paul's, 1999), 189.
16 Tacey, *Spirituality Revolution*, 30.

In creation and its care redemption is best understood. Much current Christian theology has separated creation from redemption, regarding these as separate ideas and processes. Generation Y sees redemption through the lens of the care for, and healing of, creation.[17] Their ideas are creation centered.

Politically Engaged

Youth spirituality is not about believing doctrine, practicing disciplines or following a person - it is about changing the world.[18] Generation Y have lost belief in national politics to solve the world's problems.[19] There is profound disillusionment with the current system.[20] Generation Y are often accused of apathy towards political involvement and yet they are highly engaged in aid and development work and have founded organisations such as OakTree, where the CEO must retire at age 25.[21]

Generation Y are not apathetic regarding politics, only national politics as we know it, where politicians seek to undermine one another and make sure that no good is done which may not result in reelection, prioritising reelection over the good of humanity as a whole. When a politician promotes change well, such as Barack Obama in the 2008 US Presidential election, young adults worldwide are supportive.[22]

Young adults see that spirituality is transformational rather than simply informational, and that transformation involves change that must involve action.[23] Generation Y's desire to be authentic leads them to see a failure to do right when the opportunity is given as equivalent to doing wrong - inaction is as bad as wrong action. For today's young adults spirituality is seen to be worth nothing if it does not engage with social justice and equality for all people.[24]

---

17 Frank Fletcher, "Imagination for the Australian Spiritual Journey," in *Developing an Australian Theology*, ed. Malone, Peter (Strathfield: St Paul's Publications, 1999), 266-267.

18 In 1991 Strauss and Howe identified Generation Y as one for which civic responsibility and citizenship with a strong theme. William Strauss and Neil Howe, *Generations: The History of America's Future, 1584-2069* (Quill, USA: William Morrow, 1991).

19 Huntley, *World According to Y,* 104.

20 Tacey, *ReEnchantment,* 6.

21 Huntley, *World According to Y,* 104-105.

22 Huntley, *World According to Y,* 115.

23 Tacey, *Spirituality Revolution,* 59.

24 Tacey, *ReEnchantment,* 189.

Holistic

Spirituality must be holistic.[25] The lives of Generation Y are often fragmented and rushed, yet they desire lives which are whole and unhurried.[26] Emerging spirituality breaks down barriers between public and private, personal and political, national and international. It is a holistic spirituality. Ignoring the dualism of modernity, it disregards conventional boundaries.[27] For young adults only a holistic life is authentic: one must be their true self at all times and in all places.[28]

The idea of finding a "true" self is synonymous with being authentic, yet it is not a self-indulgent activity but a process through which one might find God. Just as panentheism sees that God is present in nature, so too can the likeness of the holy be found in each person. One's true self will be that which best expresses one's uniqueness and experience of God.[29]

Contrasting emerging spirituality and traditional Christianity

When emerging spirituality meets traditional Christianity there is confusion. Contrasting the values of each group side by side may help us to better grapple with the misunderstandings and misinterpretations.

Absolutes and Relativity

Twelve years ago a university Christian student group ran an outreach campaign based around the topic of absolutes and relativity. This campaign was given support from churches Sydney-wide, cost thousands of dollars, and brought in top speakers and debaters. The student group used university wide marketing to raise awareness of the campaign and caused debate in all segments of the university campus, even quickly spreading to other campuses in the city.

The campaign slogan was "Absolute God." There were lectures on AbsoluteJustice, AbsoluteLove, AbsoluteReality, AbsoluteSex, AbsoluteLife, AbsoluteFact and AbsoluteTruth. Other students ridiculed Christians in university publications. Churches were seen anew as arrogant, intolerant and irrelevant.

---

25 Dallas Willard, "Spiritual Formation in Christ is for the Whole Life and the Whole Person," in *For All the Saints: Evangelical Theology and Christian Spirituality*, edited by Timothy George and Alister McGrath (London: Westminster John Knox, 2003), 47.

26 Michael Mason, Andrew Singleton and Ruth Webber, *The Spirit of Generation Y: Young People's Spirituality in a Changing Australia* (Mulgrave, VIC: John Garratt, 2007), 49.

27 Tacey, *Spirituality Revolution*, 79.

28 Michael Riddell, *Threshold of the Future* (London: SPCK, 1998), 131.

29 Tacey, *Spirituality Revolution*, 82.

Why did this campaign generate such strong reactions? It was coming from a modernist mindset, promoting absolute knowledge and truth to a postmodern people who gave no credence to absolutism. The campaign assumed that modernist absolutism was a necessary prerequisite for conversion to Christianity. Modernism is not a necessary prerequisite for a person to follow Christ. Modernism did not even exist until very late in the story of Christianity.

The churches and Christian leaders, still steeped in the modern worldview, honestly believed that they were serving the university community by communicating "the truth." Yet they had underestimated the power of worldview. This student group proclaimed the gospel through their own modernist worldview. In the first decade of the twenty first century Christianity was proclaimed in a culturally insensitive and destructive way. The Christian community unwittingly promoted their own worldview rather than the Gospel. They brought that message from above rather than from below.[30]

The spirituality of Generation Y is not one based on the absolutes of modernity but, rather, the relativism of postmodernity. For Generation Y, absolutes show the highest levels of intolerance and therefore cannot be loving. This is a generation which sees bias as unavoidable. Everything is known only from our perspective. To hold to an absolute is to disenfranchise a person who holds a perspective or belief different from one's own.[31] This rejection of absolutes and embrace of tolerance is one of the major differences between those in the church and Generation Y.

There are, however, ideas to which Generation Y hold strongly: they believe in relativism absolutely; they believe in the importance of love absolutely; they believe in caring for others and the environment absolutely. Different ideas and perspectives can be taken into consideration but those who do not believe in climate change or who judge people on the basis of religion or ethnicity are considered to be either uneducated or wrong.

Most young adults are critical of religious institutions and consider them to be intolerant, divisive and producing more harm than good within society.[32] The concept of tolerance is at the heart of ethics for young Australians. Living in the midst of a

---

30 Coming from above relates to the Gospel being forced upon people by those in power. The Gospel from below involves Christians holding an attitude of humility and service while sharing the Scriptures David J Bosch, *Transforming Mission: Paradigm Shifts in Theology of Mission* (Maryknoll: Orbis, 1991), 484-485.

31 Judith Bessant and Rob Watts, *Sociology Australia* (Crows Nest: Allen & Unwin, 2007), 91.

32 Hughes, *Shaping Australia's Spirituality*, 45.

multicultural society, they have learned to accept, embrace and encourage differences and diversity.

Generation Ys are suspicious of truth claims, preferring to find truth in everyday life.[33] Often these ideas of truth emerge from stories, though Generation Y reject the concept of an overarching meta-narrative.[34] They listen to the stories of different peoples, believing that if truth exists it makes itself clear through narratives. As Riddell comments: "the concept of truth they are reacting to is objective, rationalistic, individualistic and linear. Stories, on the other hand, are subjective, synthetic, relational and playful."[35]

Change and tradition

For today's young adults change is the only constant. The rate of change in the twenty-first century continues to accelerate. Change and innovation is normal for today's young people.[36] When something does not change it is considered an aberration.

Emerging spirituality's focus on justice, the environment and equality necessitates change; change in individuals, communities and nations.[37] Change which produces life and wholeness. For a spirituality to be healthy it must change.[38]

Traditional churches are resistant to change.[39] Young adults consider this a problem. In their eyes change is standard, yet it seems that the churches call for transformation in the lives of people while neglecting or postponing institutional, structural and cosmetic changes themselves.

The deficit of change within the church leads young adults to conclude that the church is, in fact, uninterested in transforming the world, it is inauthentic. Young adults desire a place to serve and speak into the church, yet the changes they see as vital are neither heard or enacted.[40] They therefore leave the church, disenfranchised and frustrated.

---

33 James Miller, "The Emerging Postmodern World," in *Postmodern Theology: Christian Faith in a Pluralist World*, ed. Fredrick Burnham (San Francisco: Harper&Row, 1989) 12.
34 Stanley Grenz, *A Primer on Postmodernism* (Grand Rapids: Eerdmans, 1996), 45.
35 Riddell, *Threshold of the Future*, 105.
36 Mark McCrindle, *The ABC of XYZ: Understanding the Global Generations* (Sydney: UNSW, 2009), 189.
37 Riddell, *Threshold of the Future*, 108.
38 Margaret Guenther, *The Practice of Prayer* (Cambridge: Cowel, 1998), 14.
39 Tacey, *ReEnchantment*, 16.
40 Tacey, *Spirituality Revolution*, 109.

Wholeness and dualism

The modernist worldview broke down ideas and subjects into their smallest components.[41] The postmodern worldview seeks to put together much of that which it perceives has been disconnected, undermining the agenda of modernity to classify and separate. The public and private worlds merge into one for Generation Y. As has been noted, authenticity is of paramount importance to young adults.[42] Authenticity comes as a result of wholeness. Yet for many in the religious traditions the idea of wholeness is difficult. For the church there are stark contrasts between secular and spiritual, good and evil, right and wrong, the body and the spirit. These contrasts are not considered valid by younger Australians who seek to merge these ideas together, believing that we are all connected in a web of relationships, not only people but all of creation.[43] Within this activist spirituality there is no distinction between the secular and the spiritual, between the body and the spirit. If God is immanent and seen in a panentheistic manner then there is no distinction between matter and spirit, for the spirit is seen through the matter and this makes the matter spiritual. The spirit/matter dualism of the modern church is removed within this new and emerging spirituality.[44]

Spirituality and religion

There is a divide between spirituality and religion in Australia. Young Australians exhibit surprise that religious people have an interest in spirituality when they consider themselves spiritual but not religious.[45] A vital factor in the formation of this divide is the contrasting modern and postmodern worldviews exhibited by the church and young Australians. Religious institutions have been shaped by modernity and exist in the modern mindset while young adults are shaped by postmodernity and ethics of wholeness, tolerance, relativity and change.[46]

The postmodern spirituality is shaped by action and ideas rather than doctrine, for those part of emerging spirituality the central and significant figure is not a priest but a prophet.[47] As we see through the Scriptures prophets have rarely found a place within institutional religion during their lifetime. The prophet is one who calls for change,

---

41 Riddell, *Threshold of the Future*, 107.
42 Hughes, *Shaping Australia's Spirituality*, 77.
43 Riddell, *Threshold of the Future*, 107.
44 Tacey, *ReEnchantment*, 198, 229.
45 Tacey, "Spirituality in Australia Today," 48.
46 Celia Kourie, "Crossing Boundaries: The Way of Interspirituality," in *Religion & Theology*, Vol 18 (2011), 11.
47 Tacey, "Spirituality in Australia Today," 50.

who calls for justice and mercy. These are not easily welcomed by religious institutions who hold to the traditions of the past and see God active within the past or within the boundaries of their institution. Yet if God is truly active in our world then surely God can act through different kinds of people and ideas, creatively showing us God's will and plan for our world.[48]

With the growth of postmodern ideas and ethics the gap between religion and spirituality grows ever wider. There exists a mutual misunderstanding between the church and emerging spirituality. This misunderstanding is present within both groups and stems from a lack of contact and dialogue between religion and spirituality. If the gap between religion and spirituality in Australia is to begin to close, then this mutual misunderstanding must be addressed. This is becoming an urgent matter as many churches continue to decline in size and especially in growth amongst younger generations.[49]

Overcoming a mutual misunderstanding

The importance of dialogue

Communication is a vital component of any healthy relationship. Given the lack of communication between the church and emerging spirituality it can be asserted that if a relationship exists it is not one which is healthy. There is a need for dialogical communication between the church and emerging spirituality if a relationship is to be built and the gap between religion and spirituality in Australia is to be narrowed. Bevans and Schroeder go so far as to state that "mission is dialogue."[50]

As Christians engage in mission it is vital that they seek to understand the culture or sub-culture with and to whom they seek to minister.[51] The incarnational approach to mission wherein the missionary is an insider rather than an outsider to the culture is most often the best approach.[52] This the way that God has revealed Godself to humanity in Jesus.[53] By becoming human God became an insider in our culture and experienced all that humans experience. Incarnation is the best way in which to engage in mission.

---

48 Tacey, *Spirituality Revolution*, 21.
49 Brian McLaren, *Finding Our Way Again: The Return of the Ancient Practice* (Nashville: Thomas Nelson, 2008), 126.
50 Stephen Bevans, Roger Schroeder, *Constants in Context: A Theology of Mission for Today* (Maryknoll: Orbis, 2004), 285.
51 Stephen Bevans, *Models of Contextual Theology* (Maryknoll: Orbis, 2002), 9.
52 David Bosch, *Transforming Mission: Paradigm Shifts in Theology of Mission* (Maryknoll: Orbis, 1992), 513.
53 Bouyer, Louis, *A History of Christian Spirituality I: The Spirituality of the New Testament and the Fathers* (New York: Seabury, 1960), 127.

One of the best ways to understand a culture is to come to learn their stories. As Christianity is pushed more to the margins of Australian society, many young people have only a skewed memory of any Christian stories. To enable young people to understand Christianity it is essential that we retell our Christian stories. Narrative may be the easiest way for young adults to share their ideas, beliefs and experiences with Christians. The dialogue we need is not formal two way communication but the relaxed sharing of our stories.

A narrative dialogue for Australia

Bosch notes six important factors which must be in place when engaging in a missiological dialogue.[54] Engaging these six points will help us to engage in a constructive narrative dialogue.

1. Missiological dialogue is a matter of the heart rather than a matter of the mind.

Narrative enables ideas to speak to the heart. The dialogue which must take place will not succeed if arguments are purely intellectual. Stories speak to the heart but also tease the mind; they are open to interpretation and begin a dialogue. Narratives themselves do not claim to hold absolute truth, making this a productive way for the church to express its theology to spiritual young Australians.

2. True dialogue presupposes commitment.

The aim of dialogue is not agreement but, rather, mutual understanding and respect. The church cannot and must not disengage from its commitment to following Christ. It must seek to understand the nature of following Christ in a postmodern world. The church must recognise that though young adults may not have the language to express the theology behind their commitments their commitments are nonetheless present.[55] Narrative may give form to the theological underpinnings behind the actions of emerging spirituality.

3. In dialogue the church must accept that God has preceded us and has already been present and active within those with whom we dialogue.

God is active and present in our culture and emerging spirituality is a move of the Spirit in desperate times.[56] God has always been active outside the boundaries of the

---

54 Bosch, *Transforming Mission*, 483-489.
55 Tacey, "Spirituality in Australia Today," 48.
56 Tacey, "Youth Spirituality as a Response to Cultural Crisis," 92.

church and the church must recognise the hand of God at work and approach emerging spirituality reverently as though it is holy ground.[57] Through the stories of emerging spirituality we may identify the presence of God and join in with the spiritual work which is already happening in the lives of young Australians.

4. Dialogue is possible only when conducted in an attitude of humility.

In a dialogue between the church and emerging spirituality this would involve those in the church, who are likely the older party, listening in humility to those younger than they; remembering the words of Paul to Timothy that the young ought not be looked down upon because of their youth. There cannot be judgements and absolutes in this dialogue, rather mutual respect and a thirst to understand the other is essential.

5. All religions (and spiritualities) ask and seek to answer fundamentally different questions.

The prime concern within emerging spirituality is the future of the world, as it can be shaped in the present time. Emerging spirituality is concerned with how the world might move to healing from its broken state, while the Church seems more concerned with sinfulness and holiness.[58] While these ideas are connected both of these groups begin their theology at fundamentally different points they do interrelate and for both groups to understand the "starting point" of the other would be a leap forward in mutual understanding.

6. Dialogue is "not a substitute or subterfuge for mission."

Dialogue must occur in relationships and relationships are an indispensable asset to mission. Mission is central to the call of the church, it is through missional lenses that identity of the church is most clearly seen.[59] God is serious about mission and calls those who follow Jesus to be people of missional action.[60] Mission has different models and motivators throughout Christian history. It is vital that the church engages in mission to young adults, but this cannot be completed under the guise of dialogue. It must be a separate yet interrelated process.

---

57 Bosch, *Transforming Mission*, 484
58 Tacey, *Spirituality Revolution*, 2.
59 Alan Hirsch, *The Forgotten Ways: Reactivating the Missional Church* (Grand Rapids: Brazos, 2006), 47.
60 Tacey, "Youth Spirituality as a Response to Cultural Crisis," 192.

Emerging spirituality and mission

As we engage in a narrative dialogue we may find that Christian stories with themes in creation and eschatology are related to the wholeness and authenticity sought in emerging spirituality. N T Wright states that our beliefs regarding eschatology fundamentally impact the way in which we engage with the world and suggests that the Christian hope of the New Heavens and the New Earth demand a holistic Christian response to the problems of the world.[61]

Those best suited to engage in this dialogue are likely young adults who find tension in belonging to the institutional church. These young adults will be those who yearn for a spirituality of action and adventure with God, for a spiritual journey of significance.[62] They must realise that this spiritual adventure has arrived. However, it may involve staying in the church, where they feel discontent, and challenging it to act incarnationally in an Australian context. The task will not be easy.

The temptation will be present to either move to a fundamentalist religion or to give up unique Christian beliefs in order to reach culture.[63] To succeed in their mission of bridge building, young adults must carefully navigate their faith. They ought not compromise their mission by taking either of these philosophically easier paths. Young adults must use their wisdom and creativity to counter the challenges with which they are faced.[64]

These young adults must tell and live out the stories which illustrate their faith in Christ and the call to act in desperate times, to love people no matter who they are and how they express themselves. They will need encouragement from those both within and outside of Christian institutions. Young adults who remain in the church with the hope of change may be the means of embracing those who hold to the new spirituality.

Conclusion

The modernist mindset of the Australian church is fundamentally different to the postmodernist mindset of young Australians. This difference has been misunderstood as an intellectual problem and some Christians have tried to counter the differences with intellectual debates and the dismissal of postmodernity as an intellectual

---

61 N T Wright, *Surprised by Hope* (London: SPCK, 2007), 198.
62 See Michael Frost and Alan Hirsch, *The Shaping of Things to Come: Innovation and Mission for the 21st Century Church* (Peabody: Hendrickson, 2003), 135; also Riddell, *Threshold of the Future*, 131.
63 Gollnick, *Religion and Spirituality in the Life Cycle*, 118.
64 McLaren, *Finding our Way Again*, 5-6.

partner.⁶⁵ This viewpoint misunderstands the depth to which worldview impacts our understandings of ourselves and the world in which we live.

The church has attempted to engage in mission to postmodern Australia using modern techniques and viewpoints. What must now be created is a new map from which to engage missiologically, a map through which the world is interpreted taking into account the depth of the issue of worldview on the every aspect of a person and culture.⁶⁶ Without this understanding the gap between religion and spirituality will continue to widen.

A narrative dialogue between a modernist church and the postmodernist emerging spirituality may create a much needed contextual theology for postmodern Australia. This theology would endorse ideas of holism, activism, contemplation and emphasise the new creation. It would be a theology based strongly upon eschatological ideas. Looking forward to the time when there will be no more suffering or pain or evil or poverty or injustice, where the justice and mercy which emerging spirituality seeks would be brought forth in abundance.

This contextual theology would need to be created by learned theologians, practitioners and Christian young adults who have strong connections to the wider postmodern culture. It is the young adults within the church who might form the bridge between religion and spirituality in Australia. They are those who understand and are part of both of these groups. They are those who can be incarnational in their approach to culture and to the church. These young people would have a vital role to play in the creation of postmodern Australian theology through which mission might engage.⁶⁷

From these encounters in dialogue and mission the church may have the opportunity to be involved in the spiritual formation of Australian culture as a whole. The time is ripe for this to happen. God is at work within our society. Young adults passionately pursue justice and mercy, not realising that the hope Christians have in Christ is a hope in which they share. The idea that Jesus is God, embodied and living as the perfect, holistic human, can speak strongly to emerging spirituality. Australia is ready for the story of Jesus to be told in a new way.⁶⁸

---

65 Miller, "Emerging Postmodern World," 8.
66 Alan Roxburgh, *Missional Map-Making: Skills for Leading in Times of Transition* (San Francisco: Jossey Bass, 2010), 29.
67 Tacey, *Spirituality Revolution*, 89.
68 Wright, *Surprised by Hope*, 248.

13. There is No Public Square, The Secularist Myth of Neutral Ground

Lewis Jones

The promotion of the common good is the occasion for much Christian engagement in the public square as we attempt to honour God and love our neighbour. The effectiveness of our efforts, however, depends largely on the nature of the public square. In our western liberal democracy there is a general belief that the public square is a level playing field open to all comers to make their case for the common good and let the voters decide. In order to preserve this concept of neutral territory, the powers that administer our public spaces require that all participants leave their particular traditions and accompanying presuppositions at the door, in order that arguments are formed solely on the basis of what is common to all people. The nature of our society then means that the public square isn't public after all and that Christians would do well to develop new strategies for promoting human flourishing in Christ.

The common good and liberal society

What is the common good? How can we achieve it? The Christian response to these two questions has prompted much engagement in the public square. Indeed, Christians have adopted a host of strategies for commending our vision of the common good, both formal and informal, as well as those that focus on evangelism or service. A survey would include at least the following; Christian schools and hospitals, soup kitchens, evangelistic rallies, OpEd pieces on same-sex marriage, and tea table discussions on asylum seeker policies. Of course different strategies provide different kinds of opportunities. Some allow us to articulate the simple message of forgiveness in Jesus, others do not. However, in one way or another, they are all an exploration of what "loving God" and "loving neighbour" look like as we confront the issues of the day.

In the midst of engagement in the public square, discussion inevitably arises as to what constitutes the common good in each issue or circumstance. Historically, the notion of the common good has been both the theme of the public square and the regulatory principle by which it is administered. Yet, ironically, because of the way our particular society is ordered, these twin roles of the common good serve to inhibit and undermine the effectiveness of public discussion. This chapter will explore the twin questions: what is the nature of the public square and how can Christians best commend their worldview to our society.

We will first examine the nature of liberal society and how it undermines public discussion of the common good, and after looking at the possibility of a neutral public square, we will conclude with a suggestion for the kind of society that will aid Christians in the promotion of human flourishing in Christ for the glory of God and the common good.

The nature of liberal society

Western liberal democracy is a descendant of the Enlightenment. It is not a continuation of the Enlightenment project as such, but more of a resigned response to it. One of the great dreams of the Enlightenment was a tradition-independent system of rational enquiry. It was the search for principles of rationality that transcended any particular culture, race, or religion that all rational people would naturally apprehend.

Since the Greeks it had been recognised that rationality and justice were defined by principles that differed from *polis* to *polis*, so what constituted a rational argument would depend on what was considered the common good for each city. If Athens strove after the goods of excellence, broadly the notion of virtues, then honesty would be paramount in their dealings with other cities, even if it meant their economic or military disadvantage, but if Athens strove after the goods of effectiveness, broadly victory, then dishonesty may be the right choice in order to preserve the city.

This tradition-dependent justice and rationality became of serious practical concern in Europe in the wake of the Protestant Reformation. The holy grail of a tradition-independent method of rational enquiry was going to free us from the tyranny of authoritative traditions, the disagreements between which had justified violence and war right across the continent.

Liberal society is not a continuation of that philosophical search, but rather a concession to the failure of that search. That is, while the Enlightenment was shaped by the debate over universal principles of rationality, Liberalism is shaped by a commitment to the interminability of that debate.[1]

---

1   Alasdair MacIntyre, *Whose Justice? Which Rationality?* (Notre Dame: University of Notre Dame Press, 1988), 335.

The common good in Liberalism

Liberal society sees itself as the only keeper of the truth of the impossibility of the Enlightenment dream and so the common good of Liberalism is simply the perpetuation of the liberal social and political order.[2]

Being committed to the idea that there is no way to rationally justify or refute any one conception of the good, liberal society is designed to allow each citizen to propose and pursue whatever good they please, justified within whatever tradition of enquiry makes sense to them.[3] The liberal political order exists to support the expression and fulfilment of the multitude of personal preferences of its citizens. *Beliefs* about an absolute notion of the common good that might require the government to instruct people in that good are allowed to be held, up to a point, within the bounds of one's own traditional community, but the attempt to implement that belief for the general public will necessarily be ruled out and indeed be treated as an attack on the liberal state.

Because there is no one conception of the ultimate human good nor a universal rationality, the liberal self pursues a range of goods in different spheres, each of which will likely involve different ways of evaluating goods, creating what seems an impossible task when it comes to prioritising goods within the individual. The proliferation of life coaching is one demonstration of our commitment to ourselves as liberals. We set goals for family, career, finances, property, education. To develop as a human being is to pursue pragmatic goods in multiple spheres. Because the rationality for what constitutes progress in each sphere is different, the spheres are of necessity highly compartmentalised as well.

When it comes to ordering the pursuit of preferences, there is no consistent way to decide which is more important. One need only listen to parents discussing schooling for their children to see this problem in action. "If he goes to School A, he'll have a better chance at a place in Medicine (career)." "If he goes to School B, he will be with his friends (relationships), but then School B costs more and I was planning to cut back my hours so that I could start my eBay business (parent's career)." "But then, if School A, he will just be mixing with money-driven people (values)." Which good is more important? On what basis will this decision be made?

---

2 MacIntyre, *Whose Justice*, 345.
3 Miroslav Volf, *A Public Faith: How Followers of Christ Should Serve the Common Good* (Grand Rapids, MI: Brazos, 2013), 123-124..

However, even given this difficulty, the notion of a unifying scheme, say through religious belief, still seems implausible. Philosopher of Liberalism John Rawls expresses it like this, "Human good is heterogeneous because the aims of the self are heterogeneous. Although to subordinate all our aims to one end does not strictly speaking violate the principals of rational choice…it still strikes us as irrational or more likely as mad. The self is disfigured."[4] In liberal society, to live life with a single purpose is to be a disfigured person.

The liberal individual then participates in a market of preference fulfilment and our bargaining power is our capacity to aid others in the fulfilment of their preferences. The means to bargain is crucial and the regulation of the means to bargain is the purpose of the liberal legal system. Justice in Liberalism is not about a notion of the common good, but about whether the preference market is operating well. Court decisions are decisions about whether one party has infringed on another's means to bargain, not whether the preferences being pursued by the parties are right or wrong. Our legal system is conflict resolution without a theory of human good.[5]

The liberal social and political order is a market for the expression and fulfilment of personal preferences across various compartmentalised spheres of life, the purpose of which is the maintenance of the market itself as the demonstration of its commitment to the interminability of the debate over universal principles of justice and rationality.

One of the assumptions underlying the implementation of Liberalism is that the marketplace of preferences is a level playing field, neutral ground, on which all can work, play, believe, discuss, and bargain without fear of prejudice or discrimination. This is the public square where Christians make their case for the good life and we need to understand the nature of that space, if we are going to know what kinds of goals we should have for our contributions and how to achieve them. We now turn to consider the public square, whether neutrality has been or even can be achieved, and ways Christians can respond that will honour God and love neighbour.

The dream of neutrality

There is a dream of neutrality that appears in the rhetoric surrounding the public square. It is not that anyone believes the public square is free from restrictions, but that what is common between people is all that matters. Common ground is neutral

---

4   John Rawls, *A Theory of Justice* (Cambridge: Harvard University Press), 456.
5   MacIntyre, *Whose Justice*, 344.

ground. This idea is encountered on two fronts: the perspective that common ground is all that is real, a totalising of the commonalities, and the perspective that there is no way to adjudicate between particular preferences, such that including them in the discussion leads to division, confusion, and a lack of actionable conclusions.

Similarly, there is a belief that the absence of teaching one particular belief is equivalent to not teaching any belief. For example, Richard Dawkins dreams of a time when it will be illegal to teach children religion until they are old enough to make up their own minds, or better would be to simply remove children from religious parents altogether.[6] In this way, no one is taught to believe anything and everyone can grow up free to form their own opinions based on evidence rather than authority. Of course, in this scheme, the idea of belief becomes the taboo and, if you can make it stick that someone is basing an idea on their "belief," their idea can be dismissed without consideration.

In New South Wales, there is now an option in public schools for children not otherwise in Special Religious Education to attend ethics classes. The introduction video on the Primary Ethics website states the aim of the classes is not to teach moral instruction, what to think, but ethical enquiry, how to think.

In this kind of discussion, especially about children, there is an enduring conviction that a commitment to the absence of particularities is not its own particularity. The Primary Ethics video goes on to say that what they do want to challenge is a blind acceptance of moral authority and an uncritical acceptance of moral relativism. Is this not itself moral instruction?

Secularism is the philosophy that most closely describes the liberal notion of the neutral public square. Policies are to be based, as far as possible, on what can be gleaned from what is common to all people, i.e. the physical universe and a narrow, almost anatomical, anthropology.

We will work through five different perspectives on the public square and the question of neutral ground in order to understand the difficulties and frustrations Christians face in their public engagement.

---

6 Richard Dawkins, *The God Delusion* (London: Bantam, 2006), 308, 325-329.

The problem of objectivity

We start with the fundamental philosophical difficulty confronting the notion of neutrality of any enterprise, the problem of objectivity. Every enterprise is the creation of individual persons and every person necessarily has a subjective view of the world. Thomas Nagel opens his book *The View From Nowhere* like this:

> This book is about a single problem: how to combine the perspective of a particular person inside the world with an objective view of that same world, the person and his viewpoint included.[7]

Any given person may manage to step back a little further than their neighbour so as to appreciate a marginally more objective view of the universe, but Nagel continues

> The subjectivity of consciousness is an irreducible feature of reality – without which we couldn't do physics or anything else – and it must occupy as fundamental a place in any credible world view as matter, energy, space, time, and numbers.[8]

Try as we might, we cannot free ourselves from our particular perspectives. This has two consequences for the public square. First, the public square will necessarily take the shape of the particular perspective that created it and, so, is not a neutral space. Second, if the rules of engagement in the public square inhibit the expression of your own particularities because, according to Nagel, you cannot be divorced from your particularities, you cannot participate in the public square without pretending to be someone else. People embody traditions, so the public square is not neutral toward traditions other than the one that created it.

The preference for objectivity

Liberalism also has a preference for objectivity. What is valued in liberal society is what is perceived to be objective. Indeed there are structures and disciplines that provide, by their very nature, a more objective perspective than others, e.g. government bureaucracy versus village bartering and Inorganic Chemistry versus English Literature. What this means is that liberal society is more comfortable with the procedural and scientific than with the messier world of human particularities.[9]

---

7   Thomas Nagel, *The View From Nowhere* (Oxford: Oxford University Press, 1986), 3.
8   Nagel, *View From Nowhere*, 8.
9   Vinoth Ramachandra, *Subverting Global Myths* (Downers Grove: IVP Academic, 2008), 148-149; MacIntyre, Whose Justice, 344-345.

That is, rather than adjudicate the value of various preferences, the liberal government creates and maintains procedures and structures through which its citizens can engage in those debates, if they choose. As long as people are living within those procedures, the liberal state is uninterested in the content of the debate.

A general rule of thumb across human cultures is that the public arena is where honour is accorded and power is concentrated.[10] For liberal society, that means the people most comfortable and fluent in public affairs will either be those who share the particular subjectivity or tradition of the creators of the public square or those who can easily pretend to be someone other than who they really are, who can live as someone whose tradition is not the foundation of their rationality, who can reason one way in public and another way at home.[11] As a result, all subjective viewpoints other than the dominant one become private.

The dominant subjectivity of the public arena is Secularism, a central pillar of which is that neutral ground is defined by what is common to all. That notion is, however, particular to that tradition of Secularism and, ultimately, undermines the concept of "public" in public square. That is, any individual will always be more than what is common, so the self-aware "public" find themselves excluded or, at the very least, their viewpoints distorted and unrecognisable as they are translated into the "common" language-in-use of liberal discussion.

Because Secularism, in its quest for objectivity, will only permit this pared-down humanity, the liberal self is always a divided self, being forced in the bargaining around preferences to reason without reference to tradition, to be half a person in order to be heard but unable and not desiring to escape the subjectivities of their own consciousness, relationships, loves, and dreams. It is often the Secularist who is most self-deceived about the degree of their own objectivity and in the denial of their divided self since no one can achieve that "view from nowhere," yet they must maintain they have achieved it in order to maintain power. The consequences of the divided self can be observed in the rise of emotional and psychological therapies to ease our aching souls.

---

10 Ramachandra, *Subverting Global Myths*, 148.

11 Nicholas Wolterstorff, "The Role of Religion in Decision and Discussion of Political Issues," in *Religion in the Public Square: The Place of Religious Convictions in Political Debate*, ed. Robert Audi and Nicholas Wolterstorff (Lanham: Rowman & Littlefield, 1997), 73.

Scientism

One of the consequences of the preference for objectivity has been the adoption of Scientism, another way in which public discussion is constrained. Scientism is the belief that scientific knowledge, particularly from the natural sciences, is the only or at least the highest form of knowledge. Thomas Nagel says, "Scientism...puts one type of human understanding in charge of the universe and what can be said about it."[12] If we can't demonstrate something scientifically, we will not admit it as knowledge that can affect the outcomes of our discussions. The undeniable success of the scientific enterprise in understanding and harnessing the physical mechanisms of the universe has driven some to define subjectivity out of the universe and claim that Science will finally reveal to us that our subjectivities are nothing more than the firing of neurons that themselves can be understood completely and objectively. As Francis Crick would have us believe, "You, your joys and your sorrows, your memories and ambitions, your sense of personal identity and free will, are in fact no more than the behaviour of a vast assembly of nerve cells and their associated molecules."[13]

In order for Scientism to be useful, reality needs to be defined as consisting of only those things that can be explained by Science. Again, Nagel says there is an "assumption that what there really is must be understandable in a certain way – that reality is in a narrow sense objective reality."[14] On the final page of his book, *The Magic of Reality*, Richard Dawkins makes this very claim:

So where does life come from? What is it? Why are we here? What are we for? What is the meaning of life? There's a conventional wisdom which says that science has nothing to say about such questions. Well, all I can say is that if science has nothing to say, it's certain that no other discipline can say anything at all.[15]

Scientism constrains the public square by ruling out of court all evidence from disciplines other than the natural sciences.

Presuppositions and evidence

A related distortion of the playing field has to do with the relationship between our presuppositions and the interpretation of evidence. Listen to Richard Dawkins on the

---

12 Nagel, *View From Nowhere*, 9.
13 Francis Crick, *The Astonishing Hypothesis – The Scientific Search for the Soul* (New York: Simon & Schuster, 1995), 3.
14 Nagel, *View From Nowhere*, 7.
15 Richard Dawkins, *The Magic of Reality* (London: Bantam, 2011), 257.

presuppositions of Naturalism:

> An atheist in this sense of philosophical naturalist is somebody who believes there is nothing beyond the natural, physical world, no *super*natural creative intelligence lurking behind the observable universe, no soul that outlasts the body and no miracles -- except in the sense of natural phenomena that we don't yet understand. If there is something that appears to lie beyond the natural world as it is now imperfectly understood, we hope eventually to understand it and embrace it within the natural.[16]

The point here is straightforward. Tradition-dependent rationality is unavoidable and will, given the same set of evidence, necessarily colour your conclusions relative to those who come from a different tradition. A Christian can present to Dawkins the evidence for the fine-tuning of the universe or the resurrection of Jesus and, even if he accepts them as facts, his response will be that these are natural phenomena that we don't yet understand. Our traditions render us immune from certain conclusions, which entails idiosyncratic hermeneutics for the facts about our world with which we are constantly presented.

Presupposition-dependent interpretation of evidence is not a feature of one tradition, e.g., Naturalism, but rather all traditions and must be taken into consideration when entering into discussions with those outside our own tradition.

Options in the marketplace

Returning to the marketplace of preferences, another way in which the public square is biased against the "public" is that the list of possible preferences that can be fulfilled will be limited and the power in a liberal society then lies with those who are able to determine the available choices. Alasdair MacIntyre observes that: "the consumer, the voter, and the individual in general are accorded the right of expressing their preferences for one or more out of the alternatives which they are offered, but the range of possible alternatives is controlled by an elite, and how they are presented is also controlled."[17] Again, Thomas Nagel similarly observes

> There can be no ethics without politics. A theory of how individuals should act requires a theory of the institutions under which they should live: institutions which substantially determine their starting points, the choices

---

16 Dawkins, *The God Delusion*, 14.
17 MacIntyre, *Whose Justice*, 345.

they can make, the consequences of what they do, and their relations to one another.[18]

While this limiting of alternatives is common to any society, it is of special concern for Liberalism as it alone makes the promise of a tradition-independent marketplace, but ultimately cannot escape its own tradition. Liberalism will allow into the marketplace only those preferences that do not challenge the nature of the marketplace.

Toward an understanding of Christian engagement

This chapter is more about the problem than the solution, but here are some brief reflections on what kind of society Christians might strive for and what public engagement might look like in that society.

In Miroslav Volf's book *A Public Faith*, he argues for what he calls religious political pluralism.[19] He is not interested in prescribing a single way Christianity is to engage with the state, rather he recognises that we are already living in a somewhat plural society in our western democracies, and suggests that his scheme is an improvement on what we have already, not a radical dissolution of liberal society.[20] As he lays out the options, there are two possibilities: religious totalitarianism or religious political pluralism.

Totalitarianism would be the result of the privileging of any one religion. In this vein, the liberal attempt to make public discussion a religion-free zone really only results in the privileging of Secularism, which itself becomes the favoured perspective, as much as any religion could have been.[21] The conclusion then is that, in a liberal society, anything other than a rather pure pluralism will end up in some degree of totalitarianism, whether that is religious or secular.

Nagel concurs saying "distinct individuals are still the clients of ethics, and their variety guarantees that pluralism will be an essential aspect of any adequate morality, however advanced."[22] Finishing that thought, he says:

> This is inconvenient: it may seem that political theory must be based on a universal human nature, and that if we cannot discover such a thing we

---

18 Nagel, *View From Nowhere*, 188.
19 Volf, *A Public Faith*, xi.
20 Volf, *A Public Faith*, xvi.
21 Volf, *A Public Faith*, 124-125.
22 Nagel, *View From Nowhere*, 187-188.

have to invent it, for political theory must exist. To avoid such folly, it is necessary to take on the much more difficult task of devising fair uniform social principles for beings whose nature is not uniform and whose values are legitimately diverse.[23]

The Christian voices here see the idea as fertile ground from which to engage with other traditions for the common good and to make the case for our tradition as giving the best hope for human flourishing, both temporarily and eternally.

Nicholas Wolterstorff coins the term "consocial," "a politics of multiple communities,"[24] and Vinoth Ramachandra describes this new "nation-state not as an aggregate of individuals but as a community of communally embedded citizens."[25] Any society requires a broadly shared public culture to sustain it, but in our now highly multicultural, liberal democracies there is no common shared perspective. Something is going to need to change to maintain our multicultural society. Ramachandra pictures a new shared culture as multiculturally constituted, growing "out of the vigorous interaction of majority and minority cultures, and not by their relative isolation."[26] The idea, says Volf, is that each of our multiple perspectives can "speak in the public square in a voice of its own."[27] In this society, the government would be encouraging the different traditions to be in continuous public conversation as a way of forging a "continually contested but coherent public culture."[28]

Whether or not this vision is ever realised, it is a plausible candidate for how to tweak a liberal democracy in order to level the playing field for its citizens and how to free the Christian voice to speak in public as Christian.[29] Let us now just touch on what the reality of a social order like that will mean for Christian believers.

Christians to not claim privilege

For hundreds of years, Christianity has enjoyed the privilege of public power in many places and still does in some. This new vision for an enhanced pluralism will end

---

23 Nagel, *View From Nowhere*, 188.
24 Wolterstorff, *Role of Religion*, 109.
25 Ramachandra, *Subverting Global Myths*, 153.
26 Ramachandra, *Subverting Global Myths*, 152.
27 Volf, *A Public Faith*, 125.
28 Ramachandra, *Subverting Global Myths*, 153.
29 In *A Public Faith*, Note 18 of Chapter 7, p165, Volf points out that Oliver O'Donovan argues that the rules of civic association in a liberal society will always be too restrictive for believers, causing the divided liberal self of the public and private spheres, and so declares Liberalism to be broken beyond repair.

that privilege. Christians will be one tradition among many and it will undermine the project for Christians to treat other traditions as less entitled. Christians will have to come to terms with a new status.

No preferred centre

The properties of our universe appear to be such that there is no preferred centre. Imagine 200 billion galaxies stuck to the surface of an expanding balloon. Our planet could have turned up anywhere in any galaxy and the view would be substantially the same. The same would be true for our more fiercely plural state. Society would look like a network of communities wrapped around the surface of a balloon.

Most pluralisms in history have existed within a strong, dominant culture, e.g. Corinth was firmly Greek in culture, yet full of cultures from all over the known world.[30] What makes this new pluralism different is that there would be no dominant culture other than the culture of negotiation between its communities in the pursuit of common cause for the good of society as a whole. No centre. Only margins.

Reason from your tradition

One of the features of the tweaked liberal society will be that each community is invited to reason in public from their own tradition without trying to conceal the commitments behind their arguments. We note two consequences of this new freedom. First, Christians will need to be integrated people able to apply their theological thinking to the sphere of government policy and other expressions of the common good. As a community, we have a long way to go on this. Liberalism has persuaded us to compartmentalise our lives to such an extent that we almost do not believe integration is a goal worth pursuing. Also, we have spent so long developing secular arguments for the goods we value that it will not be a simple matter to rethink how to argue our case without any restriction on what we can say.

Second, other communities will be reasoning from within their traditions, from their particular premises and presuppositions. This will require a commitment on our part to listen carefully and work hard at putting ourselves inside their tradition so as to understand and empathise with their perspective.

---

30 James Davison Hunter, *To Change the World* (Oxford: Oxford University Press, 2010), 201.

To change the world

Are we going to change the world? Are we going to change Australia? Will we reconfigure our society into a new pluralism that allows religion into the public square? In his book *To Change the World*, James Davison Hunter is pessimistic about the prospect, and rightly so, as the Bible's promises of large-scale cultural transformation are entirely eschatological. What then is our response to the liberal social order and the constrained and distorted public square? What can Christians do now to mission more effectively in our society as it is currently configured?

First, we can work hard as our Christian community to develop in our individual members a coherent and comprehensive worldview that can reason from the Bible and Theology to action on issues of the day. The starting point of the New Testament on that path is the creation of character, the inculcation of Christian virtues. We are firstly schooled in who to be before we are schooled in what to do. The virtues are themselves guides to action such that being confident in the kind of person I ought to be, I act so as to be that person.

Second, we can bypass the currently contrived public square by engaging in bilateral relations with other communities in an effort to advance the glory of God and the common good. There is no need to wait for the complete reconfiguration of society. Christians can approach the Muslim community to discuss asylum seeker policy. Christians can approach the homosexual community to discuss the nature of marriage and family. However public these discussions are, they will be conducted on terms negotiated between the communities involved, not on terms set by the constraints of Secularism and liberal self-preservation.

Christians should strive to be a distinct, coherent community. It is in our community where we learn to reason and to act and it is as a community that we witness to the world. The more consistency there is between the character of the community in which we live and the gospel we proclaim, the more persuasive we will be to those who hear the message. "By this everyone will know that you are my disciples, if you have love for one another" (John 13:35, NRSV).

14. Indie-Rock And Mission: Challenges and Possibilities of De-centred Mission in the 21st Century

T. Mark McConnell

Montreal-based indie-rock band "Arcade Fire" have been lauded as the most important band of the last decade. In terms of their cultural and potentially theological significance it has been argued that Arcade Fire is to Gen Y what U2 is to Gen X. This chapter explores the music and content of their latest album Reflektor, released in October 2013. The main influences in this album are Haitian "rara" music, the 1959 film Black Orpheus, and an essay by Danish philosopher and theologian Søren Kierkegaard entitled "The Present Age," in which he contrasts the "passionate age" with the "reflective age." These influences and the resultant themes are explored, with a final reflection framed by the Apostle Paul's interaction with his contemporary culture, and using the work of Charles Taylor, to discover ways in which this important voice from the margins might speak to and help the contemporary church as it engages in mission in the postmodern world.

Since the launch of their critically acclaimed debut album, *Funeral*, in 2003 and through the release of their subsequent three albums, the Montreal-based indie-rock band Arcade Fire have been consistently lauded by both fellow musicians and music critics. In 2007, after the release of their second album, *Neon Bible*, the Guardian newspaper described them as the "best band in the world."[1] In 2013 *Paste* magazine, dubbing their first three albums "the Holy Trinity," ranked the albums as "among the most impressive streaks of recorded rock music in the past couple decades."[2]

Despite this recognition Arcade Fire has remained somewhat on the margins of mainstream pop music, defying pop culture norms in their music, lyrics, and performances while at the same time speaking significantly into the existential, philosophical, and even theological concerns of contemporary culture. They offer an artistic and incisive cultural critique while giving expression to the longings and desires of the human heart.

---

1   Alexis Petridis, "The Bitter Taste of Success," *The Guardian*, October 26, 2007, http://www.theguardian.com/music/2007/oct/26/popandrock.alexispetridis.

2   Ryan Reed, "Arcade Fire: Reflektor," *Paste Magazine*, October 29, 2013, http://www.pastemagazine.com/articles/2013/10/arcade-fire-reflektor-1.html.

This chapter will argue that as the church engages in mission, particularly in contemporary Western culture, Arcade Fire provides an important voice from the margins that ought to be heard. More specifically this chapter will explore the music and content of their latest album *Reflektor*, released in October 2013, which speaks into the modern digital and media-soaked age. Through its main influences (Haitian "rara" music, the Greek myth of Orpheus and Eurydice, and an 1846 essay by Danish philosopher and theologian Søren Kierkegaard entitled "The Present Age") and by invoking the genre of Carnival the album deals with an array of issues such as death, love, passion, desire, the after-life, embodiment, spirituality, and the meaning of our humanity.

On the basis of this voice from the margins, the chapter concludes with a reflection, framed by the Apostle Paul's interaction with his contemporary culture, and using the work of Charles Taylor, to propose a number of issues which the church should reflect upon as it participates in God's mission in the world.

A Brief History

In 2001, Win Butler, a religious studies and philosophy student at McGill University in Montreal, began collaborating musically with Josh Deu, a visual arts student. Soon they added Régine Chassagne, another student at McGill whom Butler had noticed singing Jazz at an art opening. Although Deu left the band early on his influence in terms of visual performance has continued. Butler and Chassagne married in 2003 and additional band members were added, including Butler's brother Will.

In 2003 Mac McCaughan signed the band to Merge Records after hearing a demo tape. However, it was only when he heard them play live in a small club that he experienced the essence of the band. "It was like seeing U2 on the *War* tour when I was 15. It's not like they sounded like U2 exactly, but they had these huge anthems that the crowd was responding to right away even though no one had heard the songs yet."[3] The parallels with U2 are worth noting. It has been said that Arcade Fire is to Gen Y what U2 is to Gen X. Like U2 their songs resonate with a generation who, while rejecting organised religion, still wrestle with issues of faith, transcendence, and the big questions of contemporary life. Butler has been called "an astute theologian and philosopher"[4]

---

3   Kot, "Band of the Year: An Interview with Arcade Fire," *PopMatters*, http://www.popmatters.com/feature/band-of-the-year-an-interview-with-the-arcade-fire/.

4   Blake Baxter, "Just a Reflektor: The Spiritual and Emotional Journeys of Arcade Fire," *Saying Something* http://baxnglass.com/2013/11/08/just-a-reflektor-the-spiritual-and-emotional-journeys-of-arcade-fire/.

and the band itself "a rock band for our time."[5]

Despite what many fans would see as anti-religious sentiment in their songs, Arcade Fire's attitude to religion has always been complex and difficult to discern. *Neon Bible* most directly addresses the topic of religious life, albeit in the context of the religiosity of the United States. According to Butler the album "is addressing religion in a way that only someone who actually cares about it can. It's really harsh at times, but from the perspective of someone who thinks it has value."[6] Given Butler's religious studies and philosophy background this is not surprising.

For Butler mere scientific understanding of the world is not enough, especially when it comes to talking about meaning. As Butler has explained, "I think a lot of the human experience has to do with trying to understand what things mean, and there's not really any tools to do that unless you're thinking about it in a more spiritual or philosophical realm."[7] Such thinking occurs throughout Arcade Fire's recorded works, including their latest offering *Reflektor*.

Reflektor

Arcade Fire's fourth album, released in October 2013, is arguably their most challenging and ambitious to date. The double album departs from the more straightforward anthemic tones of past success. Rather than being music for the stadium, this is music for the dance floor, but with far from a straightforward disco feel. One review describes it well by stating, "It's an elusive, frustrating album. It is also a masterpiece… It is at once fractured and cohesive, unbalanced and symmetric."[8] It is a risky venture for a band with a consistent track record of success.[9]

---

5 Patton Dodd, "Let There Be Arcade Fire," *Christianity Today*, January 22, 2014, http://www.christianitytoday.com/ct/2014/january-web-only/let-there-be-arcade-fire.html.
6 Sean Michaels, "Inside the Church of Arcade Fire," *Paste Magazine*, November 4, 2007, http://www.pastemagazine.com/articles/2007/04/arcade-fire.html.
7 Josh Modell, "Win Butler of Arcade Fire," *A.V. Club*, http://www.avclub.com/article/win-butler-of-arcade-fire-14070.
8 Gabriel Samach, "Arcade Fire: Reflektor," *Tiny Mix Tapes*, http://www.tinymixtapes.com/music-review/arcade-fire-reflektor.
9 A number of reviewers have made parallels with U2's *Achtung Baby* and Radiohead's *Kid A*. As *Rolling Stone* magazine states, *Reflektor* is "a thrilling act of risk and renewal by a band with established commercial appeal and a greater fear of the average, of merely being liked." David Fricke, "Arcade Fire Reflektor Album Review," *Rolling Stone*, September 27, 2013, http://www.rollingstone.com/music/albumreviews/reflektor-20130927.

The album's holographic front cover artwork is symbolic of the album as a whole portraying the reflective modern digital age in all its shiny glory.[10] However, juxtaposed with the shimmer is Rodin's 1893 sculpture of Orpheus and Eurydice: the two main figures in a tragic story of love, death, music, the afterlife, escape, trust, passion, and the power of music.

In the Greek myth, Orpheus has the ability to charm anything with his music. When his wife Eurydice dies by stepping on a viper, Orpheus travels to the underworld, and due to the sweetness of his music he is allowed to return with Eurydice to the world of the living, but on one condition: he must walk in front and not look back until both have reached the upper world. Just as Orpheus reaches daylight, however, he turns to see Eurydice. At that moment she is snatched back and lost once more to death.

The story of Orpheus and Eurydice is featured on the first two songs on the second disc of the album. The first, "Awful Sound (Oh Eurydice)," may refer to the sound of Eurydice falling to the ground dead after being poisoned. In the second, "It's Never Over (Oh Orpheus)," we find ourselves in a conversation between Eurydice and Orpheus about love and trust which seems to end in a debate about whether pain and death ever end. Butler is on record that one of his favourite films of all times is *Black Orpheus*, made in 1959 by Marcel Camus, and set during Carnival in Brazil.[11] For Butler, "The Orpheus myth is the original love triangle, Romeo-and-Juliet kind of story," and it is stories such as this that get to the core of human relationships.[12]

These themes of love and death, passion and risk, are explored on the rest of the album, with two major influences in the background: a trip the band took to Haiti and an essay by Kierkegaard.

Haiti and Carnival

Straight after the band received their Grammy award in 2011 for their third album, *The Suburbs*, the band travelled to Haiti, where Régine Chassagne's family had lived until the 1960's and the dictatorship of François Duvalier, when they emigrated to Canada.

---

10 For a description of the very intentional design process of the album cover and packaging see "Arcade Fire's 'Reflektor': The Story Behind the Album Cover," May 11, 2013, http://www.juxtapoz.com/music/arcade-fires-reflektor-the-story-behind-the-album-cover.

11 As a teaser prior to the full album release, the band posted for 24 hours on Youtube the entire album accompanying the *Black Orpheus* as a soundtrack. In addition, in one of three official videos for *Afterlife*, one of the singles form the album, again *Black Orpheus* was used.

12 Patrick Doyle, "Win Butler Reveals Secret Influences Behind Arcade Fire's 'Reflektor,'" *Rolling Stone*, October 22, 2013, http://www.rollingstone.com/music/news/win-butler-reveals-secret-influences-behind-arcade-fires-reflektor-20131022.

The trip was transformative for the band; in Haiti they experienced another world. In playing to local crowds who had no background knowledge of Western music, the band had to connect through rhythm and emotion. This experience brought the band back to the core of what music was really all about.[13] The band also encountered carnival and "rara" street music with its horns and percussion. Despite the poverty and suffering of the Haitian people, the music brought a sense of joy and life, and even a spiritual encounter. In one interview Butler recounts being on the beach at three in the morning and seeing a voodoo drummer playing, with kids and teenagers dancing for four hours and starting "to get the spirit."

A Haitian musical influence and an overall Caribbean rhythmic feel can be found throughout the album *Reflektor*, but is most apparent in the song "Here Comes the Night Time." There are two version of the song. The one on the first disc anticipates the coming excitement of the night. The second version, which opens up the more sombre second disc, is more haunting with the night symbolising the ending. According to Butler, both versions are influenced by when the sun is just starting to go down in Port-au-Prince. It's a time of intensity, anticipation, and crazy energy "because most of the city doesn't have electricity so everyone is just racing to get home before dark."[14] In addition, says Butler, there is also "the nightlife thing that happens, and it's a combination of really dangerous and fun."[15]

In contrast to the spirit of the Haitian people there was the spirit of Western missionaries that Butler observed. In Haiti he saw packs of missionaries all wearing the same T-shirts saying, "Jesus loves Haiti." In response to being asked why they were there they replied that they were going to paint houses. For Butler this was strange: why not just pay a Haitian to paint the houses? For Butler there was a certain incongruity of people coming to Haiti to teach people something about God: "Just the absurdity that you can go to a place like Haiti and teach people something about God. Like, the opposite really seems to be true, in my experience. I've never been to a place with more belief and more knowledge of God."[16] For Butler the Haitian people are some of the most religious he has ever met. He notes that, "After the earthquake, people were singing songs of praise in the street. It's a strange idea that we can teach these people something."[17]

---

13 See Doyle, "Win Butler Reveals Secret Influences Behind Arcade Fire's 'Reflektor.'"
14 Doyle, "Win Butler Reveals Secret Influences Behind Arcade Fire's 'Reflektor.'"
15 Michael Barclay, "Arcade Fire Frontman Win Butler: 'Yeah, We're a Weird Band,'" *Macleans.ca*, October 19, 2013, http://www.macleans.ca/culture/arcade-fire-frontman-win-butler-on-haitian-influences-and-plan-b/.
16 Doyle, "Win Butler Reveals Secret Influences Behind Arcade Fire's 'Reflektor.'"
17 Barclay, "Win Butler."

In "Here Comes the Night Time," the Western missionaries come in for significant criticism. They preach a message of "being left behind". This is ironic since the Haitian people have been left behind a thousand times. The message is one of exclusion, one which cannot recognise the spirituality of the people or their music, or even the Spirit's prior working. The "heaven" proclaimed by the missionaries is behind a gate and the people are not allowed in. "When they hear the beat coming from the street they lock the door." The criticism continues and becomes more pointed in the direction of TV evangelists whose message comes to Haiti by satellite. Hell is not somewhere out there reserved for the Haitian people, but instead resides within the hearts of these preachers.

Music plays a key role for the Haitian people, especially in terms of their suffering. It is a matter of life and hope, and allows the experience of the transcendent. To not be able to feel such music, as the missionaries seem unable to do, it is suggested, points to death.

One of the key "musical" events experienced by the band in Haiti was Carnival. For Butler it "felt like going to the Old Testament or something like that."[18] It was like entering another world. In the words of Butler, "There's sex and death and people dressed up as slaves with black motor oil all over their faces and chains, and there's these little kids in puffer fish outfits or dressed like Coke bottles. There's big fire-breathing dragons that shoot real fire at the crowd."[19] A key element of Carnival is that most of the participants wear masks. This anonymity seems to bring a sense of freedom. For Butler, "Wearing the mask in Carnival felt like less of a division between body and spirit."[20] In other words, a sense of wholeness was experienced.

Carnivalesque and The Festive

In his 2009 book, *Gods and Guitars*, Michael Gilmore, using the work of Mikhail Bakhtin, the Russian philosopher and literary theorist, argues that *Neon Bible*, Arcade Fire's second album, has qualities of "carnivalesque."[21] For Bakhtin, in European

---

18 "*Arcade Fire - Interview with Win Butler in Brussels*", November 24, 2013, https://www.youtube.com/watch?v=yGpRqV1ClXs.

19 Doyle, "Win Butler Reveals Secret Influences Behind Arcade Fire's 'Reflektor.'"

20 *Q with Jian Ghomeshi: Interview with Win Butler and Jeremy Gara*, https://www.youtube.com/watch?v=n6JWK44Ror8.

21 See Michael J. Gilmour, *Gods and Guitars: Seeking the Sacred in Post-1960s Popular Music* (Waco, TX: Baylor University Press, 2009); and Michael J. Gilmour, "Arcade Fire's Parobolic Bible," *SBL Forum*, 2009, http://www.sbl-site.org/publications/article.aspx?ArticleId=824. Gilmour makes the claim of carnivalesque by pointing out the way in which Arcade Fire subverts the official "culture" of Christianity by, for example: identifying the album as a kind of bible; listing and numbering the songs and verses in the liner notes like Bible chapter and verse numbers; and by recording and mixing the album at "the church" in Québec.

medieval carnivals "the unofficial culture would mock official culture, temporarily resisting political oppression and totalitarian order – political, ecclesial or social – through laughter, parody, and grotesque realism."[22] In this experience, everything is turned upside down: social expectations and norms are cast off; authority is ridiculed; and the sacred is profaned. The concept does not fit the whole of *Neon Bible* and not every element of carnivalesque can be found in the album, but what Gilmore does is highlight an important aspect of Arcade Fire's social and religious critique, which is more fully developed on the ground-breaking *Reflektor*.

In his well-regarded book, *The Secular Age*, Charles Taylor, the renowned Canadian philosopher, who is also a practicing Roman Catholic, narrates the movement of Western society from a culture in which disbelief in God was unthinkable and where a sense of transcendence gave significance to an "enchanted" world, to one in which such belief is almost untenable but which nevertheless remains "haunted" by transcendence. One way in which contemporary society forges a sense of transcendence is through various kinds of "festive" events and gatherings in which people come together to escape the "the everyday order of things."[23] Taylor's notion of "the Festive" includes religious feasts and pilgrimages, but also Carnival, and, interestingly for our purposes, "rock concerts, raves and the like."

In such times of "collective effervescence" when there is a powerful shared feeling, participants experience "moments of fusion in a common action/feeling, which both wrench us out of the everyday, and seem to put us in touch with something exceptional, beyond ourselves."[24] This is often experienced as a sense of the sacred. Thus, for Taylor, that which is often experienced at a rock concert, even though non-religious, sits "uneasily in the secular, disenchanted world."[25]

These events are similar to the Carnival years gone by. Both can be powerful and moving, heady and exciting, witnessing to "the birth of a new collective agent out of its formerly dispersed potential."[26] However, unlike Carnival, in such festive events as rock concerts there is no structure and counter-structure dynamic.

It seems as if Arcade Fire know this, implicitly if not explicitly. What *Reflektor* does in terms of the album itself and the associated concert tours is to bring together the festive

22 Gilmour, *Gods and Guitars*, 57.
23 Charles Taylor, *A Secular Age* (Cambridge, MS: Belknap Press of Harvard University Press, 2007), 469.
24 Taylor, *A Secular Age*, 482–483.
25 Taylor, *A Secular Age*, 518.
26 Taylor, *A Secular Age*, 715.

rock experience with the experience of Carnival. In a number of interviews Butler has stated that one of his aims at concerts during the "*Reflektor* Tour" is to create a sense of Carnival.[27] This is to be achieved not only through the Haitian inspired rhythms of the music but also by asking those attending concerts to dress up in costume.[28] For Butler, "the point of carnival is about the crowd, not the performer."

In bringing together the experience of Carnival with the collective fusion of the rock concert Arcade Fire seem to be giving their fans a means of dealing with the sense of personal fragmentation and isolation, the loss of transcendence, and the need for release from the alienating structures and practices of "ordinary" contemporary life, a life which is now lived in the digital age. This leads us to the final influence: Søren Kierkegaard.

The Present Age

The album title, *Reflektor* comes from an 1846 essay by Kierkegaard entitled *The Present Age*. Butler explains the background to the Kierkegaardian influence as follows:

> I studied the Bible and philosophy in college and I think in a certain sense that's the kind of stuff that still makes my brain work. There's an essay by Kierkegaard called The Present Age that I was reading a lot that's about the reflective age. This is like in [1846], and it sounds like he's talking about modern times… [You] kind of read it and you're like, "Dude, you have no idea how insane it's gonna get."[29]

The context of the essay is Kierkegaard's reaction against post-Kantian Hegelian philosophical attempts to show how the truths of religion could be harmonized with the demands of reason. For Kierkegaard such attempts had the effect of replacing the core truths of Christianity with a set of abstract principles. In his *Concluding Unscientific Postscript to Philosophical Fragments* Kierkegaard states:

> My principal thought was that in our age, because of the great increase of knowledge, we had forgotten what it means to exist, and… If men had forgotten what it means to exist religiously, they had doubtless also forgotten what it means to exist as human beings; this must therefore be set forth.[30]

---

27 See, for example, "Arcade Fire - Interview with Win Butler in Brussels," November 24, 2013; "Big Day Out 2014 Interviews: Arcade Fire", https://www.youtube.com/watch?v=KQkre_8qZ-U.

28 Butler himself wears mask like make-up while on stage which has the effects of hiding his eyes, and so leads by example.

29 Doyle, "Win Butler Reveals Secret Influences Behind Arcade Fire's 'Reflektor.'"

30 Søren Kierkegaard et al., *Concluding Unscientific Postscript to Philosophical Fragments* (Princeton, NJ: Princeton University Press, 1992), 223.

In his essay, *The Present Age*, Kierkegaard developed this thinking further and reflects more specifically on the popular culture of his day. For Kierkegaard, "The Present Age is one of understanding, of reflection, devoid of passion, an age which flies into enthusiasm for a moment only to decline back into indolence."[31] "Reflection", according to Kierkegaard, is the problem. In the present age "the individual... does not have the passion to rip himself away from either the coils of Reflection or the seductive ambiguities of Reflection." By "Reflection" Kierkegaard means both deliberation as opposed to action and also, more importantly, a person deriving their identity and individuality from those around them who act as a kind of mirror. Such a mode of reflection means a lack of passion, desire and action. It means the present age is "an age of advertisement, or an age of publicity; nothing happens, but there is instant publicity about it."

The underlying principle in the passionless age of reflection is envy. Such envy creates the dynamic of levelling; bringing everyone down to the same level which stifles and hinders creativity, originality and individuality. People live in fear of being different; sameness becomes the aim.

As Butler states, the parallels with modern contemporary society are striking. Today the dominating influence of celebrity-driven popular media, as well as the power of social media, creates a sense of envy which ends up leading to a form of paralysis, passivity and inactivity. It is ultimately impossible to keep *Keeping up with the Kardashians*. Conformity to the fashions and standards dictated by such media is the norm.

The key activity in life becomes constructing one's identity through profile and status updates on sites such as *Facebook* and *Instagram*. Achieving an acceptable number of likes/loves or friends/followers becomes the new levelling process. In talking about Kierkegaard's description of the levelling process Butler states, "So it would kind of paralyse you to even act basically, and it just kind of resonated with me – wanting to try and make something in the world instead of just talking about things."[32]

In the album *Reflektor* Arcade Fire not only try to name the reality which Kierkegaard describes, they also attempt, in a carnivalesque way, to challenge the existing order and structures. In this fourth album, Arcade Fire continue their prophetic role, described by Paul Morley of *The Guardian* as being "a scholarly post-punk gospel choir merrily identifying the menace of the world."[33]

---

31   All quotes from *The Present Age* are taken from http://cliffarnold.com/thepresentage.pdf
32   Doyle, "Win Butler Reveals Secret Influences Behind Arcade Fire's 'Reflektor.'"
33   Quoted in Christian Scharen, "Secular Music and Sacramental Theology," in *Secular Music and Sacred Theology*, ed. Tom Beaudoin (Collegeville, MN: Litugical Press, 2013), 97.

Kierkegaardian Songs

The most straightforward Kierkegaardian song is the opening title track "Reflektor." The singer sings of the effects of the digital age. It is like being trapped and alone in a prism of light. In the digital world of the computer screen, which is supposed to be a form of heaven, the singer desperately wants to experience real relationship but he is trapped between the kingdoms of the living and the dead. "Now, the signals we send, are deflected again; We're so connected, but are we even friends?"

Tragically it turns out that in this online world everything is just a reflection of something else. The singer knows there is something on the other side but he just can't get to it. Even turning to religion, and specifically praying to the "resurrector," does not seem to help since it too turns our to be just a reflector. Lack of passion and action can be found in religion as much as any other sphere of contemporary life. Something more is needed. Technology will not give us passion, life, real connection or authentic existence. Most of the other songs on the album are taken up with these themes.

"We Exist" is a song of rebellion and defiance; a proclamation of existence and identity in the face of various levelling processes. The song imagines a person, a "gay kid" according to Butler, who stands out from the crowd.[34] The crowd stares through him and prays that he would not exist but they cannot ultimately deny the reality of his existence. There is much despair in this song, as with much of the album, but it does end on a note of hope, pointing to the significance of connection and relationship with each other: "Maybe if you hang together you can make the changes in our hearts."

"Normal Person" covers similar ground. What does it mean to be normal and what are the effects of defining normal? "Waiting after school for you they want to know if you if you're normal too." For Kierkegaard the notion of "normal" is a fiction that drains passion from life.

Other songs expand these themes and explore different aspects of contemporary life. "Flashbulb Eyes" confronts us with the culture of paparazzi, photoshop and selfies. What if the camera really does "take your soul"? "You Already Know" highlights the tendency to overthink. You don't need to wonder why you feel so sad, "You already know." In contrast, in "Joan of Arc" we are pointed to someone who lived their life full of passion, being willing to take action on the basis of what she believed even though this led to her death when she was only 19 years old. "Porno," highlights how passion

---

34 See Jonny Ensall, "Arcade Fire Interview: '"Hipster" Means Absolutely Nothing,'" *Time Out*, January 11, 2013, http://www.timeout.com/london/music/arcade-fire-interview-hipster-means-absolutely-nothing.

and desire have become distorted through pornography and the objectification of women. In contrast the singer longs to be seen despite the hurt that he has caused. "Afterlife" acts like a cathartic climax, bringing together the themes of desire, passion, love, and afterlife in what the most memorable dance-beat song of the whole album: "When love is gone, where does it go? And where do we go?"

Listening to Arcade Fire for the Sake of Mission

Like the statue to an Unknown God in Acts 17:23, Arcade Fire give us insight into the religious and spiritual yearnings in contemporary culture, particularly among a younger generation who are becoming increasingly alienated from organised religion and traditional forms of Christianity. Despite the claims of some secularists that "religious belief" is on the decline because reason and rationality exclude such unreasonable superstition, which Charles Taylor calls a "subtraction story,"[35] Arcade Fire points to an alternative narrative.

Taylor paints a picture of modern society inhabiting a "cross-pressured situation," one that hangs between the malaise of immanence/modernity and the memory of transcendence.[36] In the words of James K A Smith, Arcade Fire attest to the fact that:

> [O]ur age is haunted. On the one hand, we live under a brass heaven, ensconced in immanence. We live in the twilight of both gods and idols. But their ghosts have refused to depart, and every once and while we might be surprised to find ourselves tempted ... by intimations of transcendence.[37]

As has been noted, despite the band's criticism of certain forms of religious practice, Butler sees value in religion, particularly in the issues and questions it raises, such as questions about death, the afterlife, and the nature of love; issues which are directly raised on *Reflektor*.

In addition, since their beginnings Arcade Fire have attempted in their concerts to create an experience of what Taylor calls "the Festive." In an interview in 2010, Josh Due, the co-founder of Arcade Fire stated, "Rock is about the experience. It's not just about rebellion and being avant-garde. It's about interacting with the audience and having almost like a religious experience."[38] This "experiential" and "religious" sense

---

35 Taylor, *A Secular Age*, 525.
36 For example, see Taylor, *A Secular Age*, 300-304.
37 James K A Smith, *How (Not) to Be Secular: Reading Charles Taylor* (Grand Rapids: Eerdmans, 2014), 3.
38 Madeline, "Deu Discusses Past with Arcade Fire," *Ultraviolet*, November 13, 2010, http://www.theultraviolet.com/wordpress/2010/11/deu-discusses-past-with-arcade-fire/.

has been taken to another level in the Carnival theme of the *Reflektor* album and associated performances.

In this sense Arcade Fire acts as a prime exhibit in Taylor's argument. Participation in formal religious activities may have declined but this does not mean Western society is less religious. Arcade Fire show a persisting desire for transcendence. As the church engages in mission this is something that needs to be recognised. The church has a role in challenging the accepted subtractionist narratives of secularisation. Arcade Fire can help in this task. The search for transcendence is alive and well but the ghosts of the past may be found in unexpected places; in the margins of indie rock music.

In this respect Arcade Fire ask some difficult questions of Christian mission and witness, both in, and from, the West. How is non-Christian religious experience, such as that experienced in voodoo ceremonies or through Haitian rara music to be understood? When "the spirit" descends, as Win Butler sings, does this have anything to do with the Holy Spirit? Such questions have been asked, and are being asked, even by more conservative missiologists and theologians. An interesting trend is the theological work being done by Pentecostal theologians such as Amos Yong.

Taking a pneumatological approach Yong has argued for the Spirit's work in world religions.[39] This means the need for Christians to discern what the Spirit is doing and this requires dialogue. For Yong, however, this does not conflict with an evangelistic stance. Rather, dialogue and evangelism and intrinsically connected. This is the case with Christian interaction with voodoo. For Yong, the movement of the Spirit can be discerned in Haitian voodoo.[40] With its belief in "spiritual reality, the narrativity of theology, empowerment by the spirit, music and rhythms, dreams and visions [and] healing in belonging" Yong sees Haitian voodoo as phenomenologically comparable with Caribbean Pentecostalism.[41]

How might the Spirit then be discerned? For Yong, rather than being judged exclusively by whether Jesus Christ is named and acknowledged, the focus ought to be on "the signs of the kingdom." With this in mind Yong has highlighted the role of voodoo in

---

39 See Amos Yong, *Discerning the Spirit(s): A Pentecostal-Charismatic Contribution to Christian Theology of Religions* (Sheffield: Sheffield Academic Press, 2000); Amos Yong, *Beyond the Impasse: Toward a Pneumatological Theology of Religions* (Carlisle, Cumbria, UK; Paternoster, 2003); Amos Yong, *The Spirit Poured Out On All Flesh: Pentecostalism and the Possibility of Global Theology* (Grand Rapids, MI: BakerAcademic, 2005).

40 In terms of the development of modern Pentecostalism, Yong highlights the influence of William J. Seymour at Azusa Street in Los Angeles in 1906. Yong notes that Seymour grew up on a slave plantation and would have been familiar with Louisiana Creole religion, including Haitian voodoo. See Yong, *The Spirit Poured out on All Flesh*, 73, n.133.

41 Amos Yong, "Justice Deprived, Justice Demanded: Afropentecostalism and the Task of World Pentecostal Theology Today," *Journal of Pentecostal Theology* 15:1 (2006), 135.

the development of early Pentecostalism and the empowerment of black communities against racism, sexism and classism.[42] In other words, the key question has to do with the role of voodoo and its music, in "liberation" according to the values of the kingdom.[43] These are precisely the issues that Arcade Fire are raising on *Reflektor*. Thus, it might be said that Arcade Fire are doing the work of missiological reflection, but on the pages of *Rolling Stone* magazine rather than the pages of the *International Review of Mission*.

If the Spirit is at work in Haitian music and rhythms then what about the experience of "something exceptional beyond ourselves" and "fusion" felt at what Charles Taylor names as "rock concerts, raves and the like"? Can the experience which is "almost like a religious experience" as Josh Deu articulates, be considered a movement of the Spirit? In other words, if we are to look for the movement of the Spirit in today's modern urban culture should we be looking to the kind of concert experience that Arcade Fire seeks to produce? The impulse to build the statue to an Unknown God may not be a fully redemptive work of the Spirit but this does not mean we can discount it as an authentic expression of the movement of the third person of the Trinity at work in the world.

In that same Lucan narrative of Acts 17 the Apostle Paul quotes the philosopher Epimenides, "In him we live and move and have our being" and also Aratus, "We are his offspring." Like these "non-Christian" philosophers who speak, as it were, from the margins, Arcade Fire not only illustrate to us the religious and spiritual yearnings in contemporary culture, they also point to truth; particularly truth about what it means to be human. *Reflektor* offers a telling critique of contemporary culture, which the church would be wise to engage with in relation to its commitment to mission in the West.

What is under threat in the modern digital age is connection and relationship and Arcade Fire helpfully and creatively make this point. In the online world the danger of simply becoming a reflection of one's true self is great. Just as in the first century the

---

42 Yong, *The Spirit Poured out on All Flesh*, 68-80.

43 Yong cites the D.Min thesis of James A. Forbes Jr, "A Pentecostal Approach to Empowerment for Black Liberation" who tells of his experience of Haitian voodoo: "It was a great surprise to the author to get a more balanced picture of the true nature of Voodoo in Haiti. I expected to see the instruments of witchcraft. I had been taught to think of Voodoo almost totally in terms of the use of destructive power. But observation of a Voodoo ceremony and an unbiased or positive presentation of its meaning revealed that Voodoo is the form of Afro-American religion which supplied cohesion and strength for the black people of Haiti. I also learned that while witchcraft is practiced in the area it cannot be lumped in with the religious ceremonies which centre around the effort to make contact with the spirit world. It became very clear why Voodoo had to be discredited. It was largely due to the unifying power of Voodoo that the Haitian peasants were able to throw off the yoke of bondage." See Yong, *The Spirit Poured out on All Flesh*, 73-74, n.133.

church offered a radical vision of relationships in a hierarchical and sectarian culture, so in the 21st century the church faces the task of a similar radical vision but now in the context of an online digital world.

In his comments about Carnival and wearing a mask Butler has spoken about how such activities overcome the division between body and spirit. In other words, Arcade Fire are interested in challenging a basic dualism that lies at the heart of Western culture. This is not something new for them. In the song "My Body is a Cage" from their *Neon Bible* album Arcade Fire sing about this dualism more directly: "My body is a cage that keeps me from dancing with the one I love, but my mind holds the key."

A good case can be mounted that in the modern era Protestant Christianity, and in particular evangelicalism, has been part of a movement which has dis-embodied and de-ritualised Christianity thereby turning it into a "belief system." In *The Secular Age* Taylor describes this process as "excarnation." He argues:

> We have moved from an era in which religious life was more 'embodied', where the presence of the sacred could be enacted in ritual, or seen, felt, touched, walked through (in pilgrimage); into one which is more 'in the mind', where the link with God passes more through endorsing contested interpretations.[44]

Arcade Fire point to a truth about the embodied nature of our humanity and thus the need for a recovery of an embodied faith. Again, this can be taken as a cry from the margins. In our post-modern age, the mission of the church can no longer be envisioned as merely the articulation of, as Taylor says, a "contested interpretation." Rather, the mission of the church needs to include a witness to the embodied nature of our humanity in all its fullness and wholeness. Thankfully, within Christian theology, even evangelical Christian theology, there is a recovery of the significance of human physicality.[45]

This links in with Kierkegaard's critique of the reflective age in which "reflection," in both senses of the word, keeps people from passionate engagement with the world,

---

44 Taylor, *A Secular Age*, 554.

45 See for example, James K A Smith, *Desiring the Kingdom: Worship, Worldview, and Cultural Formation*, 2009; James K A Smith, *Imagining the Kingdom: How Worship Works* (Grand Rapids, MI: Baker Academic, 2013); Timothy Gorringe, *The Education of Desire: Towards a Theology of the Senses* (Harrisburg, PA: Trinity, 2002); Warren S Brown and Brad D Stawn, *The Physical Nature of Christian Life: Neuroscience, Psychology, and the Church* (Cambridge; NY: Cambridge University Press, 2012).

instead taking refuge in a "depersonalised realm of reified ideas and doctrines."[46] Arcade Fire helpfully remind us that desire and passion are part of our embodied humanity. These are not things that we are to be escape from but rather things that we are to redeem. With the line "praying to the resurrector," which turns out to be "just a reflector," Arcade Fire ask another significant question of the church, with regard to missionary urgency, "How has the church lost the revolutionary message and power of the resurrection?" Such a message, far from denying our embodied humanity, actually sanctifies it and gives it a renewed meaning. Too often the church has acted, in the words of Kierkegarrd, as a leveller; with a message of conformity. The church in mission must find a place for the celebration of human desire, passion, individuality, and creativity. This is what we hear if we are willing to listen to Arcade Fire.

Conclusion

Rolling Stone magazine, in a review of *Reflektor*, referred to Arcade Fire as "the most important band of the last decade."[47] Arguably they are also one of the most important bands for the church to hear as it attempts to engage missionally in the world. In *Reflektor* Arcade Fire provide a thoughtful critique of contemporary culture as well as certain forms of religious practices. In their music, lyrics, and performances we hear a yearning for transcendence and a sense of the sacred, a quest for wholeness in a context of fragmentation, a helpful critique of Western missionary practice, a questioning of the way accepted norms and attitudes lead to the draining of passion and creativity, and a challenging of the construction of the reflected self in the digital age. These are all crucial issues the Western church needs to engage with if it is going to stay relevant to postmodern context and come alongside what God is already doing in the world. Arcade Fire's voice, albeit marginal for most within the established church, is deeply insightful and prophetic.

---

46 Patrick L Gardiner, *Kierkegaard: A Very Short Introduction* (Oxford: Oxford University Press, 2002), 40.
47 Doyle, "Win Butler Reveals Secret Influences Behind Arcade Fire's 'Reflektor.'"

E. The Asian Horizon

Any mission engagement the…church undertakes in its region…needs to occur within the context of global partnership, mission from all continents to all continents and regional co-operation.

Ross Langmead, "Contextual Mission: An Australian Perspective" (ANZAMS conference paper, 2009)

15. Christians in the City: Challenges to Faith and Mission in the First "Urban Century"

Ash Barker

This chapter was a public lecture delivered during the triennial AAMS conference, Adelaide, October 2014 on an evening honouring the life and work of Ross Langmead.

I feel privileged to deliver this lecture in honour of my mentor, friend and hero Ross Langmead. He had always been supportive of the community we founded, Urban Neighbours Of Hope, but he also saw the scholar in me in a way I did not see myself. Indeed Ross invested seven years of his life supervising my PhD researching a Christian response to slums. It was not an easy journey to do a PhD living in a slum, on slums, and I know my crazy life tested Ross' patience to the limit.

For the last two years of the PhD I shared my desk with an elderly man who was given a Kings pardon and released from jail after over 40 years in Klong Prem prison. "Frank" had actually been a serial killer who ate his victims and couldn't return to his village. He did translation work for us and needed someone near him. What this meant, of course, was that Ross and I had to deal all kinds of interesting interjections as we held our regular Skype meetings about my latest thesis drafts. Nothing phased Ross and he would be kind to Frank and me, while pushing me to sharpen my thinking and footnotes.

Ross' death premature death shocked me and I am still in deep grief. Ross shared my PhD graduation celebration with me in July 2012 and died a year later.

I do feel a kind of new responsibility. God's work though Ross' passion for creative mission, justice and shalom is unfinished. In many ways that is why I am now going to the United Kingdom to establish the Centre for Urban Life and Mission at Springdale College, Birmingham. After 25 years in urban mission, including the last 12 in Klong Toey slum, Bangkok, a new generation of thoughtful, committed radical disciples needs to be mobilized, formed and equipped for this new urban world. I need to focus my best energies now on offering the same opportunities Ross gave me.

As we have transitioned out from UNOH and into this new role I have longed to fill Ross in and seek his wisdom. I do sense Ross keeps smiling and enjoying our journey. He knew that what we had worked on together in my PhD has implications far beyond us.[1]

This chapter, in Ross's honour, explores some of the real challenges that the urbanisation of the last few decades poses to Christian life and mission. This is very much about missions, but like all good missiology is also about real people in real places.

Pi Bla's challenges

When I first met Pi Bla, she greeted us with, "I am a Christian! Are you?" It was 1999 and I was entering Klong Slum, in Bangkok, Thailand, for the first time, about to start a sabbatical with my family. All we really knew about Klong Toey was her notorious reputation as Bangkok's largest slum and that there was only one small church for its 80,000 mostly Buddhist residents in what was then 2 square kilometers. Bla's welcome in English came as a wonderful surprise for us. She quickly found us a home to live in, helped orientate us into the community, and when we moved to live in Klong Toey permanently in 2002, Bla became part of our family and vice versa. When my son Aiden was born in 2003 Bla was right there with us in the birthing unit.

Bla loves Friday night worship at a house church we belonged to in Klong Toey, praying fervently for those in need. She knows firsthand what it is like to be in desperate need and for God to answer prayers. Born as one of sixteen brothers and sisters, when Bla was just a little girl her family's fishing village in southern Thailand could no longer sustain them. In search of work and the promise of a better life they travelled by train to Bangkok with what little that had. The dream quickly became a nightmare with only slum housing and hard, low paying work in sweatshops available. They could hardly afford small rations of daily rice. When HIV/AIDS claimed one of Bla's brothers, the family debts started to mount up.

Bla, still then a teenager, was "married off" to raise money. This kind of child prostitution of a vulnerable girl is common and it saved the family from starvation and dangerous moneylenders, but it scarred Bla. A low point was after a fire burnt down part of her slum neighborhood and her family was blamed and expected to pay compensation. The offer for Bla to go to Hong Kong and Singapore to quickly pay these debts was accepted.

---

1 An updated version of my PhD was published as Ash Barker, *Slum Life Rising: How to Enflesh Hope in a New Urban World* (Melbourne: UNOH Publications, 2012).

When Bla arrived in Hong Kong her passport was taken and she was forced to service 20-30 men a day, locked in a basement. She tried to commit suicide numerous times between servicing customers, but her captors found ways to prevent this. In desperation Bla cried out to God for help and God answered in an unusual way. Amazingly Bla was led to the Lord by one of her customers who had meet Jesus and was starting to come to faith. He felt so bad about what he was doing that he helped her escape and go back to Klong Toey.

The way Bla came to Christian faith is not recommended or in any evangelistic strategy manual, but can God use broken people to help set other broken people free! Bla's faith became real and she continues to grow in Jesus. It was a month after her return to Bangkok that she welcomed us to Klong Toey.

Just because you know Jesus does not mean crippling debts suddenly disappear. Within a few years of returning to Bangkok, Bla began to get sick and needed to do far worse things for far less money. Eventually my wife, Anji, and Bla worked together to find alternative employment via making and selling handicrafts. Skilled at finding good materials and making bracelets, this initiative soon took off for Bla. Rather than horde success for herself however, Bla invited neighbors in similar circumstances to join her and helped to found a business initiative called "Klong Toey Handicrafts." Last year over eighty women were involved and they had over $200,000 worth of sales all around the world. The fact that Bla survived and got back to Klong Toey is a miracle, but that she could share her opportunities with others is an inspiring sign of God's grace and hope.

Bla's coming to faith may be unusual, but her circumstances are increasingly the new global norm. Complex movements from rural to urban injustices, increased population growth and free flowing globalised markets are creating the rapid growth of urban areas the planet has not seen before. When the famous evangelical revivals began in the 1800s less than three percent of people lived in urban areas. The vast majority of these urban people identified themselves as Christian. This has drastically changed today as 2009 saw, for first time in earth's history, that urban-living humans surpassing the number of rural-living humans.[2] Only about 39% of these urbanites self-identified as Christians, however.[3]

---

2   United Nations, *World Urbanization Prospects – The 2009 Revision* (New York: United Nations, 2010), 2.

3   Barrett and Johnson, *Status of Global Mission - 2009*

What is especially challenging is the rise of urban slums, like Klong Toey, where over a billion people now live.[4]

Today's one billion urban slums residents like Bla are hard to imagine. To put this sudden growth into context, consider that when Christians were first called to go out into "all the world," that world contained fewer than 200 million people. It took humanity until 1804 to reach one billion.[5] The one-billionth slum resident, however, made the ratio one in every six humans today living in slums.[6] While difficult to predict, that number could double within twenty years, leading to one in five people (or two billion people) living in urban slums by 2030,[7] the entire world population of 1930.[8] By 2050, the UN-Habitat warns that "if left unchecked" slum residents could well reach three billion people.[9] Bla is not alone. Her experiences are quickly becoming the most normal human experience.

Christianity and urban contexts

Although Christian faith began with Jesus in the rural villages of Galilee, it grew to be an influential movement throughout Roman cities and urban centres. From its early beginnings in Jerusalem, to its growth in Roman colonial cities like Ephesus and its eventual status as the official religion of the Roman Empire, Christianity has a history of adapting to urban conditions and finding resonance among urban populations.

Christian faith even sees eternal life in the city of "New Jerusalem" (Revelation 3:12). Attention to the urban context in history has not been consistently however. At its best, for example, during the plagues in Roman cities when Pagan priests and most who were able to flee did so, the courage of early Christians to stay with the afflicted is credited as an important dimension in the rise of Christianity.[10] The credibility of

---

4   UN-Habitat, *The Challenge of Slums*, iv; see also United Nations, *World Urbanization Prospects – The 2009 Revision*, 2.

5   Matt Rosenberg, "Current World Population: Current world population and world population growth since the year one", http://geography.about.com/od/obtainpopulationdata/a/worldpopulation.htm

6   UN-Habitat, *Challenge of Slums*, iv.

7   UN-Habitat, *Challenge of Slums*, xxiv.

8   Rosenberg, "Current World Population."

9   UN-Habitat, "The Challenge", www.unhabitat.org/content.asp?typeid=19&catid=10&cid=928 ; see also UN-Habitat, *The Challenge of Slums: Global Report on Human Settlements 2003* (London: Earthscan, 2003), xxiv; David Barrett, "Status of Global Mission, 2009, in the Context of 20th and 21st Centuries", http://ockenga.gordonconwell.edu/ockenga/globalchristianity/resources.php_.

10   Rodney Stark, *The Rise of Christianity: How the Obscure, Marginal Jesus Movement became the Dominant Religious Force in the Western World in a Few Centuries* (San Francisco: HarperCollins, 1996), 73-94.

a Christian faith underpinning such acts rose too.[11] However, Christianity can also be seen at its worst when entwined with the dark spectre of European colonisation. Certainly this became the case when Christianity was adopted as the official religion of the Roman Empire, but also later the British, Dutch, Spanish and Portuguese Empires. Intertwining the tasks of civilising and Christianising these empires were an especially oppressive force upon indigenous populations around the world, and cities became important bases from which to pursue their colonising agendas.

Almost certainly Christianity's urban influence began to wane prior to 1900. According to Barrett and Johnson cities seem to have been tough places for Christianity to find resonance in since then. They note that in 1900 urban Christians made up over 68% of the global urban population, but by 2004 the figure was 39.67%, with projections at just 36.90% for 2025.[12]

Some Evangelicals are adapting to this new urban world. Christian populations are finding resonance and growing in many cities of Latin America, Sub-Saharan Africa and a few Asian countries. These however are now the exceptions. Urban Christianity in the West is either declining or starting to bottom out. The new, rapidly growing 10/40 Window cities (i.e., North Africa, Middle East and Asia, the countries situated between 10 degree and 40 degrees north of the equator) are dominated by Islam, Hinduism or in Bangkok's case Buddhism. This is especially so in their slum and squatter neighborhoods. In Bangkok, for example, the percentage of Evangelicals in the city could be as low as 0.3%[13] with over 1.5 million slum residents having less than 12 churches among them. Across Asia the majority of the largest fifty cities have both large numbers of slum residents and small Christian populations. It is in these 10/40 Window cities that the future relevance and faithfulness of Christian faith will be found or found out.

By contrast, some post-colonial cities with high numbers of slum residents have high rates of Christian identification. This is especially the case in Latin America, Sub-Saharan Africa and Manila. However, colonially-instigated Christianity is difficult to measure with nominalism and syncretism easily undermining active faith. If Christian community participation is one indicator of genuine Christianity, then we see mixed

---

11 Stark, *The Rise of Christianity*, 91-93.

12 David Barrett and Todd Johnson, "Status of Global Mission, 2004, in Context of 20th and 21st Centuries," *International Bulletin of Missionary Research* 28:1 (2004), 25.

13 Peter Wagner, Stephen Peters and Mark Wilson, *Praying through the 100 Gateway cities of the 10/40 Window* (Seattle: YWAM, 1995), 134.

results in urban slums. In Manila, for example, which has a Christian identification rate of 93.8%,[14] and where there are 3.3 million slum residents, Viv Grigg found that there were 677 churches in 1998 and over 1000 by 2004, but only 3% of these were in slums.[15] Grigg did find higher rates of churches in slums in other post-colonial cities like Lima, Peru. Lima has 2.7 million slum residents and 594 churches, and 90% of these churches are located in the slums.[16]

In the slums of post-colonial cities with high rates of Christian identification there are reports of both high and low levels of church participation. It is difficult to make a generalised statement about the state of Christianity in the slums of these cities. What we from the International Society for Urban Mission *can* say is that, to our knowledge, there are no reports of high rates of church participation in the slums of post-colonial cities where there are *few* Christians overall.

Urban slums are especially prevalent in large numbers in cities where one of three "other" major religions (Buddhism, Islam and Hinduism) are a majority. We can see, for example, that Bangkok slums have over 1.5 million residents, are mostly Buddhist, and have fewer than 12 churches. Large Muslim cities like Dakar (Sengal) have over one million slum residents but few Christians, as 89% are Muslim.[17] Hindu cities like Delhi have 1.5 million slum residents but few Christians (78% Hindu).[18] Majority Hindu, Muslim and Buddhist cities all have very few Christians, but many have large numbers of slum residents.

Where urban poverty is most concentrated – and that includes where the most slum-residents live – Christianity is struggling most. The 10/40 Window has been highlighted as a geographical area where poverty is highest and Christianity is weakest. This region also accounts for over 630 million slum residents. That is, approximately 63% of all slum residents or almost two out of every three slum residents.[19] Yet Christians comprise only 8.5% of the population in that region, a total of 352 million.[20] Given that

14 Johnson and Ross, *Atlas of Global Christianity*, 246.

15 Viv Grigg, "Where Are the Churches of the Poor?" *Urban Leaders*, http://www.urbanleaders.org/weburbpoor/04Context(CX)/Global%20Movements/where%20are%20the%20churches%20of%20the%20poor/Churches%20of%20the%20poor.htm

16 Grigg, "Where are the Churches Of The Poor?".

17 Earth Observatory, "Dakar, Senegal", http://earthobservatory.nasa.gov/IOTD/view.php?id=8886; Johnson and Ross, *Atlas of Global Christianity*, 244.

18 Jeremy Page, "Indian Slum Population Doubles in Two Decades," *The Sunday Times*, http://www.timesonline.co.uk/tol/news/world/asia/article1805596.ece; Johnson and Ross, *Atlas of Global Christianity*, 246.

19 UN-Habitat, *State of the World's Cities 2006/7*, 72.

20 Johnson and Ross, *Atlas of Global Christianity*, 136.

over 140 million of these Christians live in Eastern Asia (which includes South Korea and China),[21] the numbers become far starker for the other parts of Asia and North Africa that have higher numbers of slum residents. Indian cities like Mumbai, for example, have 3.2 million slum residents, Delhi 1.8 million and Kolkata 1.5 million,[22] and those cities have tiny percentages of Christians. Similar stories can be told throughout Asia, Middle East and Northern Africa, where all three urban conditions – rapid urbanisation, post-colonialism and the existence of another world religion in the majority – help to ensure a large number of slums, but with few Christians living in them.

Christian Responses

It is no exaggeration to say that Christians could well be being found wanting in this new urban world. In an interconnected world, rapidly growing urban slums are a challenge to everyone's global security, equality and stability, but Christians have a special mandate from God to seek God's will done on earth as in heaven (Matthew 6:1). Evangelical faith and mission is especially challenged in how to respond to this new, urbanising earth. It is estimated, for example, that only 1 in 500 international missionaries and less than 10,000 national Christian workers focus on slums. Many of our Christian aid and development agencies are now very effective in rural areas, but most struggle in urban slums with even our largest like World Vision spending only 1.3% of their 2004 global budget on slum projects.[23] We also know personal relationships are a key part of sharing faith, yet as Todd Johnson of the Centre for Global Christianity reports, among Muslims, Hindus, and Buddhists – the three largest religions other than Christianity and where the growing cities of the 10/40 window dominate – less than 14% (or 1 in 7) had personal contact with a Christian. It is not an exaggeration to say evangelical engagement is mostly missing the action in some of the most important, demographically growing cities today.

Bla's life shows what God can do in an urban slum like Klong Toey. Despite the darkest of circumstances, it is not impossible for real transformation through Jesus to shine through.

---

21 Johnson and Ross, *Atlas of Global Christianity*, 140.
22 Jeremy Page, "Indian Slum Population Doubles In Two Decades".
23 The Urban Working Group, "The Keys to the City: Finding New Doorways to Urban Transformation—A Report and Recommendations", (Draft: 2007), http://www.transformational-development.org/Ministry/TransDev2.nsf/A6748A23BB21C3F08825725700707E73/$file/Urban%20R&D%20Report%20-%20Summary%20(Draft)%20-%20Jan%209,%202007.pdf.

Will a new generation of Christian workers rise up to submerge themselves deeply, relationally and strategically to be part of seeing more of this happen?

Many urban Christian activists on the front line today resonate with Jeremiah 29:7: "But seek the shalom of the city where I have sent you into exile, and pray to the Lord on its behalf, for in its shalom you will find your shalom" (NRSV with "shalom" substituted for "peace"). This promise of shalom – the well-being found in the harmony between God, people and place – is remarkable because the city in these verses in which God's people have been asked to live, pray and seek shalom is none other than Babylon, a city that has the most villainous qualities in the biblical narrative.

Perhaps God is calling more of his people to seek the shalom of the world's cities again, even in the most challenging of places? It may be that in seeing God at work in the lives of people like Bla we have the chance to find our own shalom.

I encourage you to do all you can to stand with Christians in slums seeking wholistic transformations. The so called "New Friars" communities are very accessible and include groups such as Word Made Flesh, Servants to Asia's Urban Poor, Servant Partners, InnerCHANGE and Urban Neighbours Of Hope with teams in both Western and Majority Worlds.[24] The International Society of Urban Mission (ISUM) is another that brings together diverse urban Christian activists, scholars and leaders to seek shalom in cities, with a special concern for Majority World cities. The World Evangelical Alliance (WEA) Theological Commission sponsors the annual ISUM Summit and the New Urban World journal which helps network, research and mobilise Christians to better engage urban poverty.[25]

---

24 Scott Bessenecker, *The New Friars: The Emerging Movement Serving the World's Poor* (Downers Grove, IL: InterVarsity Press, 2006).

25 Newurbanworld.org. Key references on the topic of this chapter are: Barker, *Slum Life Rising*; Todd Johnson and Kenneth R. Ross, *Atlas of Global Christianity* (Edinburgh: Edinburgh University Press, 2010); UN Habitat, *The Challenge of Slums: Global Report on Human Settlements, 2003* (London: Earthscan, 2003).

16. A World of Peripheries
Scott Litchfield

Between the dynamic cities and nation states of South East Asia there are many areas that fall "through the cracks." Located "on the margins" in border areas these communities have none of the prosperity and global economic connections of their close neighbours. Today they are connected by roads and have access to mobile communications technology, but they remain on the periphery of the societies around them struggling for justice and cultural identity. This chapter looks at the global and social realities for those living on the margins and uses the concept of "creating space" as a critical missional approach with those living on the peripheries. This space is an emotional, spiritual and psychological encounter between mission workers and those who find themselves living in the borderlands.

A Reflection

The borderlands of South East Asia have been of interest to me for over 20 years since I first moved to live here. As an Australian we have no land borders with another nation and so the concept of two nations meeting at a common border was new. Long before I became interested in the missiological significance of these regions I was captivated by the interactions of people from two or more places at the border crossings and the various actors taking a role in what I observed. I visited the golden triangle region of northern Thailand where Thailand, Laos and Burma touched. Notorious by reputation because of the drug trade, by the early 1990s it was already a burgeoning tourist site artificially created for visitors. The nearby crossing at Mai Sai, between Thailand and Burma, was a far more interesting place to be. The markets on both sides of "no man's land" were fascinating for what was on display and what was sold "out the back."

Trade is a common presence at all border crossings. I remember visiting crossings in the mountains between Thailand and Burma or Thailand and Laos where "tribal people" wearing traditional clothing coming from either side of the border to trade their respective products together dominated the commerce. There were also Thai business people who brought consumer goods from the Thai cities to sell/trade for the often unrecognisable agricultural products offered by the local mountain people. I can still clearly see the sight of very short, time worn tribal women, dressed in traditional clothes, bargaining with lowland Thais with their fancy utes (pickup trucks) waiting to be filled with a seasonal product destined for the waiting market back in the cities and towns of the lowlands.

This coming together of two cultures is far more than just an interaction of national backgrounds and ethnicity. It is a picture of globalisation and developed market economics coming into the realm of the centuries old meeting of local communities for trade. At a fundamental level there is a mutual need for each other and trade together is a way of expressing that.

For many people however, border crossing points are also places where there is no mutuality, where the exploitation of human beings takes the place of the age-old practice of trading together. On the Thai-Cambodian border Cambodians are trying to find the allusive income they struggle to source in their home provinces by crossing to Thailand, documented and undocumented, to work and make a difference for their families. The 7am opening of the crossing between Cambodia and Thailand at Poipet, a border town of some size in northern Cambodia, is an amazing process that sees adults and children pass the glitz of the eleven Casinos in "no man's land" to face a day, week or many months of work in whatever form that may take. In the mix are the porters, the men who push trolleys back and forwards across the border for $2-3 a day. For some Thailand offers labouring work in the fields or on construction sites, or the chance to work in restaurants and the service industry. This can often see young women tricked by unscrupulous brokers as their restaurant job becomes work in a brothel in the back streets of Bangkok or another Thai city. Children cross to beg on the Thai side of the border, in the local town or further afield in Bangkok. The Casinos stand silently watching this daily movement of humanity knowing that later in the day Thais will enter their doors to try their "luck."

The walk back to the town from the border, through a local slum community, sees those left behind making breakfast on charcoal fires boiling rice that will probably be the only food on offer until family members return with money. The old look after the very young. School age kids are already on the way to school dressed in the white shirts and blue shorts or skirts of government schools across the country. Other children are sitting around going nowhere, perhaps waiting to be called for work; or perhaps they have no documents to get into school, or their parents cannot afford the 25 cents needed each day to pay the teacher. For some education or sport offer a way out, but for the majority it is only a matter of time before they too are in the group crossing the border at 7am.

The town is full of people from across Cambodia – some looking for a better life working in the Casinos or in the service industry of restaurants, markets and guesthouses, others escaping something from their past, and yet others getting things in line for their next deal in human misery. It is sometimes hard to find a "local" – born in Poipet – in a town full of people from "somewhere else." But it is here, in this incredibly mixed and at times dark social context, that the light of Christ is shining. Little glimpses of the transforming power of the good news can be seen in border communities across the globe.

Introduction

In this chapter I have begun with some personal reflections from the borderlands of South East Asia (SEA). I will now move to consider some of the broad global influences on life at the periphery, consider the place of power and social structures in maintaining the status quo for those on the margins, and then look at the importance of creating "space" that becomes the locus of missional engagement. To finish I will reflect on some possible future directions for life in the borderlands of SEA and what it would take to be in mission there.

The "borderlands" and "peripheries" of SEA are geographically located between nation states, and also places of emotional and social liminality. These communities often attract the dislocated and migrant who leave home to find something new. "Dislocation is a term used to describe the experience of those who have relocated from a familiar to an unfamiliar place" and can be characterised as being "voiceless, invisible and powerless."[1] In the borderlands there are those on the way somewhere else who are just passing through; those that were going somewhere else but circumstance has caused them to stay for a while; and those for whom the border community is their place of birth.

Whilst the focus of this chapter is the borderlands communities of SEA, I hope that some of the ideas I consider are applicable in other social contexts of marginality.

The Global Considerations

During the colonial era the church used the expansionism of colonial powers as a means to also expand the church. This can be seen in both Catholic and Protestant colonial contexts. At the same time the church was also often called into an "in

---

1 Sophia Park, "The Galilean Jesus: Creating a Borderland at the Foot of the Cross," *Theological Studies*, Vol.70 (2009), 420.

between" position as it protected or supported the colonialised peoples from the colonial powers. Today, in our globalised context the church needs to take a similar place in-between the globalising economic and social forces and those communities that are negatively impacted by globalisation.

Globalisation has radically changed the way people interact around the world. Hierarchies can be circumvented and in many cases replaced in the global patterns of interaction by "flows and networks."[2] This means many of the traditional structures and social norms have been incorporated with or, in many cases, superseded by new approaches to social interactions. Some initial assessments of power in this new globalised context indicate that multiple actors have more influence and power than the previously dominant bipolar "centre" and less dominant "non-centre" construction. In part this is because globalisation creates multiple centres, but it is also because individuals have the ability, with a combination of the right resources, personal knowledge, and opportunity, to become players in a global or at least regional context.

The other significant development in the last decade is the global influence of the internet, social media and Information and Communications Technology (ICT) networking. Significant global uprisings that have led to regime change in a number of countries have been enabled by internet communications and wider networking has clearly had an impact in other social settings where groups are seeking change.[3]

Those on the periphery are those who cannot or do not want to engage with the centres. Peripheries are found in every place that sees people and communities unable to enter into the prosperity and lifestyle available to those who live at the centres. An example of this are the millions of poor rural workers employed on construction sites around Asia. They are building state of the art commercial, residential and shopping complexes but they live in incredibly poor and dangerous conditions on the building site during the life of the project. Then on completion of the project they are left homeless and need to find another building site or return to the village. They are within touching distance of the "centre" but remain very much on the periphery.

---

2   This comes through a number of works by Arjun Appadurai about Globalisation and Manuel Castells writing on the global communications context starting with his book *The Rise of the Network Society* (Oxford, UK: Blackwell) in 1966.

3   There has been an ongoing discussion about the actual impact of social media on social movements and uprisings around the world. Whilst the extent of this is hard to assess, there is no doubt that social media has had a significant impact. See http://www.washington.edu/news/2011/09/12/new-study-quantifies-use-of-social-media-in-arab-spring/ and http://www.theatlantic.com/technology/archive/2011/09/so-was-facebook-responsible-for-the-arab-spring-after-all/244314/

Power Dynamics and Social Structures

The most common model of mission in much of the world is from the centre to the margins. This approach has strong historical roots in colonialism where the establishment of centres or stations formed a base from which colonial expansion could proceed. The expansion of Christian activities alongside colonialism is historically linked and so the model "from the centre to the margins" was common in the colonial era. Globalisation offers the opportunity for a similar approach, perhaps even more so because of advances in communications technology that increases the likelihood of activities based in the centre reaching out to the peripheries.

In the recent declaration *Together Towards Life* at the WCC meetings in South Korea in 2013, the concept of "Mission from the Margins" was developed and fundamentally challenges the centre to periphery approach. "Mission from the margins calls for an understanding of the complexities of power dynamics, global systems and structures, and local contextual realities."[4] In our globalised world an understanding of power structures is even more important than in previous eras because of the increased complexity of multiple centres. The declaration identifies some important understandings for seeing mission initiatives "from the margins." It counteracts injustice and critiques the model of mission being from the powerful to the powerless, from the rich to the poor, and from the privileged to the marginalised.[5]

If power structures are not addressed in the thinking and approach of missional activities it can lead to outcomes that do not challenge the forces that marginalise and dehumanise others as it tends to keep the oppressive status quo in place. At times this is justified by those individuals who are a "success" in moving from the margins to the centre usually through education or employment opportunities. The practice used in many mission contexts of identifying a few key young people (usually the smartest but also often the most loyal and compliant), training them up in Christian faith, and sending them off for education in the city is still alive and well in the mission endeavours of churches in South East Asia. It is based on the flawed assumption that they will then be future Christian leaders who will influence many for the Gospel. The problem is that on most occasions these people from the margins then embrace the "life" at the centre and they are unable or dis-inclined to return to the periphery. The status quo is then maintained. The centre has won. It has rescued a few from the

---

[4] *Together Towards Life: Mission and Evangelism in Changing Landscapes*, CWME-WCC, 2013, paragraph 37.
[5] *Together Towards Life*, paragraph 38, see also "Introducing Mission from the Margins," *International Review of Mission* 101:2 (Nov 2012).

margins while maintaining its power and position. Mission that does not challenge the power structures "has generally aliened with the privileges of the centre and largely failed to challenge economic, social, cultural, and political systems which have marginalised some peoples."[6]

The WCC declaration says: "The aim of mission is not simply to move people from the margins to centres of power but to confront those who remain the centre by keeping people on the margins. Instead churches are called to transform power structures."[7] Transformation of social contexts is complex because it needs to see systemic change that can only come about through a deep, concerted and resilient challenge to the powers. This is a long process, can be disheartening, and because it challenges those individuals with power, it can be personally very dangerous to the churches and mission workers involved.

Creating Space on the Peripheries: Hope and Transformation

"Living in a globalised world where time and space have been compressed, where those who have and those who have not are driven further apart, a truly intercultural way of doing Theology between the local and the global is required of us."[8] This space identified by Schreiter is where ministry on the margins occurs – between the local and the global and on the periphery. Life at the centre is increasingly life without space as Schreiter's image of time being "compressed" is felt no more acutely than in the centre. The space at the peripheries however, is where "home" is created even in the transience of having no permanent dwelling. Elaine Padilla's reflection on *Shekhinah*[9] provides an image of home as a "'no-place', a 'nowhere' or utopia (*ou topos*) in the sense of "that which can become" can help redefine migratory experiences with regards to home and identity."[10] Ministry in this space on the peripheries is with and amongst those who Maria Lugones identifies as her people "the only people I think of as my own are transnationals, liminals, border-dwellers, 'world'-travellers, beings in the middle of the either/or."[11]

---

6   *Together Towards Life*, paragraph 41.
7   *Together Towards Life*, paragraph 40.
8   Robert Schreiter, *The New Catholicity* (New York: Orbis, 2004), 133.
9   *Shekhinah*, the Hebrew word for "to dwell" or "to abide", "through time emerged as a wandering divine presence in the desert". Padilla explains "Although *Shekhinah* is not the same as what Christians understand by the Holy Spirit, she resembles the Spirit in being a figure of the divine, one that is mobile and nomadic and one that opens earthly realities to the infinite that is beyond." Elaine Padilla, "Border-Crossing and Exile: A Latina's Theological Encounter with Shekhinah," *Crosscurrents* (December 2010), 530.
10 Padilla, *Shekhinah*, 530.
11 Maria Lugones, "Purity, Impurity, and Separation", cited in Padilla, *Shekhinah*, 529.

In this space, where ministry and mission happen on the margins, we need to create a sense of identity and home for people on the move. As they sense home and have place and identity they can begin to understand the good news of Jesus. Daniel Groody in his theological reflections on migration sees Jesus' *kenosis* as being a critical part of the witness of mission workers as they minister at the margins. The important example of the "self-sacrifice, self-emptying, and self-offering for the sake of others" seen in Jesus' life is critical because it breaks the power nexus that so often overwhelms and dis-empowers those on the margins.[12] Sophia Park's reflection on John's gospel, especially chapter 19:23-30, has some great insights about the nature of this "space." She describes it as a place where "[an] uprooted person is re-rooted in herself, others and God, and finds no security outside the in-between space."[13] For Park friendship is a key aspect of this new community, based on equality and Jesus clear friendship with his disciples, "an individual's friendship with Jesus is the fundamental requirement for being a member of the community."[14] As community and a sense of place is created in the borderlands and peripheries the Holy Spirit can begin to work in the hearts and minds of the marginalised persons as they meet and share life with Jesus followers and each other.

The concept of a "third space" is deeply entrenched in post-colonial thought and is at the basis of my thinking about space at the margins. Originally conceptualised by Homi Bhabha, Paul Meredith, writing from the Aotearoa/New Zealand context, summarises the concept of Third Space:

> Thus, the third space is a mode of articulation, a way of describing a productive, and not merely reflective, space that engenders new possibility. It is an "interruptive, interrogative, and enunciative" (Bhabha 1994) space of new forms of cultural meaning and production blurring the limitations of existing boundaries and calling into question established categorisations of culture and identity. According to Bhabha, this hybrid third space is an ambivalent site where cultural meaning and representation have no "primordial unity or fixity" (Bhabha 1994).[15]

---

12 Daniel Groody, "Jesus and the Undocumented Immigrant: A Spiritual Geography of a Crucified People," *Theological Studies* 70 (2009), 315; Rosalind Brown, *Being a Deacon Today: Exploring a Distinctive Ministry in the Church and in the World* (London: Canterbury Press, 2005), 33.

13 Park, "Galilean Jesus," 421.

14 Park, "Galilean Jesus," 428.

15 Paul Meredith, "Hybridity in the Third Space: Re-thinking Bi-Cultural Politics in Aotearoa/New Zealand" (Paper Presented to Te Oru Rangahau Maori Research and Development Conference, 7-9 July, 1998, Massey University), 3. Meredith refers to Bhabha 1994: Homi Bhabha, *Location of Culture* (London: Routledge, 1994).

Finding Identity

The critical development that occurs in these spaces at the peripheries is that people can begin to find who they are – their identity. At the level of identity and culture Post colonial thinkers, particularly Bhabha, have developed the concept of "hybridity" to explain the coming together of two cultural backgrounds in a person's life. Recognising that bi-cultural is not an adequate description of the reality of having two cultural influences in one's life, hybridity helps describe the coming together of two cultures to create a mix.[16] But I want to go beyond a mix of cultures to Virgilio Elizondos use of *mestizaje* which sees the formation of a new identity, a "third" cultural identity which is more than a mix of two, more than the "sum of the parts." Individual and group realisation of their cultural background and current social context combines to help see the possibilities of how life can be.[17]

Another area of study that has similar understandings of the coming together of multiple cultures to produce a new cultural identity is the concept of Third Culture Kids (TCK).[18] TCKs are children who have grown up outside their passport country and identify with their parents or "home" culture, and the host culture of the country where they live, as well as the expatriate cultural influences of their peers from around the globe.

Mestizaje, TCK and hybridity are diverse and yet complimentary concepts that provide insight on what is possible for people as they come into the "third space" created in the borderlands of South East Asia. Coming from many cultural and sub cultural contexts the created space on the peripheries allows for them to begin to find themselves again and form a new identity and community.[19]

The Importance of Creating Space

Justice and Peace need to be evident on the margins. This is best developed through action that sees those in ministry standing alongside marginalised communities as

---

16 See Bhabha, *Location of Culture* and many other books and articles.

17 Virgilio Elizondo has written widely about *Mestizaje* and brings many of his thoughts together in the book *The Future is Mestizo: Life where Cultures Meet* (Boulder: University Press of Colorado, 2000, originally published in 1986).

18 See http://www.tckworld.com/ and http://en.wikipedia.org/wiki/Third_culture_kid for two good overviews of the TCK concept.

19 How much this happens across ethnic groups is questionable because of the mis-trust and racism across the region built over hundreds of years of war and subjugation. It is certainly possible amongst people of diverse social groups from with the same country as they meet at the border and perhaps eventually, through spiritual change and transformation, across "national ethnicities."

they seek justice in the face of injustice.[20] In their powerlessness the marginalised find support with each other and those in solidarity with them. From slow and tentative beginnings it is possible to see transformation as trust is built and relationships develop. This comes not through the project and the resources shared but human interaction with others who believe in them. There is a place for prophetic ministry on the margins "[that] will demand that we develop the tenacity to keep on speaking for those who can not speak for themselves."[21]

Awareness of the "local" in the face of globalisation is critical for those creating space for others. As marginalised communities face the forces of globalisation they often feel insignificant and irrelevant. Finding the Divine and the precious in what is often looked down upon by others is a powerful statement to those we relate with on the margins. Being able to "see" God's presence in those so often unseen by the majority of the world is a gifting of the Spirit. Listening well, long and deeply is critical to be effective in these contexts. Coming from outside the marginalised context means we come with presuppositions and, regardless how well prepared we might be, we are never prepared for the reality of life in the borderlands. But we can learn.

Approaching the mission task in the space created with humility and meekness makes us able to listen, to take the time needed to recognise God at work, and find how we can be a part of God's plans for that community. It can be hard to take the time to listen and learn in a world so full of expectations for quick outcomes and clear results. To appease this trend we can resort to "resource" transfer through a project based development response, but true transformation in lives and communities comes by sharing life together through friendships of mutuality. In friendship "we allow ourselves to be disarmed, we become both vulnerable and strong. The only weapons then at our disposal are those of the spirit. We choose the way of Jesus, laying aside all the earthly resources that give us power - in order to be present to those we love."[22] As Anthony Gittins articulates so clearly "in our following Jesus we are made whole, and in our encounter with the broken our brokenness finds healing."[23]

---

20 Geevarghese Coorilos, "God of life, Lead us to Justice and Peace: Some Missiological Perspectives," *International Review of Mission* 102:1 (April 2013), 16.

21 Brown, Being a Deacon, 37.

22 Christopher Heuertz and Christine Phol, *Friendship at the Margins: Discovering Mutuality in Service and Mission* (Downers Grove: IVP, 2010), 97.

23 Anthony Gittins, *Bread for the Journey: Mission as Transformation and Transformation as Mission* (Eugene: Wipf and Stock, 1993), 161.

What are some of the characteristics of ministry in the space at the peripheries?

Firstly, it is critical that the mission workers see people coming as individuals and getting to know them as they are and not simply as members of ethnic or social groups within society. Often those on the margins are there because they have been rejected by or unable to fit cultural expectations in another social context.

Secondly, mission workers should not start with a preconceived understanding of what will happen in the space they are entering into and how their interactions with people on the margins will unfold.

Thirdly, ministry in this space needs to take time to see what develops and be willing to build understanding and then relationships with the people they are serving. As noted earlier in Sophia Park's work friendship is a critical aspect of ministry in this space as she writes "a new kinship or parental friendship is forged from the communal dynamics of a friendship with Jesus" and "for the community of the dislocated, serving each other in a friendship grounded in equality and mutuality functions to empower the member."[24]

Fourthly, hospitality is a critical component of ministry at the margins. Food, a warm welcome, and acceptance, help create a space where people feel comfortable and able to explore who they are, where they fit, and what God is doing in their lives.

Lastly, ministry in the space at the margins must be based on the work of the Holy Spirit in the social context and within the lives of those living in these places. Whilst recognising the role of the Holy Spirit might seem obvious for any missional activity, it is more critical on the peripheries because of the transient lives of the people living there, and a lack of institutions and formal organisations that bring structure and shape. By recognising the work of the Holy Spirit we are acknowledging the spiritual nature of the mission task at the borders because of the specific spiritual brokenness, fear and anxiety that is in the lives of many who seek refuge in the space we create. As Jonathan Ingleby describes so well "What Jesus offers is the healing community. A place where the pained, the demoniacs, the moonstruck, the paralysed of our society can come and find their illness begin to mend."[25]

---

24 Park, "Galilean Jesus," 428.

25 Jonathan Ingleby, *Beyond Empire: Post-colonialism and Mission in a Global Context* (Bloomington, IN: Author House, 2010), 114.

Future developments in the Borderlands of South East Asia

The Greater Mekong Sub-region (GMS) has been conceptualised for 20 years and recognises the environmental, social, and economic interconnectedness of Burma, Thailand, Cambodia, Laos, Vietnam, Yunnan Province and Guangxi autonomous region in China (added 2005). In more recent years ASEAN has been working on a common Economic Community (AEC) set to be inaugurated in 2015. Both these concepts, especially the AEC, have the potential to radically change life in the region. The development of "economic corridors" throughout the GMS identifies the possible impact of the flow of goods across national borders. Alongside the movement of goods is the movement of people (documented, undocumented and forced) across borders and through communities on the margins. Sleepy border communities of the past will be changed into international crossing points of increasing significance and the wealth of the global economy may overwhelm the local economies. The presence of casinos, gamblers, drugs, prostitution, and migrants will create social problems in communities with little capacity to cope.[26]

As we think about mission in these contexts we need to be "ahead of the game" and prepare to have cross-cultural workers ready and able to minister at the margins – tri and bi-lingual, "globally" aware, "locally" sensitive, and with time to invest at the grassroots. These workers could be locals with some wider experience, those coming from within ASEAN countries, or other internationals. They need to be well equipped for ministry in a complex social context that is being shaped by the ebbs and flows of global influences but also constantly engaging with the local community that is dealing with rapid change.

At a time when mission workers are generally making shorter time commitments we need longer from them.

At a time mission workers are generally less trained and less equipped for mission at the margins the social complexity of the peripheries demands better-equipped workers.

When internet and communications technology makes neat "packages" of the gospel possible we need "local" theologies generated from the grassroots.

---

26 http://www.ide.go.jp/English/Publish/Download/Brc/08.html and see also Shrestha Omkar and Chongvillaivan Aekapol, eds, *Greater Mekong Subregion: From Geographical to Socio-economic Integration* (Singapore: Institute of South East Asian Studies, 2013).

And, at a time when English is a dominant global language – we need linguistically skilled workers able to operate in two or three languages with those they connect with so that real depth can be achieved in communication together and lasting transformation can happen.

Conclusion

Missional engagements in the borderlands of SEA, and other borders or marginal contexts, must be considered with an appreciation of the global forces and regional influences impacting the social context at the margins. These forces and entrenched oppressive power structures combine to create injustice and inequality at the margins and borders leaving communities at times ravaged by displacement and exclusion.

By creating space for people on the peripheries that allows them to find a new identity and brings them closer to the hope found in God, new communities of faith can begin to challenge the status quo and bring change to both individual lives and the wider community. Missional engagement that starts "at the margins" with outsiders coming to live amongst, learn from and share life and "good news" with those they meet, has the potential to become "mission from the margins" as these communities then go beyond themselves to share with others.

In a "world of peripheries," as there are peripheries everywhere, missional engagements amongst, with and alongside the marginalised, empowered by the Holy Spirit, bring hope to those who feel invisible and unloved. They find identity and God's strength to find new ways forward.

17. Contextual Theologising on the Doorstep of Asia: Mission and Marginalisation among the Irupara Hula People of PNG

Graeme Humble

As Australia surveys the edges of its northern horizon towards Asia, it first encounters a nation of a thousand tribes. The nation of Papua New Guinea (PNG) straddles the divide between Australia and its northern Asian neighbours. PNG has long been the focus of Australia's attention regarding national security (especially the threat from Asia during World War Two), and more recently in its attempts to maintain territorial integrity with regard to refugees arriving by sea through Asian countries (leading to the establishment of the Manus Detention Centre). Furthermore, PNG's booming economy is buoyed by the investment of numerous Asian and Australian companies in the mining, timber and fishery industries. It is within this intermediate Melanesian context – neither Asian nor Australian – but one that is vital to both regions, that this study addresses the crux of Ross Langmead's passion – contextual mission and contextual theology. An in-depth case study of the Hula people of Irupara village on the southern coast of PNG outlines contextual factors that contributed to their marginalisation as a people, and also their subsequent recovery of identity as a people. Within the perspective of the restoration of their dignity, the case study engages Hula indigenous themes to underpin a contextual theology that expresses the gospel in familiar indigenous Hula ways. Such a case study in contextual theologising is instructive to all mission practitioners and missiologists as they engage in mission not only in Australia, but also in bridging beyond Melanesia toward the Asian horizon.

Introduction

A visitor to the maritime village of Irupara on the south-east coast of Papua New Guinea could be forgiven for believing that life has always been peaceful and placid for the local Hula people.[1] Their houses, either fringed by coconut palms on the strandline or built on hardwood poles a little offshore, enjoy magnificent vistas and glorious sunsets as they overlook the Coral Sea. Life appears to be good. Nearby gardens provide a relative abundance of fresh produce, sago swamps and coconut palms supply basic ingredients for the local delicacy *pariwa*,[2] while the distant reefs furnish an endless source of the Hula favourite staple food – fish of all varieties.

However, life has not always been this way. The occasional visitor is beguiled by the tropical tranquillity and picturesque location of Irupara village, located on the Papuan coast 110 kilometres southeast of Port Moresby. In order to understand the current nature of life in the Hula villages, it is necessary to investigate the historical impact of the early missionisation and colonisation processes on the cultural identity of the Hula people group.[3]

Mission, Military and Marginalisation

When the first London Missionary Society (LMS) missionaries arrived in Papua in the 1870s, the Hula people's reputation as aggressive warriors hovered as a constant threat over the villages strung along the Papuan coastline.[4] Hula military prowess is epitomised in the story of perhaps their most well known and revered ancestral warrior, Kila Wari of Alewai village, whose influence ranged more than 100 kilometres in either direction along the coast from Hula.[5] The story of his treacherous demise as revenge for his killing of a man in the neighbouring village of Babaka, is still retold with great enthusiasm.

1   The people and language are commonly referred to as *Hula*. See Nigel D. Oram, "Culture Change, Economic Development and Migration among the Hula," *Oceania* 38: 4 (1968), 243. Internally, the people refer to themselves as *Vula'a*, a term also used by some anthropologists. See Deborah Van Heekeren, "Giving-for-Being: The Religion of Vula'a Exchange," in *Religious Dynamics in the Pacific*, ed. F. Douaire-Marsaudon and G. Weichart (Lexington: pacific-credo Publications, 2010), 173. Alternatively, early colonists, missionaries and other anthropologists used terms such as *Bula'a, Bulaa, Hulaa* and *Vulaa*. See R.E. Guise, "Aboriginal Vocabulary of Bula'a," *Annual Report of British New Guinea from 1st. July, 1890, to 30th June, 1891; with Appendices* (1892), 108-114; Alfred C. Haddon cited in Charles G. Seligman, *The Melanesians of British New Guinea* (Cambridge: Cambridge University Press, 1910), 19-20; Bronislaw Malinowski, *The Dynamics of Cultural Change* (New Haven: Yale University Press, 1989), 76; Nigel D. Oram, "The Hula in Port Moresby," *Oceania* 39: 1 (1968), 1. I choose to use the popular appellation *Hula*, as the term *Vula'a* is only used by Hula people speaking among themselves (Dennis Kana, Personal Discussion with Graeme Humble, Pacific Adventist University, 9 October 2011).

2   *Pariwa* is a sago and banana pudding saturated in coconut cream.

3   Hula village is the largest of the Hula villages, often referred to as "the big village." Other villages in the Hula people group are Irupara, Alewai, Kaparoko, Alukuni and Viriolo.

4   J W Lindt, *Picturesque New Guinea* (London: Longmans, Green, and Co, 1887), 60, 113; Nigel D. Oram, *The Mystery of Guise: Conflict between Missionaries, Colonial Administrators and Foreign Traders During the British New Guinea Protectorate: A Biography of Reginald Edward Guise* [Microform], ed. Pacific Manuscripts Bureau (Canberra: Australian National University, 1998), 2.

5   Deborah Van Heekeren, "The Kila Wari Stories: Framing a Life and Preserving a Cosmology," in *Telling Pacific Lives: Prisms of Process*, ed. Brij V Lal and Vicki Luker (Canberra: Australian National University E Press, 2008), 22.

It was within this context of feuding and intertribal warfare that the Hula came into contact with traders, adventurers, missionaries and colonists in the early 1870s. Needless to say, such traditional lifestyle practices were not consistent with either the values of Christianity or those of the British colonisers.

In subsequent years various aspects of Hula culture, such as intertribal raiding, headhunting and cannibalism were outlawed by the British administrators, and with military backup, they eventually disappeared. The LMS missionaries attempted to introduce functional substitutes for these customs. For example, they saw "the gentlemanly game of cricket as a substitute for fighting ... [in order] to sublimate native aggression,"[6] and as a replacement for other practices also deemed inappropriate by the missionaries, such as lewd dancing.[7] Elsewhere in the Pacific alternative functional substitutes for the notorious Solomon Island headhunting canoes had been suggested such as canoe racing, fishing and trade.[8]

At first glance, the necessity of such interventions appears to be fairly innocuous. However, while not negating either the British jurisprudence or the Christian basis for the eradication of these traditions, the demise of these violent cultural practices had unforeseen effects on the Hula self image and their identity as a people. The relatively sudden extraction of cultural practices left a vacuum which I contend lead to a crisis of identity and subsequent marginalisation of these coastal peoples.

Paul Hiebert reminds us that culture is an integrated system of values and behaviour,[9] while Bronislaw Malinowski states that there is an organic connection between cultural components and their disappearance can result in "the destruction of the whole cultural identity of a people."[10] Commenting on the effect of the suppression of headhunting by the colonial administration in the Solomon Islands, Alan Tippett observed that "all these multitudinous activities were undoubtedly tied together in a configuration, and the loss of the central feature did cause disintegration of the way of life."[11] The anthropologist Murray Groves writing about the Hula people's nearby Motu neighbours, noted that while there was conflict between the Motu and the

---

6 Allan Jones, "Hula Since 1850: A Social History of a Papua New Guinea Village" (Advanced Diploma in Teaching Thesis, Salisbury College of Advanced Education, 1974), 183.

7 Frank Lenwood, *Pastels from the Pacific* (London: Humphrey Milford, Oxford University Press, 1917), 166-167; Oram, *Mystery of Guise*, 5-6.

8 W H R Rivers, ed. *Essays on the Depopulation of Melanesia* (Cambridge: The University Press, 1922), 109.

9 Paul G Hiebert, *Anthropological Insights for Missionaries* (Grand Rapids: Baker, 1985), 30.

10 Malinowski, *Dynamics of Cultural Change*, 53.

11 Alan R Tippett, *Solomon Islands Christianity: A Study in Growth and Obstruction* (South Pasadena: William Carey, 1967), 153.

missionaries over the Motu dance, "in that conflict, not merely dancing, but the entire social system ... [was] at stake."[12]

While Groves recorded that the Papuan cultures were confronted by Christianity, he also admitted that the ultimate demise of traditional indigenous practices, particularly in the urban areas, was due to "changing economic, political and social circumstances."[13] Regardless of the agent of change, this does not detract from the fact that the survival of the coastal cultures was threatened. Malinowski likened this deprivation effect to the mutilation of a society, whereby the excised practice had satisfied an essential need in society.[14]

In the case of the Hula, the practices of intertribal raiding and headhunting provided opportunities for identity formation and leadership development, through the emergence of courageous warriors who were necessary for a community's survival, a situation which Tippett also observed in the neighbouring Solomon Islands.[15] In Papua, the warrior's status and identity were "displayed [in] chest markings related to their exploits in the headhunt," and "sometimes special tattoos could be added to the girl if her father, brother, or a close relative killed another man."[16]

Consequently "the prohibition on all forms of murder meant that social status could no longer be established by headhunting. The tattooing that publicised a man's reputation as a fearless headhunter therefore became redundant, leading to the eventual demise of the art of Hula body tattooing."[17] In reality this meant that warriors had lost their identity and their ability to develop as leaders, while younger men had to seek alternative ways of establishing their identity. The value of young women as potential brides was diminished, as their male relative's tattoos were now merely a historical record frozen in time on their aging skin, with no possibility of additional tattoo marks to signify their prowess as headhunters.

The social status attached to the tattoos, their meaning and their concomitant "bragging rights" were not valued in the new society introduced by the colonists or the mission. Thus the removal of a central cultural value in Hula culture contributed

---

12 Murray Groves, *The Motu of Papua: Tradition in a Time of Change* (Vancouver: Webzines of Vancouver, 2011), 41.
13 Groves, *Motu of Papua*, 44.
14 Malinowski, *Dynamics of Cultural Change*, 53.
15 Alan R Tippett, *Introduction to Missiology* (Pasadena: William Carey, 1987), 201.
16 Lars F Krutak, *The Tattooing Arts of Tribal Women* (London: Bennett and Bloom/Desert Hearts, 2007), 101-102.
17 Graeme J Humble, "Contextualization and Christianity in a Changing Traditional Society: Maritime Redemptive Analogies in Hula Culture" (Doctor of Intercultural Studies diss., Fuller Theological Seminary, 2012), 40.

to their marginalisation and the subsequent diminution of their identity as a people. Diversification was necessary if they were to retain their sense of honour and identity as a people.

Forging a Renewed Identity

The Hula people repositioned themselves in the new society by the diversification and redevelopment of their skills in at least three distinct ways. First, they capitalised on other traditional strengths. The Hula were (and are) known as people of the sea, and in particular, as expert fishermen and for their proficiency in building and racing canoes. Second, they adapted to the new colonial system through education and provided key personnel to help service the colonial infrastructure. Third, they accepted the teachings of the missionaries and became participants in spreading the gospel.

Capitalising on Traditional Strengths

In pre-colonial times, when the southeast trade wind, *avurigo* (known in Motu as *laurabada*) whisked their Motu neighbours westwards on *hiri* trading expeditions in their *lakatoi* sailing canoes, the Hula fishermen also sailed west on *vili* fishing expeditions to supply the remaining Motu villagers with fresh fish.[18] On their return, the Motu traders rewarded the Hula fishermen with copious supplies of sago and canoe logs.

The Hula people enjoy a long reputation as successful fishermen. In 1880 Octavius Stone observed that "the Hula natives are great fishers with nets, which are exceedingly well made, and are superior even to those used by the Motu tribe;"[19] they were referred to as the "fishing village of Hula;"[20] while in 1888, Samuel McFarlane observing the Hula, wrote that "fish are mostly caught by nets, though often by line and hook, and sometimes by spear. I have seen them catching sardines in a very ingenious way."[21] In 1915, in a rather casual observation, Malinowski wrote "in a boat [at Port Moresby] we went near the *lakatois* from Hula – strange picture of home life on the water; they offered me a fish."[22] Referring to the period 1907-1941, Allan Jones observed that "as

---

18 Kenneth Stanley Inglis and Nigel D Oram, *John Moresby and Port Moresby: A Centenary View* (Port Moresby: Government Printer, 1974), 11.

19 Octavius C Stone, *A Few Months in New Guinea* (London: Sampson Low, Marston, Searle and Rivington, 1880), 140.

20 Lindt, *Picturesque New Guinea*, 100.

21 S McFarlane, *Among the Cannibals of New Guinea: Being the Story of the New Guinea Mission of the London Missionary Society* (Philadelphia: Presbyterian Board of Publication and Sabbath School Work, 1888), 122.

22 Bronislaw Malinowski, *A Diary in the Strict Sense of the Term* (Stanford: Stanford University Press, 1989), 76.

in the past, fishing continued to be the key to Hula's economy."[23]

The Hula built both on their historical relationship with the Motu people and also on their reputation as expert fishermen, by supplying fish to the burgeoning colonial town of Port Moresby that was developing on the Motu lands. There are records of Hula fish hawkers in Port Moresby in the late 1920s, where they continued to provide fish into the 1930s for the local Motu people during their *hiri* expeditions;[24] they fished for the Australian soldiers and provided canoes and nets for the military forces during World War Two.[25] The reputation of the Hula people as expert fishermen has continued from colonial times until the present – they are acknowledged as "seasoned seafarers whose quest to fish the oceans see no boundaries."[26] Weather permitting, every day the Hula fishermen continue to provide a wide variety of fish to the Koki and Malaoro markets in the city of Port Moresby. The Hula people, by capitalising on a traditional strength, were able to extend it to the extent that their identity has been established as major suppliers of seafood for the capital city of Papua New Guinea.

The Hula people are also known for their proficiency in building and racing canoes. Their canoe construction skills seem to have developed since colonisation, as the Keapara people provided the Hula with canoes in exchange for fish.[27] Their canoe-making skills are now so highly developed and valued that they are often contracted by opposing teams to construct their racing canoes.[28] The Hula people also have a long heritage of passionate canoe racing. An early reference to their appetite for canoe racing appeared in a 1947 Australian Patrol Report, where a brawl between the competitors was also recorded.[29] More recently a prominent PNG travel journalist reported that "the Hula people are champions in this sport [of canoe racing – not brawling!],"[30] while at the prestigious 2011 canoe races at Ela Beach in Port Moresby, the first five places in the A-grade race were won by the Hula canoes.[31] Once again,

23 Jones, *Hula Since 1850*, 197.

24 Nigel D Oram, *Colonial Town to Melanesian City: Port Moresby 1884-1974* (Canberra: Australian National University Press, 1976), 56-57.

25 Oram, *Colonial Town*, 67.

26 David Nalu, "The Viriolo Magic: A Fishing Village Outside Port Moresby," *Paradise: Inflight with Air Niugini* 6 (2010), 41.

27 Seligman, *Melanesians*, 20.

28 Dean Ani, Telephone Conversation with Graeme Humble, Port Moresby, 26 September 2011; Kala Aufa, Interview by Graeme Humble, Ela Beach, PNG, 16 September 2011.

29 S G Middleton, "Central (Abau) Patrol Report No. 7, of 1946/47," *Papua New Guinea Patrol Reports*, 1947.

30 Skerah, "Hula: A Perfect Getaway," *Paradise: Inflight with Air Niugini* 6 (2009), 43.

31 Miria Ikupu, "2011 Hiri Moale Festival Program - Vanagi/Canoe Race," *Post-Courier* (September 15, 2011), 32, 49; Kila Nao "Stanley Shows His Class," *Post-Courier* (September 20, 2011), 35.

by focusing on a traditional area of expertise, the Hula people have established an enviable reputation that has endowed them with a national identity and the status of being the most skilled skippers and builders of racing outrigger canoes along the Papuan coastline.

Colonial Adaptation

The second major way that the Hula people were repositioned in the new society was through the incorporation of its values through education. An LMS mission station and school was established at Hula by Polynesian missionaries in the 1870s.[32] This "unwittingly opened the doors to usher in a new culture with its accompanying technology."[33] By 1916 it was reported that "from Port Moresby to Hula the work of the Mission is strong all along the coast, the schools being efficient and reasonably advanced."[34] Nigel Oram contended that the Hula were "one of the best-educated village populations in Papua"[35] due to their advantageous situation of having "the mission head station in the village which provided them with greater educational opportunities."[36] By the early twentieth century, the Hula school was considered to have the best teachers and resources.[37]

Education in the mission schools equipped the students with the necessary skills that enabled them to adapt to the colonial system and thus become eligible to be absorbed into its workforce. By so doing, they provided key personnel to help service the colonial infrastructure. Hula men were conscripted during World War Two, and were also employed as clerks and craftsmen.[38] However, they generally refused menial jobs and preferred to remain unemployed than take on employment as unskilled labourers.[39] The Hula school is attributed with educating "many Papuans [who were at the time of writing] in prominent public life" as well as training a number of teachers, pastors and nurses.[40]

32 Ron Crocombe and Marjorie Crocombe, eds. *Polynesian Missions in Melanesia: From Samoa, Cook Islands and Tonga to Papua New Guinea and New Caledonia* (Suva: Institute of Pacific Studies, University of the South Pacific, 1982), 132.
33 Jones, *Hula Since 1850*, 87.
34 Lenwood, *Pastels*, 167.
35 Nigel D Oram, "The London Missionary Society Pastorate and the Emergence of an Educated Elite in Papua". *The Journal of Pacific History* 6 (1971), 128.
36 Oram, *Culture Change*, 271.
37 Jones, *Hula Since 1850*, 196-197.
38 Oram, *Hula in Port Moresby*, 5.
39 Oram, *Culture Change*, 260.
40 Oram, *Culture Change*, 262.

Although the Hula had lost part of their identity due to the clash between their traditional values and those of both the colonial powers and the mission, both were also instrumental in assisting the Hula to regain a new sense of worth and identity through the provision of education and a diversity of employment opportunities. The traditional leadership development lost due to the prohibition of intertribal raiding had been replaced by inculturation for leadership in the new colonial context. A number of their people, educated in the Hula school, had been propelled from the margins into diverse leadership positions in both the PNG public and private sectors.

Mission Mobilisation

A third major way that aided the Hula people in forging a renewed identity was their acceptance of the teachings of the LMS missionaries and becoming active participants in promulgating the gospel message. The pioneer Polynesian teachers Taria and Gativaro and their wives introduced Christianity to the Hula in 1876-1877.[41] Despite the massacre of four Polynesian mission teachers and their families by a jealous neighbouring village in 1881,[42] the Hula people "were the first people in the area to adopt Christianity with enthusiasm and to welcome new ways."[43] By 1918 every activity in the village revolved around church life, to the extent that the LMS claimed that the entire village had been converted to Christianity.[44]

Church-related activities replaced the traditional feasts. Jones notes that "the pastor and the deacons became increasingly important in the social structure of the Hula, and with the election of three deacons from each clan, these men were, in effect, the heirs of the pre-contact hereditary clan leaders, church and custom had combined."[45] During the course of time, many Hula men were engaged in leadership positions in the church, where they were variously referred to as teachers, pastors and later, as ministers.

Nigel Oram traced four generations from five Hula families into the 1960s and found that between them they had produced 21 pastors.[46] There is no doubt that many

---

41 Crocombe and Crocombe, *Polynesian Missions*, 132.

42 Garry W Trompf, *Melanesian Religion* (Cambridge: Cambridge University Press, 1991), 147; Garry W. Trompf, *Payback: The Logic of Retribution in Melanesian Religions* (Cambridge: Cambridge University Press, 1994), 294; Oram, *Mystery of Guise*, 7.

43 Oram, *Culture Change*, 254.

44 Jones, *Hula Since 1850*, 181.

45 Jones, *Hula Since 1850*, 182-183.

46 Oram, *London Missionary Society Pastorate*, 117.

more names could be added in the intervening 50 years if this longitudinal study was extended. He also noted that pastor's children featured prominently among the first intake of students at the University of Papua New Guinea – 14 out of the 58 students were pastor's children.[47]

Although traditional leadership patterns and training were disrupted when tribal warfare and feuding were outlawed, the activities of the church that permeated Hula social life provided an alternative viable functional substitute for leadership development both within the church and the wider community. This effect has continued to rebound through subsequent generations, some of who have emerged as part of the educated elite in PNG.

The Village of Two Sabbaths

The previous sections of this chapter have focused on the impact of the LMS on the Hula people and its assistance in "demarginalising" them. In this section I evaluate the contemporary practice of Hula Christianity within the seaside community of Irupara from another perspective. This village hosts congregations from both the United[48] and Seventh-day Adventist (SDA) Churches. It has been called the "village of two Sabbaths" where the United Church worships on Sunday while the Seventh-day Adventists worship on Saturday.[49] It is within this context that I will trace how this somewhat marginalised and insignificant coastal village has contributed to the proclamation of the gospel and ministry across PNG in diverse contexts, albeit from an SDA viewpoint.

It has been regularly stated that half the population of Irupara village are members of the United Church while the other half worships at the SDA Church.[50] My Irupara informants claim that the current situation is probably more like two-thirds of the village professes allegiance to the seventh-day Sabbath, although this has not always been the case. "The LMS remained the sole Christian entity in the Hula area until 1944 when Lui Oli, having become a Seventh-day Adventist in 1938, returned to his home village of Irupara and established a Seventh-day Adventist congregation."[51]

---

47 Oram, *London Missionary Society Pastorate*, 117.

48 The United Church formed in 1968 when the London Missionary Society, Presbyterian and Methodist Churches merged.

49 Michael Goddard and Deborah Van Heekeren, "United and Divided: Christianity, Tradition and Identity in Two South Coast Papua New Guinea Villages," *Australian Journal of Anthropology* 14:2 (2003), 153; Deborah Van Heekeren, "Celebrating Mother's Day in a Melanesian Village Church," *Pacific Studies* 26:3/4 (2003), 35.

50 Oram, *London Missionary Society Pastorate*, 119.

51 Humble, *Contextualization and Christianity*, 45; Lui Oli, "Saved from a Spear for Service: My Story in Papua New Guinea," *Journal of Pacific Adventist History* 6:1 (2006), 28.

Over the intervening years, the congregation has experienced growth through what Donald McGavran called the homogenous unit principle.⁵² While this principle has been critiqued in the missiological literature, the Irupara context was, and continues, as a monocultural homogenous unit where the Hula language predominates, and was thus eminently suited for evangelism and church growth via this methodology.⁵³ On a return visit to Irupara in 1950, Lui Oli shared his faith "in the homes ... [of his] family members, [where] five brothers, three sisters and ... [his] parents" joined the growing congregation.⁵⁴

A visitor to the Irupara SDA church would note its similarity to many other Papuan Adventist churches. Its architecture, order of service, content and worship style generally reflects a traditional Adventist format and is reflective of the influence of Western missionaries on indigenous leaders at training schools elsewhere in Papua. In a similar commentary, the anthropologist Eva Keller remarked that Adventist church services in Madagascar, "follow a ritualised procedure."⁵⁵ While the church and its services are valued by attendees, a visiting anthropologist's first impression on attending an Irupara service was "its tendency to replicate the structures of Western Christianity," and that her "experience as an invited guest on the occasion of a particular Saturday service resembled the hyper-reality of a visit to Movie World or Las Vegas."⁵⁶

A recent missiological study of Adventism in Irupara has suggested a more contextual approach, whereby elements of Hula culture are employed as conduits for the gospel.⁵⁷ It is recognised that it may take a period of time to transition to an expression of Christianity that is dynamically informed by Hula cultural insights, and more will be said about these insights later in this chapter. While not incorporating all aspects of Hula culture, the adaptation of appropriate aspects of Hula culture into church life will validate Hula culture as a legitimate conduit for conveying the gospel in an Adventist context, while at the same time enhancing the image of Adventism as being able to

---

52 The homogenous unit principle proposed that it should not be mandatory for people to cross either racial, linguistic or class barriers in order to hear the gospel. See Donald A McGavran, *Understanding Church Growth* (Grand Rapids: Eerdmans, 1980), 198.

53 See Rene C Padilla, "The Unity of the Church and the Homogeneous Unit Principle," *International Bulletin of Missionary Research* 6:1 (1982), 29; John R.W. Stott, "Twenty Years after Lausanne: Some Personal Reflections," *International Bulletin of Missionary Research* 19:2 (1995), 50.

54 Oli, *Saved from a Spear*, 28.

55 Eva Keller, "Towards Complete Clarity: Bible Study among Seventh-Day Adventists in Madagascar," *Ethnos: Journal of Anthropology* 69:1 (2004), 95.

56 Deborah Van Heekeren, "Being Hula: The Appropriation of Christianity in Irupara Village, Papua New Guinea" (PhD diss., University of Newcastle, 2004), 142.

57 Humble, *Contextualization and Christianity*.

be expressed in any culture. Such a transition will help restore the dignity of the Hula people within their culture, thus minimising their marginalisation as a people and as a congregation of believers.

Case Study: The Oli Family

Mention has already been made of the pioneering work of Pastor Lui Oli in establishing the SDA Church in Irupara. This village has contributed many skilled and professional people who dedicated their lives in cross-cultural mission throughout the diverse people groups of PNG, across a variety of Adventist ministries; for example, mission carpenter David Kana (now retired); mission treasurer, Kila Rupa Kila (deceased), who served in various places in PNG and in Vanuatu (Kila was my first contact with a person from Irupara, when he worked in Goroka, PNG); current lay ministry workers: the bursar of Pacific Adventist University (PAU), Mrs Karo Matainaho; PAU telephone technician, Gereana Kila; PAU security manager, Reuben Alu; PAU nurse, June Wala, daughter of Pastor Wala Iga, the fish caller;[58] PAU cabinet-maker, Naime Kana; Central Province SDA education director, Peter Iga; teacher, Alu Laka and the list continues. The contribution of these mission workers is disproportionate to the size of the village (estimated to be between 500 and 600),[59] and corroborates, as Oram noted, the value of education, mission schools and church communities in producing Christian leaders.[60]

However, as this case study focuses on the Oli family, I noted earlier that Lui Oli's five brothers and three sisters, together with their parents Oli Veleke and Manu Raka accepted the Adventist faith shared with them by Lui.[61] Many became mission workers. Lui himself became a prominent leader in the SDA Church throughout PNG, holding a number of highly responsible administrative positions.[62] In his retirement at Irupara, he planted an Adventist congregation in Hula village. Lui died in 2010, aged 87, but his legacy continues.

Lui's son, Walter Oli, followed in his father's footsteps and until his retirement served as an Adventist pastor and senior administrator in various places across

---

58 Deborah Van Heekeren, "Naming, Mnemonics, and the Poetics of Knowing in Vula'a Oral Traditions," *Oceania* 84:2 (2014), 173.

59 Deborah Van Heekeren, "Giving-for-Being: The Religion of Vula'a Exchange," in *Religious Dynamics in the Pacific*, ed. Françoise Douaire-Marsaudon and Gabriele Weichart (Lexington: pacific-credo, 2010), 176.

60 Oram, *Culture Change*, 262.

61 Oli, *Saved from a Spear*, 28.

62 Oli, *Saved from a Spear*.

PNG. Another of Lui's sons, Gideon Oli, held the positions of Secretary of the Prime Minister's Department of Papua New Guinea and the Chief of Staff of the Office of the Prime Minister. He is a high-ranking official. In his current role he was tasked with the creation of the Office of the National Events Secretariat where he is involved in frequent international high-level negotiations and organising state visits for foreign dignitaries to the PNG government. Gideon lives in Port Moresby with his Australian wife Helen.

Lui's nephew, Peter Oli (son of Lui's brother Alama Oli), is an Adventist pastor and has served in various senior administrative roles across PNG. Another brother, Joseph Oli (now deceased), trained for ministry and also took up numerous senior church administrative responsibilities across the nation. Reuben Alu, the PAU security manager previously mentioned, is the son of one of Lui's sisters, Arena, who joined Lui in his faith. Another nephew, Stephen Oli (son of Lui's brother Veleke), is considered the eldest descendant in the chiefly Oli line and as such, is the "gatekeeper" for major happenings in Irupara village. He began his career as a lawyer, later becoming a magistrate, has served as the Deputy Chief Magistrate of PNG, and is currently a National Judge in the PNG judicial system.

The genogram of the Oli family is complex with multifaceted interrelationships through intermarriage with other Irupara families. However, as incomplete and complex as it is, this descriptive genealogy serves to demonstrate how a once marginalised and apparently insignificant beachside village has contributed to the proclamation of the gospel through strong pastoral and administrative leadership, while also providing a wider service to the diverse communities scattered across the 800 or more people groups in modern PNG.[63]

Restoring Hula Dignity via a Christian Contextual Approach

I have already alluded to a recent missiological study of Adventism in Irupara which recommended a contextual approach, where familiar elements of Hula culture are used to convey gospel content and meaning.[64] The use of such an approach has the potential to not only convey gospel truths, but also has the capacity to restore the dignity of the Hula people. Hula culture, although battered by colonisation, modernity and missionisation, still remains as a viable and living mechanism with the capacity to

---

63 Jackson Rannells and Elesallah Matatier, *PNG Fact Book: A One-Volume Encyclopedia of Papua New Guinea* (Melbourne: Oxford University Press, 2005), 94-95.

64 Humble, *Contextualization and Christianity*.

deliver spiritual truths in a unique Hula way. The Hula people do not need to rely on Western forms of communicating the gospel.

The study employed an ethnographic approach in an attempt to discover cultural bridges within Hula culture for the communication of gospel truths. More specifically, it attempted to locate redemptive analogies, similar to the approach that Don Richardson discovered with his famous *Peace Child*[65] experience in Western New Guinea.[66] From this investigation a number of potential responses were suggested, namely, the adoption of the redemptive analogy methodology into the life and outreach of the church, and the attendant adjustments that will need to be made to accommodate such a change. This methodology is not only inclusive of Hula-specific contextual expressions of Christianity, but also has the potential to restore Hula dignity and guarded cultural pride in sharing the gospel in the Hula way.

Because the Hula are a maritime people, the research focused on the discovery of elements specific to their seaside context that were capable of being used as tools for the conveyance of the gospel. Six redemptive analogies were identified, each relating to the ocean as an integrative motif. None of the analogies were as stunning as Richardson's *Peach Child*, but each of them was significant. Les Henson cautions against focusing merely on the discovery of momentous redemptive analogies at the risk of missing out on the "many illustrations and seemingly insignificant cultural bridges that might have made a real difference to … the communication of the gospel."[67]

Of the six redemptive analogies, three were related to matters of survival in a maritime context (the sea as a provider, cleanser and protector); two focused on Hula identity associated with the sea activities (fishing and canoe-racing); and one involved community relationships (sea-house building). It is not possible to delineate all six redemptive analogies: these can be accessed in detail in the research results.[68] The two maritime redemptive analogies that focus on Hula identity will suffice as illustrations of the process and value of such an approach that assists in "demarginalising" Hula culture and restoring it to a place of dignity as a cultural courier of the good news.

---

65 See Don Richardson, *Peace Child* (Ventura: Regal, 1974).
66 Western New Guinea is now the Indonesian province of Papua, not to be confused with PNG's southern coastline which is also known as Papua.
67 Les Henson, "Cultural Bridges and Momina Traditional Religion: Seeking a Key Redemptive Analogy and Missing Many Cultural Bridges," *Evangelical Missions Quarterly* 44:2 (2008), 224.
68 See Humble, *Contextualization and Christianity*.

Fishers of Men: A Redemptive Analogy

Fishing is such an integral part of Hula identity that one of my informants stated that "fish is the life in here,"[69] while another responded that "our bank is the sea, and our gold is fish."[70] Yet another claimed that "you can never be a good Hula man if you don't know this art of fishing,"[71] and a retiree insisted that fish was "the lifeblood of Irupara."[72] In the earlier section "Capitalising on Traditional Strengths" I have previously described the role and value of fish and fishing in Hula life. The Hula are a sea-loving people who draw their identity from their expertise as fishermen.

The Hula people's reputation and appetite for fishing resonates with the fishing events recorded in the gospels, and as such provides a powerful redemptive analogy for the Hula. Jesus' early disciples were fishermen: the brothers Andrew and Peter, as were the partner brothers James and John (Jn 4:18-22). They identified as fishermen to the extent that after the bitter disappointment of Jesus' crucifixion they elected to go on a fishing expedition, initiated by Peter (Jn 21:2-3). It had been Jesus' intention in calling the disciples that they would serve redemptively as "fishers of men" (Mt 4:19). Despite reversion to their former occupation as fishermen, Jesus provided for their needs with a huge haul of fish followed by a fish barbecue on the beach, after which he recommissioned Peter and the disciples as fishers of men – to reach out and gather people for his kingdom (Jn 21:15-17).

The use of the "fishers of men" analogy in church life and outreach touches on a number of themes pertinent to Hula life. Further, within a fishing context, it restores sharing the gospel story of Jesus Christ to its rightful place as the centre for mission. It also demonstrates the potential that Jesus saw in a marginalised group of diverse, dispirited fishermen.

Winning the Race: A Redemptive Analogy

The sea plays an integral part in forming and maintaining Hula identity. As well as fishing, both canoe racing and canoe making have been vital to Hula self-perceptions of their identity. One of the Hula men I interviewed stated that the Hula are "experts in canoe making and canoe racing"[73] and another declared, "canoe making is one of the important things in Hula life at Irupara. If we do not make canoes we cannot go

---

69 Iga Iga, Interview by Graeme Humble, Irupara, 28 April 2011.
70 Dennis Kana, Interview by Graeme Humble, Irupara, 27 April 2011.
71 Reuben Alu, Focus Group Interview by Graeme Humble, Pacific Adventist University, 13 June 2010.
72 Guma Kalawa, Interview by Graeme Humble, Irupara, 02 May 2011.
73 Wari Kila, Interview by Graeme Humble, Pacific Adventist University, 03 December 2009.

out fishing."[74] An Irupara fisherman assured me that the Hula have a "big name" (or reputation) among the villages of the southern Papuan coast – both for their canoe racing skills and their competence in constructing race-winning outrigger canoes.[75] The value of canoe construction and canoe racing to the self-identity of the sea-loving Hula people has been previously described in the earlier section "Capitalising on Traditional Strengths."

Hula canoe races correspond in a redemptive manner with the footraces mentioned in the New Testament (NT).[76] While the race locations differ (sea as opposed to land), the details of the NT race context provide striking parallels to the Hula ocean races, such as the exhortation for participants to minimise performance hindrances; encouragement to persevere and not to veer off course and so on. Competitors are reminded that while the race may be difficult, persistence will result in a finished race that will be rewarded with a winner's crown from Jesus, the race judge (Heb 12:3; 2 Tim 4:7-8).

Application of the "winning the race" redemptive analogy to Hula personal life and church ministry will use a much enjoyed Hula pastime to connect with spiritual truth. It focuses the participants on Jesus, who sustains their faith and rewards those who complete the race. While race participants may feel marginalised due to some form of impediment, the analogy places Jesus at the centre of mission both during the course of the race and at the finishing line. It provides hope for anybody, regardless of their diverse backgrounds, to enter and win the race, regardless of the number of other competitors. In this it is similar to Hula village races, where every race contestant is valued and receives a prize.[77]

Implications for the Wider Church

The expression of Christianity in a culturally specific form that is relevant to the Hula people carries with it implications for the wider church. While "communicators must take seriously both the local contexts and the global theological themes that Christians face everywhere," they should also remember that local churches are part of the wider body of Christ.[78]

---

74 Kinikava Alama, Interview by Graeme Humble, Irupara, 02 May 2011.
75 James Kokoha, Interview by Graeme Humble, Irupara, 29 November 2009.
76 See 1 Corinthians 9:24-27, Hebrews 12:1-13 and 2 Timothy 4:6-8.
77 Raka Pala, Interview by Graeme Humble, Hula, 08 December 2009.
78 R Daniel Shaw and Charles E. Van Engen, *Communicating God's Word in a Complex World: God's Truth or Hocus Pocus?* (Lanham: Rowman and Littlefield, 2003), 217.

As the Hula Christians endeavour to relate Christianity to their local context, others outside that context may ask "Could heresy result from an overzealous contextualised apologetic?"[79] This is a vital consideration for all contextual theologies, and in this instance for the Hula, because their local contextualised expression of the gospel may be misperceived or misconstrued by outsiders. In seeking to develop a Christian Hula ethnotheology, they must at the same time avoid developing an isolating ethnic theology.[80] Consequently, the local church will need to interact freely with churches in nearby language groups and also with its denomination's administrative leaders in order to avoid potential misunderstandings or isolation from the wider church.

As the Hula people interpret Scripture from their perspective, their diverse insights can inform the wider church – their "local theological perspective ... contributes to global understanding."[81] Particular Hula insights can serve to enrich the global church by contributing towards a metatheology of "different theologies, each a partial understanding of the truth in a certain context," while at the same time, in a reciprocal relationship, the Hula church can remain informed theologically on a wider perspective through its association with the global church.[82] This will assist "the Hula church progress beyond an introspective localised Hula theology to a biblical theology in the Hula context that connects to the regional and global church family."[83]

Conclusion

This case study which traces the context of the Hula people's initial loss of identity and subsequent reinvention of their identity, particularly as it relates to the place of contextual theologising in that process, holds potential insights for mission within all people groups, regardless of their ethnicity.

---

79 See Alister McGrath, *Heresy: A History of Defending the Truth* (London: Society for Promoting Christian Knowledge, 2009); Brad Gill, "Review of Heresy: A History of Defending the Truth," *International Journal of Frontier Missiology* 26:1 (2010), 54.

80 See Charles H Kraft, "Toward a Christian Ethnotheology," in *God, Man and Church Growth*, ed. Alan R Tippett (Grand Rapids: Eerdmans, 1973), 109-126; Charles H. Kraft, *Christianity in Culture: A Study in Dynamic Biblical Theologizing in Cross-Cultural Perspective* (Maryknoll: Orbis, 1979), 292.

81 R Daniel Shaw, "A Samo Theology of Mediumship: A Case Study of Local Theologizing and Global Reflection," in *Religion and Retributive Logic: Essays in Honour of Professor Garry W. Trompf*, ed. Carole M. Cusack and Christopher Hartney (Leiden: E.J. Brill, 2010), 66.

82 Paul G Hiebert, "Metatheology: The Next Step Beyond Contextualization," in *Anthropological Reflections on Missiological Issues*, ed. Paul G. Hiebert (Grand Rapids: Baker, 1994), 101.

83 Humble, *Contextualization and Christianity*, 190; Shaw and Van Engen, *Communicating God's Word*, 217; R Daniel Shaw, "Beyond Contextualization: Toward a Twenty-First-Century Model for Enabling Mission," *International Bulletin of Missionary Research* 34:4 (2010), 212.

While the course of history has seen dramatic changes impact Hula culture since colonisation, it is impossible to reverse the process. It must also be recognised that Hula culture is not static. It is a dynamic entity that continues to respond to the ever-changing context in which the Hula people live. This is also true for most cultures. Nearly all have been affected by the forces of globalisation. All face issues that disrupt their traditional identities to some extent, while many rebound, as did the Hula, with identities that have adapted to their new contexts. A Christian contextual approach to theologising that engages indigenous themes carries the potential to assist not only the Hula, but to mutually assist all disenfranchised cultures in re-establishing their dignity and identity.

As I researched Hula culture, I was also conscious of the danger of conflation or the concertinaing of time that could lead to the fusing of Hula traditional culture and Hula current culture into one entity. Consequently, the current study has outlined the various processes of change that marginalised and affected the Hula culture.

On the other hand, the Hula research has highlighted the resilience of Hula culture by discussing the intrinsic abilities it possesses to restore its dignity via a Christian contextual approach. However, in order to do this, the Hula people, and all peoples who opt to use such an approach, will need to be mindful of their heritage and its associated cultural values. They will need to accept the challenge to intentionally utilise their own indigenous cultural redemptive analogies for ministry and mission. In this way they will assist their people in avoiding further marginalisation and the total loss of their identity by absorption into the facelessness of globalisation. Their dignity will be maintained and reinforced as it engages the gospel in culturally specific ways that not only minister to their own people, but also provide a diversity of theological insights that strengthen the wider church. Consequently, such an approach to contextual theologising is instructive for all mission practitioners and missiologists as they engage in mission beyond Melanesia toward the horizons of Asia and beyond.

18. "God called us here for a reason" Karen and Chin Baptist Churches in Victoria: Mission from the Margins of a Diaspora Community

Darren Cronshaw, Stacey Wilson and Meewon Yang, with Ner Dah, Si Khia, Arohn Kuung, and Japheth Lian

Approximately 8,500 Karen and Chin Baptists have migrated to Australia over recent years. These people groups of Burma (Myanmar) are majority Christian but many are displaced because of intense persecution and injustice. Karen and Chin migrants have settled mainly in Melbourne, Perth, Brisbane and Sydney and formed approximately fifty new congregations. This is a significant source of growth for Australian Baptists, and presents new opportunities and challenges for ministry in a multicultural society. This action research project collaboratively researches the life and ministry of Karen and Chin Baptist Churches in Australia with interviews of key church leaders. It affirms the strengths of Karen and Chin congregations, and identifies their challenges and opportunities for mission. The project particularly explores implications for broader mission beyond Karen and Chin migrants and implications for ministry of second-generation Chin and Karen young people. It is a case study of mission to, through and by and beyond the margins of a Diaspora community.

Introduction

Westgate was one of the first Baptist churches to welcome refugees from Burma (Myanmar). The first Karen family to arrive was Reginald and Pau Lu Lu and four children. In January 2000 Melbourne hosted the Baptist World Alliance (BWA) Congress. Rev Arohn and Esther Kuung, a Chin couple, escaped persecution by travelling through the Indian-Burma border, adopted identities and joined the India delegation to BWA. They sought and were granted asylum as refugees fleeing persecution. Rev Kuung is now pastor of Chin Baptist Church meeting in Sunshine. Both the Karen and the Chin people had experienced the persecution of the Burmese military and given the nature of the tension and the uncertainty of life, one could understand that different groups might have had uncertainty about the extent to which they could trust other groups. But on 14 February 2000, Reginald and Pau Lu Lu welcomed Arohm and Esther into their very small home. In fact, a double bed and wardrobe filled the space in the small shed that was to become their home for five months. For those looking on, what was so powerful was the sense that those who had received hospitality were quick to show hospitality to the newest group of refugees, despite they themselves living in a small crowded space with very little resources. When Arohm and Esther moved on to their own home, they also continued to house and help other refugees as they arrived.[1]

Over recent years, approximately 8,500 Baptists born in Burma have migrated to Australia, a significant portion of the 21,761 people born in Burma who are now living in Australia.[2] The diaspora from Burma are majority Christian but many are displaced because of intense persecution and injustice. Diaspora migrants from Burma have settled mainly in Melbourne, Perth, Brisbane and Sydney and formed fifty-three new Baptist congregations, including twenty-four in Victoria (and thirteen in Queensland, nine in Western Australia and six in New South Wales). Victoria has 5,608 people born in Burma, of whom 2,280 (40.7%) are Baptist and 4,117 (72.5%) have arrived in the decade 2001-2011.[3] This is a significant source of growth for Australian and specifically Victorian Baptists, and more continue to arrive every year, which presents new opportunities and challenges for ministry in a multicultural society.

This project researches the life and ministry of Diaspora Karen and Chin Baptist Churches in Victoria, Australia, and identifies challenges and opportunities for mission. We particularly want to explore implications for broader mission beyond Karen and Chin migrants and ministry for second-generation young people. Methodologically, this is an action research project – a cooperative project of Baptist Union staff and Karen and Chin Baptist church leaders researching together how to best foster mission.[4] This chapter is an initial overview, to be followed up with further

---

1   Newton Daddow, Swinburne University Chaplain, Interview with Darren Cronshaw, 10 September 2014.

2   These are 2011 census figures, which also show 23,230 who identify as Burmese, presumably including those born in other countries and refugee camps on the Thai-Burma border or in India and Malaysia. State of Victoria, *Victorian Community Profiles: 2011 Census, Burma (Republic of the Union of Myanmar)-Born* (Melbourne: Office of Multicultural Affairs and Citizenship, 2013), http://www.multicultural.vic.gov.au/images/stories/documents/2013/Censusfactsheetscommunityprofiles/commprofiles/49-burma.pdf, Table 1.

3   Victoria, *2011 Census, Burma*, Table 4 and 9.

4   Enoch Wan suggests action research is an ideal methodology for investigating how to motivate and empower diaspora peoples for mission. Enoch Wan, ed. *Diaspora Missiology: Theory, Methodology, and Practice* (Portland, OR: Institute of Diaspora Studies of USA, 2014), 107-115.

exploration of mission to, through, with, by and beyond Karen and Chin people as a Diaspora community.

Karen and Chin Victorian Baptist churches

Victorian Baptist Churches have embraced multiculturalism for many years. There are 70 Baptist congregations in Victoria that worship in Languages Other Than English (LOTE), representing around a third of all Baptist Churches. The two largest language groups are Chin and Karen from a Burmese background. Chin and Karen congregations usually meet within their own language groups but it is becoming more common for them to join in partnerships or have combined membership with English-speaking churches; especially for the Karen congregations. Many also attend the English-speaking services as well; especially the young people who are becoming more fluent in English.

Karen and Chin refugees come from a context of intense religious and political persecution and suffering and human rights violations, and often have had to wait in Thailand or Malaysia for 5-10 years seeking asylum.[5] Refugees from Burma to Australia are mostly affiliated with Baptist as a denomination, due to the strong missionary work of Baptists in Burma. When they arrive, they often quickly establish a connection with a Baptist congregation, but they – especially Chin groups – also embrace people from different denominational backgrounds. The main congregational marker and attraction is the tribal language group rather than a particular denomination. The Burmese community is spread throughout Melbourne (west and outer-east), Geelong and Bendigo in fourteen Chin Baptist congregations, nine Karen Baptist congregations, and three Kareni congregations that network with BUV.

Some Karen and Chin describe their settlement in Australia as temporary, until they are able to return to Burma. They see themselves as a pilgrim people, in exile in Australia in a country of safety and freedom, in stark contrast to the persecution and political instability in Burma.[6] But most want to make a permanent new home in Australia. Church leaders are aware of the need for helping their people engage productively with their adopted community, just as Jeremiah encouraged the Hebrew exiles to build houses, plant gardens, grow families and, 'seek the welfare of the city

---

5 Ner Dah, "Reading the Kingdom Teaching of Matthew from the Context of Myanmar" (DTheol thesis, MCD, 2009), 12, 25-41; Ronald Lal Din Suah, Pastor Melbourne Mizo Church, Interview with Darren Cronshaw and Stacey Wilson, Camberwell, 15 August 2014.

6 Rev Za Tuah Ngur, Australia Zotung Church Pastor, Interview with Meewon Yang, Footscray, 29 August 2014.

where I have sent you into exile, and pray to the Lord on its behalf, for in its welfare you will find your welfare' (Jeremiah 29:5-7). Rev Ronald Lal Din Suah, pastor of Melbourne Mizo Church in Ringwood, commented: 'We came with a little box and try to grow a little flower without roots in this country, but with that attitude it does not lead us far.' He encourages his congregation to make the most of opportunities to get to know their community and neighbours, to learn English and seize opportunities, and to be open to the mission they as a church are called to. Rev Suah often says: 'God has called us here for a reason.'[7]

Diaspora missiologists express the conviction that people are moving across the world as part of God's purposes.[8] To advance the Kingdom of God, therefore, will mean being aware of these diaspora movements and identifying and empowering their mission potential. What, then, is the missional purpose for the Karen and Chin diaspora in Victoria and Australia, what are the associated challenges and opportunities, and what do they need to fulfill the next stage of their missional potential?

Mission from the margins of a Diaspora community

In examining the challenges of the Diaspora from Burma it would be easy to stay focused on the troubled political situation in Myanmar, or unpack the amazing stories of resilience among Karen and Chin, or develop strategies for assisting new arrivals, but the focus of this chapter is empowering Karen and Chin for cooperating with the mission of God. Diaspora missiology differentiate mission to a diaspora group, mission through a diaspora group, and mission by and beyond them.[9]

Mission to Karen and Chin

Karen and Chin are majority Christian groups, so mission to them is not necessarily primarily evangelism but hospitality, advocacy and community development.

One way of supporting Karen and Chin is through BUV's Refugee Airfare/Assistance Loans Scheme (RAALS). This Humanitarian program offers a no interest loan for a family to pay for the air ticket of a relative who has obtained a visa to re-settle in Australia. It has enabled over 500 refugees to Australia over 10 years. It has extended to car loans as transport is a crucial need for refugee families.

---

7   Suah, Interview.
8   J D Payne, *Scattered to Gather: Embracing the Global Trend of Diaspora* (Manila: LifeChange, 2010), http://www.jdpayne.org/wp-content/uploads/2010/10/Scattered-to-Gather.pdf; Wan, *Diaspora Missiology*.
9   Wan, *Diaspora Missiology*.

Another expression of care and mission to Karen and Chin people is sponsoring them for a Global Special Humanitarian Programme Visa (sub-class 202). Croydon Hills Baptist Church people have sponsored ten Karen families. Margaret Moran, as Karen Support Worker, is appreciated as a strong advocate of the Karen people. She and others from the church have written many letters of support for newcomers in their applications for no interest loans and airfare assistance, and for supporting families in Visa applications. Croydon Hills Karen and English-speaking congregations together run The Hope Project, which has directed more than $120,000 in material aid and supports visiting team projects to Karen in the Thai-Burma border refugee camps for people from their own and neighbouring Australian churches.[10]

Back in Australia, employment opportunities are a vital need for Karen and Chin migrants. The challenges of language and varying levels of English language literacy make seeking and obtaining work difficult. There is also a sense of responsibility to provide for not just for family in Australia, but also financially support family members in refugee camps or back in Burma. A variety of social enterprises are currently being explored in partnership with the BUV, Baptcare and local churches.

"Eleven41" cleaning is one of the first social enterprise businesses. Bendigo Baptist Community Care was concerned by the isolation of many Karen, particularly the women. In consultation with local leaders and Bendigo businesses, they helped start the business in 2011. It offers training and support as well as employment, and has grown with domestic and commercial contracts to 12 part-time Karen cleaning staff. Through the Victorian Training Group they teach a Certificate II in Cleaning Operations and Certificate III in Asset Maintenance, which has trained 100 Karen. Tha Wah states:

> It is not just that they get a little bit of work, the good thing is that they get a certificate so that later, in say five years when they understand more English they can apply for jobs. They will be more confident about themselves; they have experience, and a qualification. That is a very good thing.[11]

With the help of start-up capital from, Baptcare, 'Eleven41' social enterprises are now also in Werribee, Croydon Hills and Cloverdale. The name comes from Luke 11:41 where Jesus tells the Pharisees of the day that in order to be clean on the inside we must be generous to the poor.

---

10 http://thehopeproject.org.au/about/about-history
11 Tha Wah, Church secretary, Bendigo Baptist Karen Congregation, Interview with Stacey Wilson, 14 August 2014.

One of the biggest challenges of integrating into Australian culture and employment is learning English. Table 1 shows 40.5% of Burma-born people in Victoria who speak another language report speaking English well or very well, but 37.1% say they speak English not well and 11.2% not at all.

Table 1: Proficiency in Spoken English, Burma (Republic of the Union of Myanmar)-born, Victoria: 2011, 2006[12]

Proficiency in spoken English (Self-assessment)	Persons	% of total
Speaks English only	541	9.7
Speaks other language and speaks English:		
Very well	758	13.5
Well	1,514	27.0
Not well	2,079	37.1
Not at all	627	11.2
Not stated	86	1.5
Victoria	5,605	100.0

Rev Dr Si Khia of Lautu Chin Baptist Church reports that with limited English skills, church members cannot acquire qualifications to get jobs even though they have practical work skills such as electrical works or carpentry.[13] Helping Burma-born people learn English is thus a major need. But newcomers also need assistance with government agencies, housing, employment, driving instruction and business development.[14]

Westgate Baptist Community (Yarraville) congregation has supported the Burmese community, both Chin and Karen, for over 20 years. They host a Karen congregation and Baptcare provided a grant to assist Westgate in running two Chin Refugee Women's groups, operating since 2008. These groups focus on all forms of integration, including language, literacy, accessing services and using public transport. Stresses for Karen and Chin include culture shock, financial pressure, anxiety, loneliness, isolation and facing materialism. A supportive community of peers as well as expert help is important for supporting new arrivals.[15]

---

12 Victoria, 2011 *Census, Burma*, Table 7.

13 Si Khia, Pastor Lautu Chin Baptist Church, Survey Questionnaire, 5 June 2014.

14 Cf. Randy G Mitchell, "Case Study 8: Diaspora Missions in Minnesota: Local Actions with Global Implications," in *Diaspora Missiology: Theory, Methodology, and Practice.*, ed. Enoch Wan (Portland, OR: Institute of Diaspora Studies of USA, 2014), 294-297.

15 Robert D Schweitzer et al, "Mental health of newly arrived Burmese refugees in Australia: Contributions of pre-migration and post-migration experience," *Australian and New Zealand Journal of Psychiatry* 45 (2011), 299-307.

English-speaking churches relate to Karen and Chin churches in different ways – from renting space to partnering to being one church with two congregations. English-speaking congregations can help and support Chin and Karen churches with friendship and space for worship, and with practical help with English and access to community services. But there is also a lot that English congregations can learn from Karen and Chin. They often have a resilience and perseverance in their faith that is inspiring. No doubt there are aspects of understanding God and Scripture that will be a Karen and Chin gift to the Baptist Union of Victoria and broader Australian church. Margaret Moran says that the Karen congregation at Croydon Hills has enriched the broader congregation immeasurably, and has helped them develop a cultural diversity that is also attractive to many other cultures.[16] Partnership with culturally diverse congregations can be mutually enriching.

There is a limitation in the prepositions of diaspora missiology as "to", "through", or "by and beyond", since a fourth important preposition "with" is missing. Perhaps this is implied, but practicing mission "with" one another – Karen and Chin churches with English-speaking and other Australian churches – is a critical underlying value for mission in a post-colonial context.

Sharing and learning from one another has been Westgate's experience. Their early impacts of the life of refugees from Burma continue to reverberate today. Mid 2014, a group of 12 Westgaters took a trip to Kuala Lumpur to share education and health resources through teachers and nurses in Chin programs in refugee area of KL. Their reports on their return pointed to the transformation in their own lives as they reflected on the faithfulness, courage and resilience of the refugees still languishing in really difficult circumstances.[17]

Mission through Karen and Chin

Some Australian churches have a mission to and alongside Karen and Chin people, but the biggest opportunity for Karen and Chin ministry is through Karen and Chin churches, and this begins with welcome and hospitality. Rev Dr Marc Chan, Multicultural Inclusion worker for BUV, reported that Western Australia Chin Christian Church joined the Baptist Union in October 2007 and grew from 20 to 500 adults in seven years:

---

16 Margaret Moran, Karen Support Worker, Interview with Meewon Yang, Croydon Hills, 3 August 2014.
17 Daddow, Interview.

They have a very simple but effective way of helping new migrants/refugees. Through their contact with government agencies, they receive notice of new families migrating to WA. The Church leadership assigns a family to take care of the newcomers. They will be met at the airport and taken to pre-arranged/emergency accommodation. The Church will give the new arrivals a love offering to help them during the first week of their arrival here. The family looking after them will organise for the Pastor to visit the new family and they will have a welcoming service at their home. They will be provided transport to attend Church on Sundays and also for other group meetings until they can provide their own. They are also helped to access government agencies to help them settle here. This has been instrumental in more than 95% of those newcomers staying in the Church.[18]

Most if not all Karen and Chin congregations likewise help newcomers with logistics and offer a caring community. With a strong communal ethic, Chin and Karen churches naturally are strong on caring for one another through crises and difficulties – whether the challenges of newly arriving or the stresses of unemployment, illness or grief of death.[19]

The hospitality and activities of church life meets social and other needs for many Karen and Chin new arrivals. As well as multiple worship services, Karen and Chin churches organise sport, conferences, music and socials. A two day Baptist Union of Victoria Multicultural Soccer Tournament has been staged three times, with eight to fifteen church teams including Chin and Karen. Chin Baptist churches in Victoria invite guest speakers to teach and encourage Chin churches, and also share the Gospel with the general Chin community. For example, Victorian Chin Baptist Church (VCBC) in Mooroolbark ran a week Summer camp in January 2013. They invited an American guest speaker who addressed culture and spirituality. The Chin Christian Council in Australia (CCCA) hosted a youth leaders' conference in January 2014, which similarly focused on culture and Christianity. Perth Karen Baptist Church has been sponsoring well-known music bands who perform secular music and as part of their concerts share their faith journey and invite those attending to come to Church on Sunday where they will also be performing – this time songs with Christian messages. Karen and Chin churches have ministered to the wider Burmese community by inviting them together to celebrating important cultural events and customs.

---

18   Marc Chan, "Burmese in Western Australia – 2014," unpublished report.
19   Suah, Interview; Ronald Lal Din Suah, "Relational Justice in Hosea," PhD thesis, Ridley College, 2014.

> Karen and Chin peoples often want to maintain and celebrate their culture. Karen leaders Rev Moo Hei and Jordan Pe comment that the main focus of Croydon Hills congregation includes spiritual growth, welcoming others and language and culture maintenance: Growing together spiritually; deepening our relationship with God and at the same time, providing a safe place for the Karen community as they settle into their new life. We feel God has brought us here for a purpose; for a new future. We need not to forget the living God and always be grateful for Australia which has been like coming into the Promised Land. We are God's ambassadors here to welcome others and protect culture, language and worship.[20]

They hold a sense of destiny about being a diaspora people in Australia: "God has brought us here for a purpose; for a new future." They take pride in welcoming new arrivals and helping protect their culture, and that is part of their mission and the reason they are here in Australia. However, mission cannot be limited to preserving their culture and is not just about mission to Karen and Chin.

Many of the pastors interviewed expressed a deep sense of God's divine purpose in the Burmese diaspora to Australia. Their coming to this place is part of God's plan for their lives and as such they are excited to live out God's kingdom here. Tha Wah, Karen Church Secretary at Bendigo, said:

> A lot of people say this is our God who sends us here … after we came here we got a lot of people support, we never knew each other before and now we are very good to each other. People who believe and understand God think it is just amazing that God prepared them to leave that situation step by step.[21]

Tribalism, women's roles, second-generation and leaders

One of the ongoing challenges of mission through Karen and Chin people is their linguistic and cultural diversity, but this is also an opportunity for profound witness and growth. Karen have one main uniform language, Sgaw Karen; and Pwo Karen, spoken by the Newport congregation. Chin peoples are far more complex. Of the fourteen groups in Melbourne, there are nine different language groups: Falam, Haka, Lautu, Matu, Mizo, Teddim, Zo, Zomi, Zotung.[22] Different Karen and Chin, even

---

20 Moo Hei, Pastor Croydon Hills Baptist Karen congregation, and Jordan Pe, elder, Interview with Meewon Yang, Croydon Hills, 3 August 2014.

21 Wah, Interview.

22 Karen Pastors Network, Focus Group with Meewon Yang and Stacey Wilson, Anglesea, 30 August 2014.

when they share the same language, come from or through different countries, refugee camps and churches. Church members are inherently fragile in relationships with each other and their churches. Thus leaders are not interested in presenting challenging issues that may threaten or disrupt their hard work in building community. This helps explain the commitment of the churches to meet together, for worship but also for community support. Chin and Karen leaders also appreciate support from BUV in leadership training, and in hosting them together despite sub-cultural and language differences.[23]

Apart from tribal differences, there are also differences of expectation with gender roles. Karen and Chin women in Australia are exposed to more egalitarian relationships, work opportunities, theological education and church leadership. This encourages women to embrace a more active place in church life, but goes against cultural norms. Pastor Pancha Tintuep shares her hope to share a vision for women contributing alongside men in church and society, in Australia and Burma:

> In the church I am sharing how important men and women are in the eyes of God, and how we are both valued by God. Don't see [women] as human sees but see as God's people, all made in God's image. ... I want to go back and encourage lots of women in what they can do. No one can stop what they can do if God permitted them, then they can do anything.[24]

The shift in the roles and opportunities available for women can be challenging for families and church communities, but is also an opportunity for empowering women alongside men for mission.

Another big challenge of mission through Karen and Chin is the second generation of migrants. Of 5,607 Burma-born people living in Victoria in 2011, 1,742 (31%) are aged 0-25 and another 1,271 (22.7%) are aged 26-34; a very young population. The Burma-born population has less 0-4 and 5-9 year olds proportionately than the Victorian population, about the same 10-14 year olds, and then spiking with significantly more of every five-year bracket from 15 to 39.[25] Of all Burma-born people in Victoria, 63.3% are a couple family with children (compared to 47.1% in Australia's population) and

---

23 Barnden, Email.

24 Pancha Tintuep, Pastor Zotung Baptist Church, Interview with Meewon Yang and Stacey Wilson, Camberwell, 25 August 2014; cf. Lee Cheng Koh, Pranee Liamputtong and Rae Walker, "Burmese refugee young women navigating parental expectations and resettlement," *Journal of Family Studies* 19:3 (Dec 2013), 297-305.

25 Victoria, *2011 Census, Burma*, Table 6.

11.6% are one-parent families (compared to 10.6%).[26] The needs for youth, young adult ministry and young families ministries among Karen and Chin churches is high.

Apart from the numbers of young people in Karen and Chin churches, there are challenging dynamics for second-generation migrants. Chin and Karen parents and elders are eager to maintain their culture and way of doing things. The Karen Pastors Network recalls a common statement from their community that echoes this concern: "If you have lost your language you have lost your identity."[27] This is a challenge for Karen and Chin churches as they try to maintain their cultural identity, but without isolating themselves and alienating their children who want to learn English and adapt to local/Western culture with different gender roles, parenting styles, expressions of respect and career expectations.

There is a hope that the second generation can make the most of education and opportunities in Australia, but also use that to give wider expression to the strengths and gifts of Chin and Karen cultures. Rev Saw Ner Dah describes the importance of helping the second generation to maintain a connection to their cultural roots: "If you put all colours together that will be a messy colour but if you have red colour and your own colour, then you can mix with others you can be helpful and creative with your own identity."[28]

Rev Suah acknowledges that if they do well with their next generation, the church will continue; and if not, the church may decline. He wants to start a second service for his youth group in English, but older members and leaders see this as a threat and compromise to young people not learning Mizo language. Unfortunately the young people do not currently understand church in their dialect, and in future years are more likely not to understand.[29]

Yet Karen and Chin migrants hold out great hope for their children and what they may be able to achieve. Pancha Tintuep comments: "My thoughts and my ideas will not be the same as my daughters when they grow up. But I have lots of hope, how after ten years, how our children will turn out. These kids will lead the church and I am excited."[30]

---

26   Victoria, *2011 Census, Burma*, Table 27.
27   Karen Pastors, Focus Group.
28   Saw Ner Dah, Survey questionnaire.
29   Suah, Interview.
30   Tintuep, Interview.

It is important to develop pathways for leadership development and opportunity through Karen and Chin churches, and this can be supported by Karen and Chin networks and by the Baptist Union. A strategic question is how can emerging leaders be identified and developed?

Pastoral leadership is one of the leadership challenges. Some congregations have struggled to find suitable leadership. For example, Karen Pastors in Burma can only be ordained if they are over 40, married to someone with theological training and have children. In most situations only ordained people can preside over communion, baptism and benediction. Churches commonly get into conflict over leadership issues. TransFormation is an initiative run at Whitley College – the Baptist Theological College. The course provides theological education at a level suitable for those with limited English. More than 500 students have attended the course over the last ten years, and the majority of these have been Burmese. The BUV has raised funds for scholarships, and the course has provided an important bridge into the Union's life. It has also been a means of developing a pathway towards ordination for four Burmese pastors.

Thus tribalism, women's roles, second generation continuity and leadership development are some of the challenges for Karen and Chin churches in Australia, but there are also huge needs in Myanmar. The primary way Karen and Chin churches understand and practice mission is by supporting churches, missionaries and students back in Burma. For example, Mizo Christian Fellowship in Croydon supports four missionaries and two college students who work in Burma in rural mission areas, often reaching out to neighbouring non-Christian groups.[31] Rev Thomas Mung commented that mission is broad but Chin churches tend to focus on their home country:

> Our only focus until now for us has been to support local people to do mission in our home country. This may be the case as a result of the lack of both vision and money. We are more concerned about our own people who are suffering under a bad political and governing system.[32]

There is a lot to focus on as Karen and Chin cooperate with God in mission through them to their own people in Australia. Their migration to Australia is still relatively new – in most cases less than ten years. An immediate concern is to take care of those

---

31 Suah, Interview.

32 Rev Thomas Mung, Pastor Chin Christian Church Melbourne, Interview with Meewon Yang, Footscray, 29 August 2014.

coming here from refugee camps, Malaysia and India. They are also concerned about those who remain in their homeland and frequently provide for their needs. Churches in Australia are constantly being asked for donations from those in Burma. Individual members "here in the lucky country" are expected to financially support families, churches and missionaries "back home." This is part of "mission through" Karen and Chin and keeps a connection with a needy mission area, but also puts pressure on local church finances, particularly financial support of the pastor.[33] It also potentially limits the vision for local and global mission that reaches beyond their own cultural group(s).

Mission by and beyond Karen and Chin

Mission for Diaspora groups involves mission "to" people who come to our context, mission "through" them to their own people here and abroad, but also mission by and beyond them – to other cultural groups in their neighbourhoods and for mission globally. Mission by and beyond Karen and Chin people happens as they engage in cross-cultural mission themselves.

There is a growing interest among Chin and Karen churches for the witness through them to their new adopted community. Even when their English is limited, Karen and Chin believers often see their way-of-life and their work as a witness to Christ. Many are eager to learn how to appropriately witness to neighbours. They see this as part of the purpose God has brought them to Australia. While it is challenging for them to adapt and they still feel very strong links to their homelands, this sense of purpose gives then hope. Rev Ronald Lal Din Suah said: "When we come here, many people think that God is leading us, using the 'primitive' people to preach to the 'civilized' people … if we think that way it helps our mission work, it gives us more meaning."[34] At this time the needs of their own people are great and most of their energy and effort is going into their community ministry. However they look forward to a time when they are able to broaden their mission. Lung Ceu reflected: "Our hope for the future to be able to work in Australia, but at the moment we are very very small, and really need to look after our people first. But this is what we hope for."[35] They recognise the mission field they now live among in Australia and look forward to the ways that God may use them here.

---

33 Chris Barnden, Email to Darren Cronshaw and Meewon Yang, 1 September 2014.
34 Suah, Interview.
35 Lung Ceu, Advisor (deacon), Australia Zophei Chin Baptist Church, Interview with Stacey Wilson, August 2014.

The youth pastor of Victorian Chin Baptist Church in Mooroolbark ran an innovative outreach event a few years ago – a Burmese cultural evening with food and entertainment, widely advertised throughout the community, showcasing Chin culture and making contact with hundreds of Australian neighbours. This event was helpful for celebrating Chin culture among Chin young people but it also helped the church to connect with its broader community and helped the community to understand Chin culture and faith.

As well as local outreach, as Karen and Chin churches mature, they want to develop as mission-sending churches. We need principles for training and commissioning Karen and Chin believers for mission beyond their own cultural groups. Diaspora missiology involves a multi-dimensional approach; from and to every nation and not merely from the West to the rest. In God's economy, migrants are often able to reach other cultures that Westerners are less able to connect with, thus functioning as "bridge peoples." Payne is optimistic about the mission potential of migrants, refugees and students. He uses the acronym REPS to discuss how to Reach, Equip, Partner and Send. Mobilising a migrant group for mission may involve sending missionaries back to their own people, but it may also involve sending them to other cultural contexts.[36]

For Karen and Chin churches in Victoria, it feels like early days and most new migrants are focused on settling rather than thinking about going overseas again. In 10-15 years time pastors hope they will be able to send some of their young people, and hope to see some committed to mission work in mission or Asia but they do not feel they are yet in that position.[37] There are four Mizo missionary couples from India working with the Baptist mission Global Interaction in Asia.[38] There are not yet many (or perhaps any) missionaries from Australian Karen and Chin churches serving overseas. Many people support Karen or Chin missionaries in Myanmar, but not yet their own missionaries from here to other countries.

Saw Ner Dah embodies the passion for mission by and beyond diaspora groups from Burma. He describes how Myanmar Baptist Convention (MBC) aims to grow in holistic mission and engage in international mission.[39] He also challenges the churches to move beyond being defensive and inward looking and to be open, inclusive

---

36 J D Payne, *Strangers Next Door: Immigration, Migration and Mission* (Downers Grove, IL: InterVarsity Press, 2012); reviewed by Darren Cronshaw, in *Mission Studies* 31 (2014), 467-468.

37 Suah, Interview.

38 Barnden, Interview.

39 Dah, "Reading the Kingdom Teaching," 49.

communities.⁴⁰ From his reading of Matthew and Kingdom ethics, his conclusions include a call to holistic mission beyond themselves:

> We need to maintain the vision of inviting all to follow Jesus, even though the natural tendency is to hide away for survival and draw the boundaries more clearly against the enemy. … We need to continue to care for the displaced, the imprisoned, the hungry, the ill, the homeless, the refugees and those whose hope is being smashed, for in this we are caring for Christ himself and being the salt and light of the gospel.⁴¹

Leadership and mission training

There is a lot that the broader Australian church can learn from Karen and Chin churches, but Karen and Chin churches may also be able to learn from others in the broader church about cross-cultural mission – both to faithfully witness to their new Aussie neighbours, and to mobilise and send missionaries to other contexts.

Many Chin and Karen local church lay leaders come from a rural background and out of need are thrust into leadership in Australian churches. This is a positive trend for their inclusion and experience. They also, however, need training and resourcing for their new roles.⁴² Karen and Chin churches welcome input on leadership and teamwork. BUV training days for Karen and Chin leaders have covered topics such as leadership in multicultural Australia, hearing about migrant experiences and successful stories, Duty of Care, Financial Management, building broader Burmese community networks and celebrating diversity and unity. BUV also hosts Karen and Chin Pastors' Network meetings that function as a peer-support group over a meal sharing stories and resources, especially about spirituality, advocacy and social enterprise. Apart from the value of learning, bringing these leaders together in one place is powerful for mutual encouragement.

Another critical area of training that needs development is training for mission. Karen and Chin churches in Victoria are often strong in community and highly committed to worshipping together, usually multiple times a week, but this limits opportunities for developing English language proficiency and building relationships with other Australians. Karen and Chin believers need a new understanding of what mission is – in terms of their own local witness and not just sending finance for others to do

---

40 Dah, "Reading the Kingdom Teaching," 302.
41 Dah, "Reading the Kingdom Teaching," 303.
42 Barnden, Interview.

mission.[43] Pastors encourage people to live their lives as Christians and if people ask, say and show you are a Christian. Language continues to be a big barrier for many. Pastors hope the second generation will grow in local mission awareness and practice better. Because BUV Karen and Chin leaders' training days and pastors' networks are eagerly welcomed and are so well attended, these gatherings may be ideal forums to continue to explore how best to foster mission to, through, and by and beyond the margins of this Diaspora community.

Conclusion

Karen and Chin Baptist churches in Victoria are still young and face many challenges – helping find work for the unemployed, helping newcomers adapt to the new environment and cultures, negotiating a relationship with English-speaking churches, navigating role expectations for pastors and leaders including women, and watching the second generation being attracted to things other than church. However, these churches are growing and demonstrating tenacity in faith and have a lot to teach other established Australian churches. Is this part of the purpose of their migration to Australia? Or do they also have a role in cooperating with God in reaching not just their own people but other Australians of diverse cultures.

Rev Suah says he has a sense of destiny that God has sent them here, because God has something for them to do. It is not just Burmese politics, action of UNHCR or leftover Karma punishment or reward, but relocation to Australia is part of God's purpose. The Western world is declining in Christianity. He shares a sense of destiny with a growing number of other Chin and Karen leaders that "God is sending us back to evangelise Australia, to evangelise the West who evangelised us" and that is part of why "God has called us here for a reason."[44]

---

43 Barnden, Interview.
44 Suah, Interview.

19. A Korean Woman: A Marginal Perspective for a Multicultural Society

Pauline Kim van Dalen

I am a Korean New Zealand woman living in New Zealand as a migrant for the past 13 years. My gender and socio economic background while living in Korea and my marriage to a person with a heritage of more than two cultures living in New Zealand have created much complexity and given me multi-layered marginal experiences. As society is increasingly growing in diversity my experience is shared by many but is yet to be given true voice and appreciated for its contribution. To reflect upon my multi-layered marginal experiences theologically in order to offer what I hope will be a helpful perspective I use Korean-American theologian Jung young Lee's framework of "in-between," "in-both," and "in-beyond."

Searching for identity is everywhere. From the second half of the twentieth century until today we have seen certain social groups reclaiming their identity from the negative and stigmatised one granted them by dominant systems, culture and nations.[1] Instead of accepting an inferior identity placed by others upon them, through "growing and sharing consciousness" they define their own identity as individuals and as a community.[2] Thus to rectify past and current injustice, listening to the lived-experiences becomes crucial. Jung Ha Kim, an Asian-American theologian has put it this way:

> To a person or community in need of recovering a sense of subjectivity due mainly to historical erasure, invisibility, and constant misinterpretation, self-reflections and autobiographies are viable means of reclaiming wholeness, rather than producing privacy.[3]

In searching for my identity as a first generation Korean-New Zealander, I have

---

1   Large scale political movements like class movements, disability movements, ethnic movements, feminist movements, gay and lesbian movements, and post-colonial movements have taken place in the latter part of 20th century.

2   This is called identity politics. Jenny Plane Te Paa , "Theology Education? Identity Politics and Theological Education," in *Anglican Theological Review* 90:2 (2008), 224.

3   Jung Ha Kim, "But Who Do You Say That I Am?" (Matt 16:15): A Churched Korean American Woman's Autobiographical Inquiry," in *Journeys at the Margin: Toward an Autobiographical Theology in American-Asian Perspective*, ed Peter G. Phan and Jung Young Lee (Minnesota: Liturgical Press, 1999), 111.

found much resonance with Asian-American marginality experiences. Many Asian-American theologians find autobiographical or narrative theology fitting because the stories of people become their source of theology. According to David Ng, an Asian-American theologian, social, historical and cultural contexts are lenses through which we interpret our faith and the Bible.[4]

In 1995 Jung Young Lee, a Korean-American theologian published a book called *Marginality: The Key to Multicultural Theology* drawing from his own and other Asian-American stories. He defines three places people who are caught up in two cultures live: in-between, in-both and in-beyond. A person caught up "in-between" two antagonistic worlds experiences many negative traits. The contemporary attempt to find positive qualities of that marginal space is termed "in-both." An attempt to view marginality holistically beyond the negative and positive is called "in-beyond."

Korean migrant history in New Zealand is only about 25 years old, while Korean American immigration history is nearly 120 years old. Political refugees, students and labourers made up Korean immigration to America while New Zealand has operated a "filtering" system, accepting highly educated Korean professionals or affluent investors into the country. Mindful of this context, in this chapter I will explore my autobiography using Lee's in-between, in-both and in-beyond frame in order to offer theological reflection which might benefit the wider community in the land I call "home."

My story

> My theology is not just a story of my life. It is the story of my faith journey in the world. It is my story of how God formed me, nurtures me, guides me, loves me, allows me to age, and will end my life… It is my story of seeking to understand how God acts in my life and in the lives of those who are part of my life…Theology is certainly autobiographical, because I alone can tell my faith story.[5]

My experience of multiple-faceted marginalisation has been challenging and painful, but simultaneously, freeing. My story is a microcosm of many others' stories, which is a part of global history. Yet I am encouraged to believe that my story holds unique value in a sense that no other but I can tell my story and this forms my theology and

---

4   David Ng, "A Path of Concentric Circles: Toward an Autobiographical Theology of Community," in *Journeys*, ed. Peter Phan and Jung Young Lee, 86.

5   Jung Young Lee, *Marginality: the Key to Multicultural Theology* (Minneapolis: Fortress, 1995), 7.

relationships with the divine and all others. I reflect in this space with personal stories, while being very aware of the fact that I am still on a journey of finding *who I am* as an integrated whole person and seeking true reconciliation within myself and with others. I endeavour to reflect well to offer something constructive to those who might find my perspective helpful.

A life in-between

I am a Korean woman

I am a Korean woman who grew up in South Korea. The country's history is marked by much unspeakable suffering and pain. I am married to a person from outside of my culture. I have been living in New Zealand for the past thirteen years. Together these facts add interesting aspects and complications to my life.

As a child I lived in a multi-generational home where four generations lived under the same roof: my paternal grandparents, my grandmother's mother, my parents and my father's siblings and my brother. The most treasured possession of my grandfather was a book of family genealogy which he kept in a cupboard with a lock and often cited.

My grandfather was orphaned shortly after birth during the Japanese occupation. He went to the Korean War as a young man in his mid 20s, leaving behind his wife and a newborn baby son, my father. My grandmother was born to her Korean parents and grew up in Japan until she was nine years old when the family went back to Korea when it regained its independence in 1945. Shortly after their return her father died. She was married off at a young age to relieve the burden of feeding "another mouth" in her family. My grandparents survived through the Japanese colonisation of Korea and the subsequent civil war that divided the nation into North and South but lost two children to malnutrition and illness, an experience shared by many others of their generation.

My family culture was made up of a mix of Shamanism, Buddhism and Confucianism. They balance each other and harmonise well together in Korean households.[6] I was told that my great grandfather, my paternal grandmother's father was a Feng-Shui master/diviner who advised people where to bury their dead. I remember when I was young that sometimes my grandmother called for a shaman to come and perform exorcism in our house. She also used amulets to avert evils around the house. She took

---

6   Jung Young Lee, "Shamanistic Thought and Traditional Korean Homes," in *Korea Journal* 15:11 (Nov 1975), 48.

me with her to the Buddhist temple regularly to donate offerings and do rituals, like burning incense and bowing before statues of Buddha many times. The Confucian idea of masculinity and femininity was very clear and strictly applied in our daily living. Male superiority was practised and female submission was demanded, even if the male authority was often not exercised in a healthy manner. Everyone was under this rigid hierarchical family structure at home.

My family came from a low socio-economic background. I grew up in an area of poverty which used to be called the "moon villages," since they were often on a hilltop, which gives a closer view of the moon. My grandparents moved from a rural farming community to a city during the Korean industrialisation period in early 1960s. They worked long and hard, wasting nothing because they knew starvation and devastation first-hand.

Many of our neighbours lived quite a dysfunctional life. Homes full of domestic violence, extreme financial hardship and broken family relationships, gang members, occult groups, fortune tellers and shamans were some of our neighbours. I personally knew two girls who ran away from home and became prostitutes.

My father went to the Vietnam War as a young man, survived, and came back. But life was never the same. He joined in the workforce after he came back but he found it hard to work and live a normal life and wasted all the money his parents and my mother worked hard for on huge alcohol consumption. He was a notorious member of a gang in the region. Consequently, we struggled financially to live day to day.

When it came time for me to go to university my family was not able to financially support me. There was no such thing as student allowance or a student loan available, so tuition and other expenses were normally paid by the family. My family, including the extended family tried to persuade me to go to a local university on a scholarship, but I resisted and went to a Women's University in Seoul instead.[7] They celebrated when my father's cousin, a male from a wealthy family, got accepted to a university in Seoul, but did not celebrate my achievement.

During my university years I was without food some days and struggled to even pay the bus fees worth 50 cents. Most of my classmates in university came from families of upper-middle to high class. No one struggled financially like I did. I went to classes

---

7   Ewha Womans University. It was one of the first universities established in Korea. It later became the hub of feminism in South Korea.

during the day and worked almost every night while others were busy studying for their future. As a result, my grades were poor and my health deteriorated.

As mentioned above, my father suffered from the after-war effect. I learned later that it is called Post Trauma Stress Disorder. He was hyper-vigilant because he perceived those around him as potential threat. Domestic violence and alcohol abuse were part of our daily life. I was mistreated and threatened with death as an unborn child. My mother attempted suicide shortly after my birth. When I was about nine years old she had to flee from home for her safety, so my brother and I were without our mother for almost four years. We became the target of my father's rage.

My mother came back to be with her children despite the abuse and violence. When I was sixteen years old she got stabbed in her back by my father with a butcher's knife. She could have reported him for attempted murder but chose not to. In Korea there is a thing called the "red line." Instead of a birth certificate we had a family census paper which showed the head of the household and immediate family members under him, a legally married wife and children. If the father or the head of the household had any criminal record, a red line would be crossed over his name. It meant the future of the children was doomed because they have to live as the children of the "red line" wherever they go and so experience social discrimination.

My mother wanted us to have a future so she chose not to cause any "red line" to be drawn on the family census paper. She was not equipped with any financial or relational resources to raise us up on her own. Additionally she did not want us to be the "children of a divorced woman" and suffer from another form of social discrimination. She wanted us to have a mother for she knew firsthand what it is like growing up without one. Her mother died during childbirth when she was only 5 years old. She had lived with two or more stepmothers who treated her very harshly and an apathetic father. For her children's sake, she endured day to day in living hell.

Without family status or financial security I was a vulnerable woman in Korean society. Misogyny was deeply and thoroughly embedded in the culture. Traditional sayings, proverbs, folk tales and songs and classic literature depict the Korean view of women and its attempt to stereotype and control women. For example: "Women's fate is a calabash fate" (her fate is locked into who she marries); "Women and dried Pollack need good beatings every three days" (for tenderising purpose); "Man is the ship, woman the port" (Men can come and go as they please while women wait on him); (A married woman should be) "Blind for three years, then deaf for three years, and then mute for three years"; "Educated women live troubled lives"; "Women's income is as thin as a mouse's tail"; and "Women's greatest enemy are women".

Confucian teachings on women are based on this well-known idea of "innate and fundamental female inferiority and male superiority (男尊女卑)". Therefore, a woman should obey three men in her life: firstly her father while she's unmarried; secondly her husband during marriage; and lastly her son after the husband passed away (三從之道). Even the word "peace (安)" pictures a woman inside the house, meaning peace is achieved when women stay within the boundary of their house. A deep sense of fatalism combined with Confucianism therefore imprisons women into a perpetual sense of inferiority and physical, psychological and spiritual passivity. Their existence and worth are defined by the dominant, "superior male".

Sexual purity for both unmarried and married women is considered more valuable than a woman's life. Traditionally a young widow would be forced to remain sexually loyal to her late husband for the rest of her life. If she lost her sexual purity even by force, she was expected to take her own life to save the "honour" of the family. Even for the few survivals of Sexual Slavery during World War II, this belief was applied so that many survivals either chose not to go back home, living in a third country, or lived with a buried past. I know even of recent stories of girls and women made sexually "impure" by force, who have been assaulted, but feel they have no power to resist the offender even in public places. As young girls, we were very aware of our "sexual vulnerability." We were told to take great caution not to cause any unwanted attention from men.

My experience of marginalisation as a female is therefore not just my own personal story but an inherited one. I was born female in a misogynous society into a poor dysfunctional family that lived through times when autonomy was taken away from the men in the society who in turn oppressed the lesser in power. My grandmother and my mother experienced this in far worse degrees, because colonisation and war added more difficulties to being female in Korea. They accepted it as their fate, yet with deep sorrow. My grandmother used to blame herself and believed it was her "fate" to have a son like my father so that she would have to live with it.

My mother was put on a shameful status among relatives and people around us just because of whom she was married to. I was put in the same place because of whose daughter I was. So here I was, not from a good family, and in addition considered not passive or submissive or humble enough in relation to the societal standard on femininity. I also did not have the "desired" feminine beauty. By Korean standards I was neither a "good girl," nor a "girl from a good family." Personally I denounced femininity since I perceived it to be weak and useless and masculinity abusive and violent.

I remember across my teenage years sincerely praying to God to make me into something neither female nor male. This led me to actively consider a homosexual lifestyle in my early 20's. I lost hope of marrying someone from a "normal family" because I knew very well that no normal parent would approve their son's marriage to a woman from the kind of family I came from. People in our neighbourhood wanted my father gone because of his destructive and shameful behaviour in public. I knew my father would do anything to jeopardise my marriage as means of control and he would try to gain financial benefit from it. I was ashamed of being my father's daughter. I felt shame was engraved on my forehead.

Parental consent for marriage is considered very important because "filial piety (孝道)" is at the centre of Confucianism in Korea. I married without my father's approval. Normally the parents – especially the girl's mother – prepare the wedding and the reception, but sadly I did not have that luxury. This heightened the sense of shame on my identity and my marriage. Why did I rush into marriage? I wanted to escape from the terrible misery I was in, since I felt there was no other "way out." So I made New Zealand my home.

What seemed the land of hope has turned out to be far from that, however. Jung Young Lee, in migrating from Korea to the United States, shared a similar experience. As he put it, "I was a stranger in the land where I now hold my citizenship,"[8] due to his physical makeup and culture. My physical appearance, mannerisms and body language and my broken English with a Korean accent all have become reasons for me to be placed in a "box" by others.

I am an absurd creature

Even before my life in New Zealand began, I had already been a marginal person in my homeland due to my gender and socio-economic status and the level of

---

8   Jung Young Lee, "A Life In-Between: A Korean-American Journey," *Journeys*, ed Peter G. Phan and Jung Young Lee, 39.

education I completed (an uncompleted university degree).⁹ My marriage to a person from a low socio-economic position with little education has added more layers of marginalisation to my own experience. He is also a child of a two and more-cultured marriage, struggling to find his identity and place in society. His father was a first generation migrant to New Zealand. His mother has experienced a very high degree of marginalisation in the areas of gender, finance and education. Like mine, his marginality is also an inherited one. He has never felt at home anywhere.

We had little to almost no awareness of the gulf of existing cultural difference between us before our marital life began, let alone of our both having fragmented and marginal identities. Consequently, our marriage has been marked by many, many conflicts. We have also been constantly harassed and hurt by the very people who were supposed to care for and love us. My husband has experienced intentional exclusion and aggravation at work because of my ethnicity. We have sought to belong to communities through personal relationships and church but have been met by experiences of alienation, humiliation, rejection and abuse.

After having lived in New Zealand for more than a decade, I feel I belong to neither Korea nor New Zealand. I have felt caught in-between the two worlds. To Koreans I am not Korean enough or do not have a husband who holds a high enough socio-economic position if a foreigner, thus I am never fully accepted into the community. To New Zealanders I am Korean because of my physical appearance and close tie to my culture and language which are still relatively unknown and misunderstood in this land. Most importantly, since arriving I have not achieved anything notable nor do I have any professional skills and position valued by the dominant in society. This has given me very little value or significance in the eyes of others.

Many nights I have acutely regretted having married someone from another culture and being marginalised, for it has caused so much struggle and pain. I know no one who can understand the enormity and the complexity of what I had lived through since conception in my mother's womb. Jung Young Lee's words capture the essence of some of my experience, however:

> The marginal person has to live in these two worlds, which are not only different but often antagonistic to each other. From these two worlds, I chose membership in the dominant society, but it rejects me because of my root in the other world. Hence, I want to be accepted by the world of my ancestry,

---

9   Lee, *Marginality*, 33.

but it also rejects me. I am unwanted by both worlds, yet I live in them. That is why *I am an absurd creature* [my italics].[10]

This experience of being caught in-between two worlds deprives the person of a sense of existence. Discussing a marginal person's experiences of "in-between," Jung Young Lee names it "existential nothingness," where a marginal person's existence holds value lesser than the pets or the paintings on the wall in the house where the social gatherings happen.[11] This has happened to me in public places and in regular social gatherings where no one has talked to me at all whenever we have met. An unspoken but clear message has been given that I have to talk and act like the dominant others if I want to be admitted to the group. During a period living in the South Island of New Zealand, in almost every group I went to I was the only non-white person. Every time I said "Hello" people simply walked away from me. I have learned to assimilate.

After a somewhat successful assimilation, I have tried to become part of communities big and small, including church. However, the more I move towards the centre of a group, actions to jeopardise my effort have taken place that have led me to choose either to stay in the margin or leave. After repeated experiences like this, I have become frozen, terribly anxious inside, and completely void of a sense of value and purpose in my life. This has had the same effect on my whole family, including my children. We have "shrunk" into "existential nothingness."

I learned about attachment theory in my tertiary education, which I found useful to help me reflect upon my experiences of ruptured relational bonding with others. Healthy attachment is an almost impossible task for those in the margins due to their insecure, almost invalid, sense of identity and repetitive attachment rupture experiences. My early attachment with parents or parental figures was highly insecure and this ongoing marginal experience has heightened the sense of insecurity in my relationship with others. Additionally, poverty as a form of marginality prevents people from having relationship in equality. When you have nothing to give back, no one wants to be around you long term. Economical marginality and social marginality affect each other.[12]

---

10 Lee, *Marginality*, 43-44.
11 Lee, *Marginality*, 45.
12 Lee, *Marginality*, 33.

Jung Young Lee points out that this marginalisation process generates "self-alienation."[13] American sociologist Everett Stonequist also argues that "The duality of cultures produces a "duality of personality – a divided self."[14] Another American sociologist Charles Horton Cooley discusses this internalised sense of self process through a concept called the "looking-glass self" where a person's sense of self is continuously fashioned by social interactions and the perception of others of "self" until the last breath.[15]

Yes, I have become a nuisance in my own eyes. Still, I have to live on, caught in this "in-between" space, suffering "cultural schizophrenia."[16] I endlessly swing between the two worlds like a pendulum, where I am perceived and treated differently. This shapes my split self-images.

Let me be honest

Having been "confined" in a "cell of confusion and utter loneliness" of marginalisation for many years, I have come to face my own darkness deep underneath. I have discovered my own strong drive for centrality and my desire for reputation, power and the approval of others. The meaning and value of my existence is rooted in my achievement and performance. I have vied for manipulation and control out of fear not love. I have been like an orphan restlessly wondering about seeking to find my way "home." Externally experienced evil in the form of marginality has helped me to face the very evil within myself. I see that I have the potential to exercise the centralist ideology that divides, labels and mistreats people. And I am sure I already might have done it many times.

Likewise, while Koreans may experience marginality as a minority group in other nations, they marginalise other ethnic minorities in Korea. I hear current news of racial discrimination at every level in Korea against people from other ethnic minorities. One of the contributing factors to this phenomenon I believe is the "White Idolisation" permeated in Korean society. People long to look and speak like Anglo-Americans and to fulfil the "American Dream." Women get cosmetic surgery to look like those in Hollywood movies. This internalised "white superiority" discriminates the ethnic

---

13 Lee, *Marginality*, 46.

14 Everett Stonequist, *The Marginal Man: A Study in Personality and Culture Conflict* (New York: Russell & Russell, 1965), 139.

15 Charles Horton Cooley, *Human Nature and the Social Order* (London: Transaction, 2007), 184.

16 L.C. Tsung, *The Marginal Man* (New York: Pageant, 1963), 158-159.

minorities, while venerating the "White." Colonialism still lives in the minds of people. "Second-class citizen" identity is well and alive today in Korean society. No one is free from this predicament of "the once being oppressed later becomes the oppressor."[17]

In-both

Moving with freedom

Now I turn to the positive interpretation of marginality. Jung Young Lee expresses this positive definition of marginality as "in-both." With the emerging global changes in political, economical, geographical, cultural and social areas, marginal people are identified as "in both worlds without giving up either one."[18] The marginal person can move freely in and out of the two worlds, experiencing both the negative and positive elements of marginality.

Despite the extent and depth of the heartbreaking experiences I have had as a marginal person, there has also been a thread of God's guidance and protection. My identity was inseparable from that of my family, which in my case was quite unhelpful, but then I experienced my European NZ friends accepting me for who I was, not for what family I came from. To many of them I was their first Asian friend. I began to understand that God saw me as a "part of a whole" as well as a "unique individual."

Another wonderful thing about being in the marginal space is that I can live in the both worlds simultaneously, perceiving things through two different lenses. I have had a taste of the beauty of the incarnation of Jesus who put aside what was familiar and comfortable and became something unnatural to him and chose to remain that way forever. He was fully God and fully man simultaneously. This is like taking off my nicely fitting clothes and shoes and replacing them with uncomfortably fitting clothes and shoes and every day trying to fit myself into them. I can, like Jesus, catch a glimpse of what it is like to be the other, seeing, feeling, touching, hearing, and tasting the world through the other's senses.

In-Beyond

Thus far I have discussed the multi-layered marginalisation I have experienced with both negative and positive sides. What then are the gifts from marginal persons to faith communities in this postmodern pluralistic multicultural New Zealand society?

---

17 Lee, *Marginality*, 150-151.
18 Lee, *Marginality*, 58.

Marginality in the Christian story

I have come to appreciate my personal journey of marginality, as it has liberated me gradually from the tyranny of a centralist ideology which manifests itself in many forms of oppression.[19] As I read the Bible I find resonance between it and my life, particularly as I read the story of Joseph in Genesis.

Joseph was betrayed and sold by his own brothers as a slave, living as a marginal person in a foreign land, mistreated and humiliated, falsely accused, thrown in the dungeon and finally was completely forgotten by the world. The rest is history. Through Joseph, the marginal person, God saved all the peoples in the surrounding region from famine. Ironically Joseph the marginal person also became the catalyst to fulfilling God's dream of building Israel as a nation. He lived in-between, in-both and in-beyond. What seemed initially to be the negative and painful experiences of one person's marginality proved to be for the good of many communities.[20]

Jesus came to this world as a marginal man who lived in-between, in-both and in-beyond. The pinnacle of His marginality was the crucible through which every marginal person is welcomed in His kingdom; the broken, the lame, the social outcast, the oppressed, the lowly. Through His own marginality and His friendship with marginal persons Jesus de-constructed the power hierarchy founded on centralist ideology. Marginality is inclusive. Marginality embraces vulnerability. Marginality knows long-suffering. Marginality draws God's attention and power, as Paul writes in 2 Corinthians 12:9: "But he said to me, 'My grace is sufficient for you, for my power is made perfect in weakness.' Therefore I will boast all the more gladly about my weaknesses, so that Christ's power may rest on me."

Invitation to marginality

I invite you to ponder this journey of marginality. I believe marginal people who have embraced their marginal identity with a holistic view, drawing from both the negative and the positive, have great potential in God's Kingdom. Historian Arnold Toynbee recognises the self-assertiveness and strong spirituality in such people.[21] Additionally, the ambivalence and conflicting cultural values they have learned to live

---

19 Nagano, Paul M., "A Japanese-American Pilgrimage: Theological Reflections," in *Journeys at the Margin*, ed Peter G. Phan and Jung Young Lee, 63-79.

20 Genesis 45:5-7.

21 Sang H. Lee, "Called to Be Pilgrims," in *The Korean Immigrant in America,* eds. Byong-suh Kim and Sang Hyun Lee (Montclair, NJ: AKCS, 1980), 48.

with, resolve and integrate can birth creative visions and energy which pave way to the "multi-coloured faith community." They understand within their very being the difficulties and the possibilities of diversity and so offer expertise of great value to their communities. Their divine gift of "otherness" waits for the day of full unwrapping and appreciation, however. Without long-suffering love that perseveres to uproot the "sins of prejudice" grounded in centralist ideology making full use of their contribution will not be possible. [22]

Are you willing?

To those who dare to walk on this journey of marginality and to enter the strange world of "otherness," I have some suggestions to offer for you to ponder and practice.

First, know thyself. Be diligent in finding who you are in your personal story, as a part of a family and your country's history, and as a part of global history. What has shaped and influenced you with particular ways of being, seeing and doing in the world?

Second, try to grasp with world history the rises and falls of civilizations and nations and their relationships with each other. It does not need to be in depth, but enough to understand those around you. You just need to sit and listen! Your friends from other cultures will gladly help you learn their history and culture. Most of the world's oldest civilizations have come from the Eastern region, and your friend is likely to be the very living breathing microcosm of some 3000 years old rich civilization!

Third, learn the beauty of empty space and silence. Traditional Korean paintings, music and architecture do not "fill in" the whole space. We learn that the "empty space" or "margin" is the important part of traditional Korean art and culture. The margin invites people to "creative imagination" and to appreciate the depth and meaning of the "unknown."

In silence, first you become more aware of yourself inwardly. And you become aware of another's facial expressions, body language and the atmosphere the person carries. Communication is far greater than mere busy verbal exchanges. As parents we learn this art of non-verbal and more creative and powerful ways of communication with our babies. Speaking of listening to the silenced voices Rosemary Dewerse points out the importance of "giving space" and "genuine listening" without agenda.[23]

---

22 Elizabeth Conde-Frazier, S. Steve Kang, and Gary A. Parrett, *A Many Colored Kingdom: Multicultural Dynamics for Spiritual Formation* (Grand Rapids, MI: Baker Academic, 2004), 50.
23 Rosemary Dewerse, *Breaking Calabashes: Becoming an Intercultural Community* (Unley, SA: MediaCom, 2013), 46.

Be intentional in listening and respecting voices of those of "little importance." You will be surprised by the treasure you discover in the most unlikely places. Everyone has a story to tell if you have an ear to listen.

Lastly, practice vulnerability with courage and step out of your comfort zone. I had a profound encounter with a German woman some time ago. We had never met before and happened to be at the same eating place and began to talk with each other. Our conversation ended up in World War II and its consequences on both her and my side of life – she as a descendant of a war criminal and I as a descendant of a war victim. I learned her agony and pain of living under the shadow of the mistakes the past generation made while as the new generation endeavouring not to make the same mistakes again. She learned the pain and suffering my grandparents, my parents and I have had to live with until today. We wept in each other's arms.

Sometime ago my husband asked me to sit with him in the lounge at our home. He sat next to me and looked me in the eyes and said, "On behalf of all the males who have hurt you in life including myself and your father, I want to ask you for forgiveness. Will you forgive me?" His wet eyes were speaking more volumes than the words his mouth uttered. At that very moment I knew he was making himself very vulnerable, because he had never said anything like it before. I did not know what to say. I turned to him and we held each other and wept without words. I glimpsed **hope**. Finally, I see the rise of dawn after having been in the dark for long, long time. A beginning of true reconciliation.

This is my story. What is yours?

Contributors

Emeritus Professor Anthony Gittins, an Englishman, has taught Theology and Culture at Catholic Theological Union, Chicago, since 1984. A member of the Congregation of the Holy Spirit (CSSp) he has, among other missional commitments, worked amongst the Mende of Sierra Leone, spent time in Pakistan and the Pacific, and worked for many years with the homeless in Chicago. He now travels the world as a respected teacher, speaker and retreat leader.

Dr Rosemary Dewerse was the Director of Missiology and Coordinator of Postgraduate Studies at the Uniting College for Leadership and Theology, Adelaide College of Divinity and Flinders University, in South Australia from July 2012 to the end of 2014. She, husband Roelant, and children Mereem and Jean-Luc – all Kiwis – were very grateful for the home they found there. In 2015 Rosemary began as Mission Educator with St John's Theological College in Auckland, New Zealand.

Fr Noel Connolly is Head of the Mission Studies Centre at the Columban Mission Institute in North Sydney. He is also the Head of Mission and Culture at the Broken Bay Institute and teaches missiology at the Catholic Institute of Sydney.

Dr George Wieland is the Director of Mission Research and Training at Carey Baptist College, Auckland, New Zealand, where he was formerly Lecturer in New Testament. His background includes cross-cultural mission in Brazil and church and community ministry in the UK. He and his wife Jo try to live relationally and missionally in South Auckland.

Samuel Chan founded "red" in 2010 to reach the Australian Born Asians (ABAs) of South Australia (and beyond) by partnering with the local Asian churches to strengthen and equip ABA ministries.

Kim Chan has attended a Chinese Migrant Church for over 10 years and has an interest in researching and writing about Asian culture.

Rev Dr Elizabeth Vreugdenhil has a PhD in Social Work and was a lecturer in Social Work at the University of NSW and Flinders University of SA. She is an ordained Minister in the Uniting Church in Australia and is interested in the confluence of missiology and the social sciences. She served in Maughan Uniting Church in Adelaide from 2004 to 2010. Now retired, Elizabeth works as Minister in Association at Westlakes United Church Adelaide, a combined Uniting Church and Churches of Christ congregation.

Rev Karyl Davison is team leader for the Eaton/Millbridge Community Project in Western Australia and a minister in the Uniting Church in Australia. Karyl came to this position in 2011 after roles in Lay Education for the Queensland and NSW/ACT synods of the Uniting Church. She is currently enrolled in a DMin in Missiology at the Adelaide College of Divinity.

Rev Jasmine Dow is an Anglican Priest in the Diocese of Melbourne. She is undertaking a PhD in the area of missiology and the Eucharist through the University of Divinity where she is the Morna Sturrock Research Fellow at Trinity College Theological School. Central to her understanding of faith in the Trinity is hospitality and Christian engagement in issues of social and environmental justice.

Dr Mick Pope is a meteorologist and ecotheologian with Ethos: EA Centre for Christianity and Society. He is also a life-long martial artist and currently practices and teaches Brazilian Jiu Jitsu at Renegade Mixed Martial Arts in Kensington, Victoria.

Immanuel Koks is a Tutor/lecturer/Educational Advisor for Disabilities at Laidlaw College. He is currently completing his Master of Arts in Theological Studies from Regent College in Vancouver Canada. His Thesis examines the way Jürgen Moltmann's Concept of the Trinity impacts our assurance of hope. Immanuel is married to Sarah, and lives in Henderson, Auckland, NZ.

Christy Capper is a doctoral student at Trinity Theological College, the University of Divinity. She is a member of Generation Y and has been involved in ministry to and with youth and young adults since 2005. Christy is an Ordination Candidate with the Anglican Diocese of Melbourne and currently works in pastoral care with international students in a residential environment.

Dr Lewis Jones is the Director of The Simeon Network, a network of Christians working in academia, a position he has held since 2006. Originally from the United States, Lewis came to Australia as a postdoctoral research associate in Astrophysics at The University of New South Wales in 1996, later completing a Bachelor of Divinity, before taking up his current role.

Dr T. Mark McConnell teaches theology at Laidlaw College. Originally from Scotland, prior to moving to New Zealand he pastored a Baptist church in Vancouver, Canada for ten years. His current research interests include: Trinitarian theology, mission in Western culture, secularisation, theology and culture, and theological integration.

Rev Dr Ash Barker and his wife Anji founded of Urban Neighbours of Hope (UNOH), a Churches of Christ missional order working in the poorest suburbs of Melbourne, Sydney, Auckland and Bangkok. They have recently left UNOH to begin work in Birmingham, UK. Ash did his doctoral studies under Ross Langmead's supervision at Whitley College, and his thesis has been reworked and published as *Slum Life Rising: How to Enflesh Hope within a New Urban World*.

Rev Scott Litchfield from Australia, is Cambodia Team Leader for Interserve, a multi-denominational mission organisation focusing on the Arab World and Asia. Scott and his wife Rachael have spent over 20 years in mission in Thailand, Australia and Cambodia. Scott is a Deacon with the Uniting Church in Australia.

Dr Graeme Humble is a former Dean of the School of Theology at Pacific Adventist University, Papua New Guinea (PNG), where he lectured in missiology and applied theology from 2007-2014. He has studied Melanesian missiology since 1986, having served in PNG on three separate occasions for a total of 16 years. His doctorate from Fuller Theological Seminary focused on exploring redemptive analogies as context sensitive evangelization methodologies among the maritime Hula people of PNG. He is currently the Director of Adventist Mission for the South Pacific, located in Sydney.

Rev Assoc Prof Darren Cronshaw is pastor of a multicultural congregation AuburnLife in Melbourne, Mission Catalyst – Researcher with the Baptist Union of Victoria (BUV) and Associate Professor of Missiology with Australian College of Ministries (SCD). Under Ross Langmead's supervision, Darren researched missional church case studies for his DTheol at Whitley College – University of Divinity, where he is now an Honorary Research Fellow. He currently serves as President of Australian Association for Mission Studies.

Rev Meewong Yang is a Korean-Australian Baptist pastor who serves as Multicultural Consultant and Pastor with BUV, teaches multicultural church at Whitley College, and is national coordinator of Australian Baptist Ministries' Multicultural Ministry Network. Meewon's Master of Theology at Whitley evaluated multicultural church models, supervised by Ross Langmead with whom Meewon has also published on the topic.

Rev Dr Ner Dah is pastor of Westgate Karen Baptist Community Church, and completed his PhD at Whitley College (University of Divinity) on 'Reading the Kingdom Teaching of Matthew from the Context of Myanmar'.

Rev Si Khia is pastor of Lautu Chin Baptist Church meeting at Spotswood Anglican Church and advisor of Chin Christian Council in Australia.

Rev Arohn Kuung is senior pastor of Chin Baptist Church, Sunshine, and supports new Chin churches in Adelaide, Perth, Melbourne and overseas. He has served as Principal of Union Theological Seminary in Burma, International Volunteer Interpreter for UN High Commission for Refugees in Kuala Lumpur and pastor for Burmese refugee communities at Westgate Baptist Church.

Rev Japheth Lian is pastor of Victorian Chin Baptist Church, meeting at Mooroolbark Baptist Church and secretary of Chin Christian Council in Australia. He is a Whitley College PhD candidate exploring 'The Life, Challenges and Prospects for Unity and Witness of the Churches in Chinland'.

Stacey Wilson is a Research Assistant with BUV and an Occupational Therapist passionate about championing inclusion of people of diverse cultures, ages and abilities in churches.

Pauline Kim van Dalen is a wife and a mother of four wonderful children who she enjoys cooking, reading and playing with. Her family is her inspiration and a faithful company in her journey of life.

www.ingramcontent.com/pod-product-compliance
Lightning Source LLC
Chambersburg PA
CBHW051937290426
44110CB00015B/2008